WE NEED TO TALK

A SURVIVAL GUIDE FOR TOUGH CONVERSATIONS

Joshua Graves

Rosenfeld

NEW YORK 2025

"I found myself rethinking past conversations with a new lens. It's a must-read for anyone looking to improve how they communicate under pressure. I loved the mix of personal anecdotes and actionable advice—I only wish I could have read it sooner."

—Chay Land
Independent product designer

"Joshua's deep understanding of conflict resolution and gift for rebuilding trust across teams makes him the perfect person to write this guide. Through real stories and a practical framework, he shows how to turn tense situations into opportunities for genuine understanding. This isn't just another book about workplace communication—it's an essential guide for anyone who wants to approach difficult conversations with confidence, clarity, and care."

—Bryan Zug
DesignOps manager

"*We Need to Talk* is a master class in navigating the conversations most managers dread but absolutely need to have. No one teaches you how to face these moments of conflict and collaboration, yet they are at the heart of great leadership and teamwork. This book is not just about strategies—it's about reshaping your relationship with conflict. It transforms 'hard conversations' from stress-inducing moments into opportunities for growth, trust, and real connection."

—Bill Carlson
Design leader

"Joshua Graves empowers us to face our most challenging and necessary conversations by first understanding our own brains. A wise and much-needed book that will give you practical communication skills for work and life."

—Katrina Alcorn
Product and design executive and author

"After the first chapter, I had to pause. I said to myself, 'Is this written for me personally? How did Josh know I needed to undo a lifetime of conflict avoidance?' This book has real tools and techniques that will change how you think about conflict, uncomfortable topics, and your reactions to them. If you want to be an intentional, powerful communicator, then this book is going to give you real-life examples and framing to accomplish just that."

—Julie Froelich
Design leader at Azibo

"Whether you're a manager, individual contributor, or someone who wants to improve how they handle workplace tensions, this book offers the tools and confidence needed to tackle hard conversations effectively. A must-read for building stronger, more resilient professional relationships in today's complex work environment."

—Lucas Dickey
Founder, Fernish and DeepCast

"This isn't about being nice—nice got us into this mess! Instead, Josh shows how kindness (the real stuff) and a clever framework called the 'Conversation Pyramid' can turn even the choppiest waters into smoother sailing. You'll learn how to approach conflict with confidence, build trust, and maybe even crack a smile along the way. So, whether you're dreading a tricky chat with your boss, your partner, or that one friend who always 'forgets' their wallet, *We Need to Talk* will give you the tools to talk it out without losing your mind—or your cool."

—Carlos Salazar
Independent product designer

We Need to Talk

A Survival Guide for Tough Conversations

By Joshua Graves

Rosenfeld Media, LLC

125 Maiden Lane

New York, New York 10038

USA

On the Web: www.rosenfeldmedia.com

Please send errata to: errata@rosenfeldmedia.com

Publisher: Louis Rosenfeld

Managing Editor: Marta Justak

Interior Layout: Danielle Foster

Cover Design: Heads of State

Illustrations: Joshua Graves

Indexer: Marilyn Augst

Proofreader: Sue Boshers

ISBN: 1- 959029-11-8

ISBN 13: 978-1-959029-11-3

LCCN: 2024952896

For Charlie and Frankie

HOW TO USE THIS BOOK

Who Should Read This Book?

If you work with other humans, this book is for you. Whether you're a leader trying to build psychological safety on your team, an individual contributor navigating tricky workplace dynamics, or someone who wants to get better at having hard conversations, you'll find practical tools here. While the examples come primarily from technology and creative fields, the framework works across industries and roles. You'll learn how to transform potentially confrontational situations into opportunities for growth and understanding, all while staying true to your authentic communication style. This isn't about becoming a conflict expert—it's about feeling confident and capable when those inevitable tough conversations arise.

What's in This Book?

This book is divided into two main sections: the foundational framework and a practical situational guide. The first part teaches you the core principles of having difficult conversations, including how your brain processes conflict, how to prepare effectively, and techniques for maintaining psychological safety. You'll learn a flexible framework that helps you navigate any challenging discussion with confidence.

The second part applies these principles to specific scenarios that you're likely to encounter. From dealing with defensive reactions to handling cultural differences, from addressing unmet expectations to mediating team conflicts—each chapter provides concrete strategies tailored to common challenging situations. Throughout the book, you'll find real-world examples and practical tools you can start using immediately.

Rather than prescribing rigid scripts or oversimplified solutions, this book gives you a versatile toolbox for handling difficult conversations in your own authentic way. Whether you're preparing for an upcoming discussion or caught in an unexpected confrontation, you'll find practical guidance for transforming potentially difficult moments into opportunities for growth and understanding.

What Comes with This Book?

This book's companion website (rosenfeldmedia.com/books/we-need-to-talk-a-survival-guide-for-tough-conversations/) contains a blog and additional content. The book's diagrams and other illustrations are available under a Creative Commons license (when possible) for you to download and include in your own presentations. You can find these on Flickr at www.flickr.com/photos/rosenfeldmedia/sets/.

FREQUENTLY ASKED QUESTIONS

Will this book give me scripts to follow for tough conversations?

No. There are no rigid scripts here (they never work in real life anyway). Instead, you'll get a flexible framework and practical tools you can adapt to any situation. Think of it as building your own conversational toolbox rather than following someone else's playbook. Want to know more? Check out Chapter 1, "Before the Conversation."

What if someone springs a tough conversation on me out of nowhere?

You don't always get the luxury of preparation. Don't worry—this book teaches you specific techniques for staying centered, asking the right questions, and keeping your cool when caught off guard. Jump to Chapter 18, "When You Don't Have Time to Prepare," for the full rundown.

How do I deal with someone who gets defensive or emotional?

In short: psychological safety and redirection. You'll learn practical ways to de-escalate tension and guide things back to productive territory. I cover this extensively in Chapter 2, "Having the Conversation," and dive even deeper in Chapter 3, "People Losing Control."

What happens when we just can't see eye-to-eye?

Not every conversation will end in agreement, and that's okay. What matters is finding a way forward while keeping the relationship intact. I'll show you how to navigate these tricky waters in Chapter 19, "When You Can't Agree," and Chapter 20, "Mediating with Multiple People."

Isn't this tone policing or trying to get me to talk like some stoic robot?

No, that isn't the intent of anything you'll read here. This book is meant to help you express yourself in ways that are both authentic and productive. By doing so, this gives you the highest chance of being effective when you engage in a hard conversation. This framework is complementary to many communication styles, whether you are more impassioned or more reserved.

CONTENTS

FOREWORD

Conflict. The very word can make us bristle, squirm, or retreat into the shadows. For many, including me, conflict has long been something to avoid—a perceived monster under the bed, best left undisturbed. Yet avoiding conflict rarely leads to progress. Instead, it can stifle creativity, prevent essential conversations, and perpetuate systems that leave many voices unheard.

As someone who's spent years helping people build more inclusive workplaces, I've seen firsthand how avoiding conflict can derail even the most well-intentioned efforts to foster belonging. Inclusive environments don't materialize out of thin air; we build them through hard, honest, and sometimes uncomfortable conversations. It's work that challenges us to step into conflict—not as adversaries but as collaborators.

That's why I'm so excited for you to dive into *We Need to Talk*. Joshua Graves has created a practical and insightful guide to help us explore our flawed relationship with conflict. More importantly, he's provided a framework to transform it into something constructive and empowering.

You're going to love Joshua's storytelling. He shares his own struggles—how a fear of conflict left him on the sidelines and how that fear stifled his ability to lead effectively. He also gives insight into challenging workplace situations via other people's real-life stories. They remind us that avoiding conflict isn't a personal failing but a learned behavior. And, as this book shows, it's one we can unlearn.

We Need to Talk will challenge you to reframe what it means to be "nice." Spoiler: it's not the same as being *kind, authentic,* or *impactful.* You'll learn why "nice" often acts as a barrier to meaningful progress and how letting go of that expectation can unlock healthier relationships, better decision-making, and more inclusive cultures where everyone can do their best work and thrive.

Whether you're a leader or an individual contributor, this book will equip you with tools to navigate conflict with grace and intention. It's not about avoiding the monster under the bed; it's about turning on the light, sitting down with it, and figuring out how to move forward together.

With Joshua's book, it might be easier than you thought possible.

—Karen Catlin
Author of the Better Allies® book series

INTRODUCTION

I absolutely was *not* ready for this. Like a little kid in a horror movie when facing the story's monster, I was *stressed*. I wondered why my hands were shaking, my stomach in knots, and my brain ready to explode with stress.

My team, tasked with building a healthcare app, had just finished presenting a demo of the app to our stakeholders. What they saw went against what the stakeholders had asked for, what the patients who used it wanted, and what I had designed. They hated it. No surprise there.

I'd seen this coming but couldn't stop it.

I mean, I *could* have stopped it, but that would have meant having hard conversations with people and not just seething in the corner. Hard pass: my body hated the thought of conflict. Like, the "lose sleep, pull hair, have a stomach in knots" kind of hate. I'd do anything to avoid conflict, even if it meant settling for worse results.

In the company where I worked, product managers had a history of giving engineers big changes without communicating them to everyone else, clients included. Engineers took any designs that came their way as suggestions, building the app how they wanted it designed. And designers were the latecomers to the projects, always trying to find their place in the chaos. To call the process *dysfunctional* was a kindness.

That night I woke up in the middle of the night like I usually did after stressful days thinking about how I felt, how much I wanted this to succeed, and how I was tired of constantly finding myself in situations like this. It left me with a choice: figure out how to have and manage hard conversations—for me, for the team, for the projects I work on—or *quit*.

I am a designer by trade and a curious observer by nature. I've been likened to a kid who asks "why" until you tell them to shut up. Learning what's behind an idea or a problem is a lifelong love of mine. So, I stepped back and did just that. Here's what I wanted to learn:

- What was my relationship to conflict (and other people's) and why was it so hard to talk to people about difficult things?

- How did neuroscience, as well as cultural and psychological factors, shape how people engage with conflict?
- How could I create a flexible, effective framework that helped navigate conflict?

This exploration led me to intense study, training, and conversations with experts. I quickly saw that my situation, apart from a few specifics, wasn't too different from what other people experience in conflict. And a staggering amount of people struggle with it. Some of them even shared their stories, a few against the advice of their therapists, for this book. I'll share the rest of my story as the book unfolds, but rest assured there is a resolution.

Mending Our Flawed Relationship to Conflict

My first stop was understanding my relationship to conflict. I was born in a place that prized being "nice"—the American South. My parents made it a point never to fight in front of me or my sister, for good reasons, leaving me to form my own opinions on conflict.

I was more or less a blank slate. I knew that working things out like kids did on the playground by pushing and punching wasn't going to be a good move either. That left me with the following perception of conflict:

- You weren't supposed to have it or didn't have it.
- You had to be nice, which meant that you didn't have conflict.
- Because you were nice, and you didn't have conflict, the only acceptable phrases were "yes ma'am" or "yes sir," even if you disagreed with them. Or "bless your heart."

So basically, I knew nothing. This outsider status gave me an advantage: if I didn't really know anything, that meant I didn't have any real bad habits. And that meant I could approach working with other difficult humans in an entirely new way.

My first realization? Being *nice* sucks. It's at the core of so many problems and has to go. *Nice* is nothing more than candy-coated emptiness. It's the well-intentioned but wildly misguided notion that leads to innumerable poor outcomes, untold resentment, and emptiness. *Nice* lands people in situations this book is written specifically to address. *Nice* doesn't want people to have hard conversations because they aren't pleasant. *Nice* stifles dissent and preserves the status quo and unfair power structures. I don't like *nice*, and this book isn't about being nice.

I'm not alone, either. If I pile up all the topics that feature in my talks, workshops, and research, you could plant a flag labeled *nice* at the top of the heap.

This book is going to help you do away with the feeling that you've got to be nice. In fact, let this tiny paragraph be a funeral for nice. Here is its tombstone, and I encourage you to have a moment of silence for it:

> Here lies Nice, who passed peacefully in 2024. You were cool. Rest in Peace.

To replace nice, you need something that gives you the confidence to go to the other person and figure it out, no matter how choppy the waters seem.

What comes after nice? It's what should have been there all along: kindness. Yelling at someone who's about to step into traffic may not be nice, but it sure is kind. The same is true at work. If someone is going to wreck the project as a result of their oversight or error, you owe it to them to be direct and call it out. Kindness empowers you to do that, niceness doesn't.

Creating a Flexible Framework to Navigate Conflict

The result of this work is a principle-driven, sturdy, and flexible system filled with tools to help you navigate conflict, no matter the level or culture that someone is from. I call it the *Conversation Pyramid*, and it contains two main sections. One inward focused, the other outward focused. See Figure I.1.

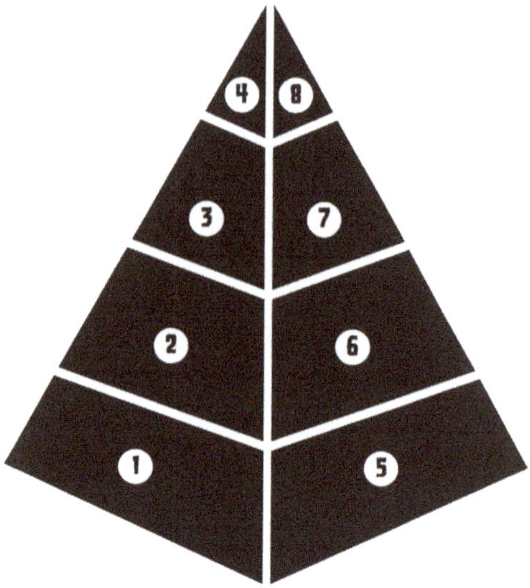

1. CHECK IN WITH YOURSELF
2. GET IT STRAIGHT
3. FORM CONCLUSIONS
4. CRAFT GOALS
5. START WITH SAFETY
6. SHARE FACTS
7. SHARE CONCLUSIONS & GOALS
8. OPEN IT UP

FIGURE I.1
The Conversation Pyramid is the answer.

The left side of the pyramid is where you're looking inward: checking in with yourself, getting it straight, forming conclusions, and crafting goals.

The right side has you looking outward: starting with psychological safety, sharing facts, sharing conclusions and goals, and opening it up to the other person.

This framework helps you navigate sticky conflicts with teammates, bosses, and fickle clients alike.

The Conversation Pyramid is guided by the following principles:

- **Be approachable.** What you'll read is informed by studies, psychology, and experience. Every word and recommendation is carefully distilled to focus on tactics over heady philosophies.
- **Focus on principles.** Technologies, processes, and situations can change, but people don't. Focusing on principles promotes flexibility and adaptability, both now and well into the future.
- **Embrace conflict.** If you really want to grow and have mutually beneficial outcomes, invest in figuring out how to best work with people. Especially those you disagree with. Your team will be better, your product will be better, and you will, too.
- **Be kind, not nice:** Remember that niceness got you into this mess. Kindness lets you be honest, respectful, and authentic—especially when it gets tough.

The Book's Structure

Chapters 1, "Before the Conversation, and 2, "Having the Conversation," set up the rest of the book. If you're in a hurry, start with those two and come back later for some extra context.

All of the remaining chapters include a real-life situation that sets up the problem.

In each situation, I detail a few ways to resolve the said situation and what to look out for so that your conversations don't go sideways.

Each situation has different solutions, but all of them draw on what you learn in the following two chapters. And each chapter ends with final thoughts to ensure that you're set up for as much success as possible.

NOTE WHAT THIS BOOK ISN'T

I don't believe in the idea of "you win" conversations. Not all conflict can or should be resolved, nor are hard conversations a zero-sum game. My goal is to get you prepared to take on anything and have the absolute best chance of having a good, healthy outcome for everyone involved.

If you're hoping for a paint-by-numbers approach to "win" conversations, you're in for some disappointment. People who sell you on the idea of checklists and surefire methods to get tidy outcomes are, at best, misguided, and at worst, they're charlatans. Those ideas make for great blog posts and well-paid keynotes, but ultimately those ideas hold up about as well as a tissue in a hurricane. There's no checklist to follow for a clean, tidy outcome in your favor. Real life is messy. Conversations are, too.

About the Situations in This Book

I've made as few alterations to the stories in this book as possible, both out of respect for those who shared their stories and for you, the person who picked up this book for practical, tactical advice based on real stories. Stories that are made up don't do anyone any good, so I didn't bother.

I limited my modifications to three things. The two easy ones were editing for clarity and changing key details in order to protect someone's identity. The third really presented a dilemma: telling these stories without playing to embedded prejudices. People of varying genders and identities contributed to this book, but including certain aspects of their identities left the door wide open to stereotyping. So, I chose a different path here.

Drawing on my love for horror movies, and the situations contained herein will undoubtedly read as horror for some, I've named every person after characters from horror movies I've enjoyed. If, when going down the list, the characters came up as women-identifying, then that's what I went with. Rest assured, these situations can—and do—happen to anyone, regardless of how they identify. My hope is you'll see this as a, err, novel solution to a thorny problem.

Lastly, I've tried as hard as I can to remove my own bias from the advice in this book by consulting with diversity and inclusion experts and BIPOC who aren't like me and having them review this book before publication. It was of paramount importance that what you read in this book be as broadly applicable as possible, regardless of your situation or background.

CHAPTER 1

Before the Conversation

This chapter guides you through the left side of the Conversation Pyramid (see Figure 1.1), which focuses on everything prior to the conversation you'll have with the other person. It gets you in the right mindset, straightens out your story, and helps you define outcomes for your conversation.

FIGURE 1.1
The left side of the Conversation Pyramid focuses on you.

It helps if you have a scenario in mind, so here's a starter:

> **Jay** (a product manager) and **Yara** (a product designer) have a conflict over scope creep on their company's new shopping app.
>
> Yara gets an email after hours and opens it. It's a notification that Jay's added some items to their app's roadmap that he believes are essential for a competitive edge.
>
> Yara feels that adding these features without proper validation and testing will compromise the usability and overall user experience of the app. She's got data indicating that no one wants those features.
>
> Jay's made unilateral decisions before without consulting Yara or the engineering team, and it had a bad effect on morale and the outcomes. The situation worsens when the stakeholders reply and say they love this.

Yara wonders why this is happening and if Jay is undermining her. Both Jay and Yara are going to talk it out one-on-one.

Check In with Yourself

It's tempting to jump to conclusions and assume that you have the solution to the problem you and your counterpart are facing. Indeed, you might, but there's a greater chance that you are missing something. So, take a moment and check in with yourself before you make a mess of things unnecessarily (see Figure 1.2). It will save you some potential embarrassment.

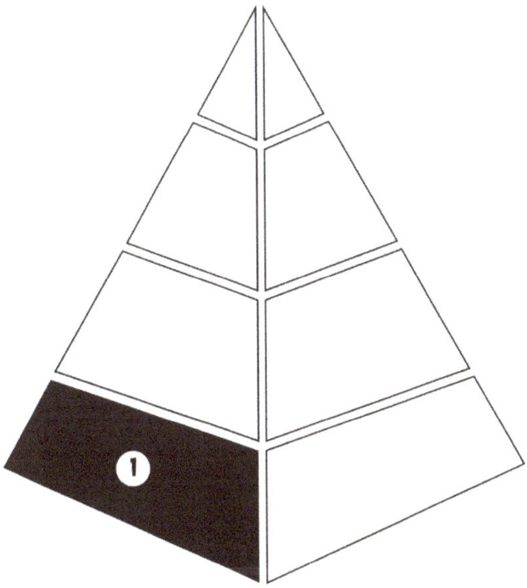

FIGURE 1.2
Step 1: Check in with yourself.

Your Brain's Structure

It's tempting to think of the brain as a singular entity, but it's more akin to a tightly networked collection of mini organs. Hierarchically, the brain is structured into three main regions: the hindbrain, midbrain, and forebrain (see Figure 1.3). Each of these regions plays a specific, integral role in our daily functioning.

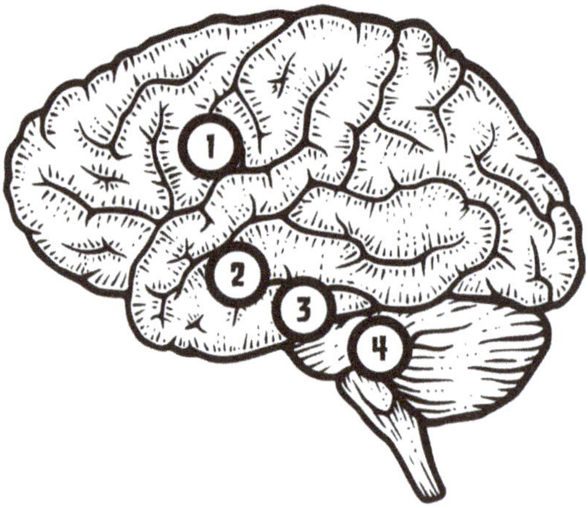

FIGURE 1.3
These parts of the human brain play a role in conflict.

1. NEOCORTEX (COGNITION)
2. MAMMALIAN (EMOTION)
3. REPTILIAN (BASIC FUNCTIONS)
4. AMYGDALA (WARNING SYSTEM)

- **Reptilian/Hindbrain:** Handles unconscious and automatic functions like regulating respiration, balance, and coordination. It's the home of the cerebellum, pons, and upper spinal cord.
- **Mammalian/Midbrain:** Bridges the gap between the hindbrain and forebrain and receives raw data from your senses and forwards it upward for further interpretation. It's the bridge between the hindbrain and forebrain.
- **Neocortex/Forebrain:** Interprets the world you inhabit and is the seat of your emotions and memories. It includes the hippocampus, hypothalamus, thalamus, and the amygdala.

Of particular interest in the forebrain is the amygdala, which is the body's early warning system that preps emergency responses and detects fear. When the amygdala senses a threat, it sounds an alarm and releases two chemicals into the body, adrenaline and cortisol (a stress hormone). The amygdala also diverts blood from other parts of the brain and puts you into survival mode. This is where your fight, flight, or freeze responses step in and take over.

The neuroscientist Joseph LeDoux calls this activation the *survival circuits*. While clear thinking is possible in this state, it takes much more effort to think and act rationally. A cartoonish oversimplification would be that you either turn into an ostrich who puts its head in the sand, or some bruiser ready to punch your way out of whatever situation you're in. (There are some fun chicken-and-egg theories that ask about the origin of this: do we think of fear and then have a physical response, or have the physical response and then think of fear? This book won't weigh in on that. Its focus is that humans end up in these states in the first place.)

Most of this book is dedicated to fine-tuning your over-reactive amygdala. It, and the survival circuits it activates, serve valuable purposes and can even be fun (see also: haunted houses, skydiving, and other thrill-seeking behavior). But what isn't fun is that your brain treats a terse email the same way as a serious, physical threat. When you find yourself or someone else awash in stress hormones, you'll have ways to counteract such an effect. I won't say it will be easy—in fact, it isn't—but what you learn here can ensure that you don't end up spending time swimming in a stew of adrenaline and cortisol when you don't need to.

Hanlon's Razor

Anxiety, fear, and a whole host of emotions will get the best of you if you aren't careful. And brains are extremely good at evaluating situations rapidly. The downside of this is that what may be an innocent mistake could turn quickly into thinking someone's out to get you, or that you'll lose your job if you don't do this or that. Yes, it is entirely possible those two scenarios are true, but are they the likeliest thing to happen? Probably not.

That's where Hanlon's razor comes in. The adage has a few forms,[1] but the gist of it is this:

> *Don't assume bad intentions over neglect and misunderstanding.*

Having a mindset like this is incredibly helpful where conflict is concerned because Hanlon's razor takes the teeth off those bad tales you (unintentionally) tell yourself, simply by prompting you to consider that maybe the other person didn't mean it. How much misery would you avoid if you assumed the other person didn't mean it?

Hanlon's razor also cuts against one other particularly unfair quirk of human nature: when people unknowingly attribute someone else's

---

1 The actual quote is: "Never attribute to malice that which is adequately explained by stupidity."

behavior to their personality, rather than external circumstances. It usually happens with people who are less like you, and it is a fundamental attribution error. It's why, for example, some men can view another man who speaks up as assertive, determined, or passionate, but they view a woman as unreasonable or angry when she does the same.

It's possible that in the sample situation, Jay is actively undermining Yara.

This isn't to say that Yara should dismiss the whole thing entirely. Actions have impacts, regardless of intent. Whether or not Jay intended to undermine Yara is beside the point, because the end result is that he jeopardized the project. Put another way, if someone steps on your foot as they walk by, they probably didn't mean it. But your foot still smarts. Behavior at work isn't any different. Everything has an impact.

Hanlon's Razor Worksheet

The next time you find yourself in a tough spot, try working through these questions:

1. Is there substantial evidence for my thought?
2. Is there evidence contrary to my thought?
3. Am I interpreting this situation without all the evidence?
4. What would I tell a friend if they came to me about this situation?
5. Will this matter in a year?
6. What's the worst that could happen?
7. How likely is it to happen?
8. If it does, how hard will it be to recover after a month, a year?

Your Role, Intentions, and Mindset

This next part isn't easy, but it's necessary work that builds on Hanlon's razor. Assessing your intentions and role in the situation requires a mountain of self-honesty. It's humbling, too—taking a clear look here highlights how people aren't as objective, logical, or fair as they might think. It isn't your fault; it's just how your brain works.

Sorting through what role you might have played in the situation and clarifying your intentions and mindset saves you from eating dirt when you go talk to your coworkers. Because you'd better believe they'll be calling out your role in this.

Your Role

The following questions in Table 1.1 help you step outside yourself and examine your role.

TABLE 1.1 YOUR ROLE

Question	Answer
How might I be contributing to this, even unintentionally?	
If I were in their shoes, what would I expect to have done to prevent it?	
Was there something I should have said but didn't?	

It's common to learn that you're not setting proper expectations—that you've expected someone to read your mind or something else. Here are some of the most obvious ways that people unintentionally contribute to their own real-life situations:

- Don't properly communicate their needs.
- Expect people to read their minds.
- Are stressed and forgetful.
- Misread the people's or project's needs.
- Don't set boundaries.
- Don't set the right goals.
- Misinterpret body language.

However, you won't always find that you've had any contribution to the situation. This is especially true if you're on the receiving end of harassment or abuse. Make no mistake here: *The harassment or abuse is entirely on the other person, and you bear zero responsibility for their actions.*

NOTE IS MY MANAGEMENT STYLE THE PROBLEM?

If you're a manager, you should also ask yourself if you are in your direct report's way somehow. Maybe you've scheduled too many check-ins or are inserting yourself into their workflow and causing a bottleneck in some way. This happens more often than you'd think with managers and their direct reports.

Your Intentions and Mindset

Having clear intentions and the right mindset are keys for success in anything you do. It goes double here. When you have a conversation with someone, you want to make sure that it benefits as many people or objectives as possible. And you want to have it for the right reasons, none of which include shutting someone down or humiliating them.

Use the following questions to help clarify your intentions:

- Who benefits from this?
- Will the work be better as a result?
- Will the team be better as a result?

If you come up short on answers, you may want to pull back.

There's also your mindset to consider.

Some people choose to frame these conversations in terms of avoiding loss or reducing pain. That's valid, because that's just how things go sometimes. But how you frame a situation influences its outcome, and if you have a chance to approach it with an optimistic mindset, you'll get a better outcome.

This isn't to say just be happy-go-lucky and upbeat. That's unkind, unrealistic, and not helpful to the people involved, and it actively works against you. That kind of delusional thinking only leads to terrible outcomes.

There's a relevant study at the University of Rochester that digs into this. The team conducting the study worked with students to understand the effects of different framings on their final exam grades. What they found was fascinating: If a student used pessimistic framing and said, "I don't want less than a C," they experienced a decrease in performance. Those who used optimistic framing and said things like, "I want to earn a higher grade," did much better. In fact, pessimistic framing depressed performance as much as positive framing increased it.

If you approach your situation with a pessimistic mindset, you may only strive to avoid loss or pain, leading to a belief that your options are limited. This can result in settling for less than optimal outcomes. But if you adopt an optimistic mindset, you'll have something to strive for. This attitude promotes creative thinking and openness to collaboration.

Conversations like the one you want to have aren't any different than the students and their exam grades. The way you frame the situation, your requests, and your goals will shape the response and success you'll have (see Table 1.2).

TABLE 1.2 PESSIMISTIC AND OPTIMISTIC MINDSET

Pessimistic Mindset	Optimistic Mindset
How can we stop the team from getting sidetracked in meetings?	What can we do to ensure that we stay focused but have a chance to explore potential problem areas?
How can we reduce employee turnover?	What can we do to ensure that employees feel supported and fulfilled at work so they'll want to stay?
How can we stop customer service from spending so much time on password resets?	How can we enable customer service to focus on the meatier problems that customers have?
How do we stop new employees from making so many mistakes?	How can we make sure that we make our onboarding as clear and helpful as possible?
How can we reduce the back and forth in the approvals process with our clients?	What can we do to ensure that the approval process is both thorough and efficient?

Put Yourself in Their Shoes

Understanding where the other person is coming from and getting a sense of their perspective is going to make for a much more productive, mutually beneficial outcome.

Cranky Conclusions

You're going to find yourself in situations that can be truly, deeply unpleasant. Maybe you're telling a direct report about their performance, chastising a colleague whose behavior is wrecking a project, or discussing any number of other unpleasant and inappropriate things. These situations can turn sour at a moment's notice and someone can get defensive, preventing any forward progress. You have the cortisol your amygdala pumps into your blood and internal stress responses to thank for that.

But you can route around that tendency with cranky conclusions, which is a set of questions that help you see where someone may go if they get defensive. In fact, it's just two questions:

- How could they pin this on me?
- What's the worst thing they can say about me?

Cranky conclusions help in two ways: they prime your brain for empathy by putting you in the other person's shoes. They also help you see the worst places where the other person could take this conversation, giving you a chance to tailor your conversation to avoid or soften the blow.

When you start your conversation, you can include a cranky conclusion to lead into your conversation if you like. More on that in the next chapter.

(And credit where it's due: cranky conclusions is inspired by the "accusation audit," a concept introduced in *Never Split the Difference*.[2] I've since evolved it for my own practice but it's important to acknowledge its roots.)

The Impact Chart

You can also get a little more granular with the impact chart (see Figure 1.4). It's a diagram that helps you make a decision on whether or not to have a conversation based on a number of factors, such as the following:

- Are you able to continue with your work?
- How impactful is it to you, the company, the project, or the client?
- Will this situation resolve itself (either they leave or the project ends)?
- How likely is it to be an issue in the future?

This tool gets you out of the "what-if" cycle that burns so much unnecessary mental energy by giving you a few outs.

2 Chris Voss and Tahl Raz, *Never Split the Difference* (New York: Random House Business Books, 2017).

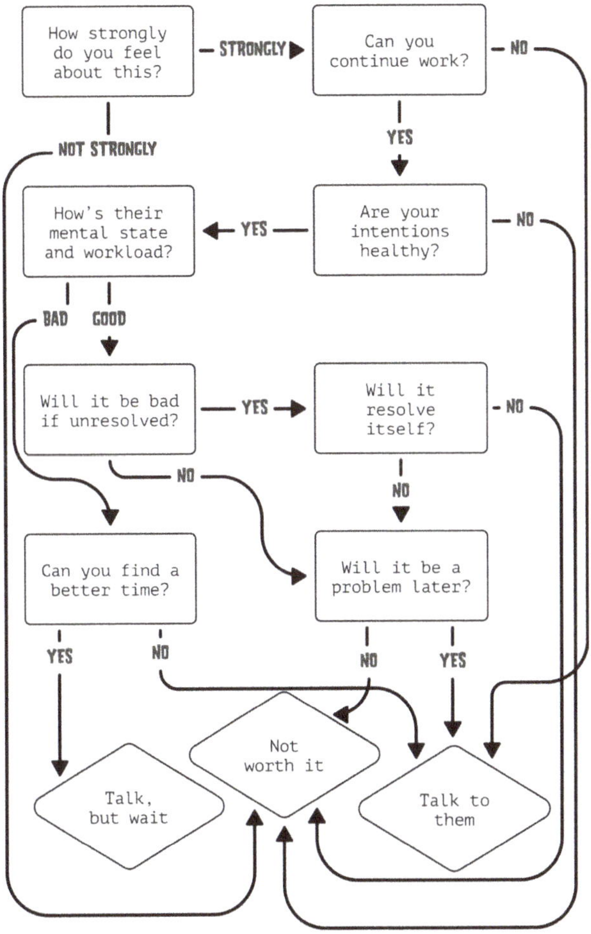

FIGURE 1.4
A flowchart showing how to know if you should have the hard conversation or not.

NOTE OUR CONVERSATION: CHECK IN WITH YOURSELF

Hanlon's razor: The team may have been overruled, and Jay had planned to discuss it with the team.

Yara's role: She may have formed a conclusion too quickly.

Yara's intentions: Yara doesn't want the product to fail, so she's going to talk with Jay. She also wants Jay to respect the agreement the team made.

Yara's mindset: She is upset, mostly about the success of the product being in jeopardy.

The impact: This decision will affect the team's morale and the product's success.

Cranky conclusions: Jay's going to tell Yara to stop being so rigid.

Get It Straight

Now that you've got your head on straight, it's time to move on and do likewise for the situation. This is a bit more straightforward on paper than it is in reality. You're going to write down the details of your situation and do a little exercise with it (see Figure 1.5).

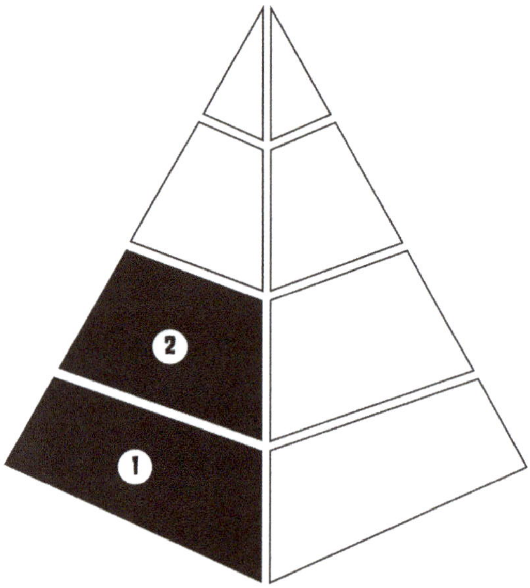

FIGURE 1.5
Step 2: Get it straight.

Write It Down

You'll want to jot down everything about the situation you can recall: what happened, how it made you feel, and the impact it had. Even the temperature in the room where you were, if you like. Just get it all down.

There's a particular emphasis here on physical writing, because it forces you to articulate your thoughts. That option may not be available to you, and it's okay—do what feels natural to you.

Separate Fact from Fiction

Once you're done, you'll separate the facts from the conclusions you've drawn about them (see Table 1.3). Both are important; right now, though, your concern is primarily the facts. The section after this focuses on your conclusions.

Facts matter most because they are objective, powerful, and the least risky parts of any conversation. They are also the most effective way to make your case because they don't contain any conclusions or value judgments. They also keep you honest.

Take a moment and highlight them or call them out in some way. A key way to differentiate a fact from a conclusion is to look at the situation like a security camera:

> *If I were reviewing security camera footage of this event, what would I see?*

Security cameras can't determine if someone is angry or said something in a snarky tone of voice. They can only report things that were observable without judgments. They also don't make assumptions.

TABLE 1.3 FINDING THE FACTS

Objective	Powerful	Least Risky
It's much easier to tell someone they didn't attend a meeting than observing that they disrespected the team by not showing up to the meeting.	Facts are more powerful than opinion because they form our conclusions. Change the facts, change the conclusion.	If you start with your conclusions, you risk the conversation backfiring by unintentionally insulting the other person.

Take a moment and read through the following examples. As you go along, underline or highlight the pieces of this entry that are facts. After you're finished, see the answers that follow.

> I got an email saying that Jay has updated our roadmap. He's on some kind of power trip going over our heads like this. He did this without consulting me or the team. And now our stakeholders are giving a thumbs-up emoji? If we do this, it's going to be an all-out disaster. We've done the research to prove that no one wants these features, and he's seen it himself.
>
> Things change, I get it. But we need to talk before making decisions like Jay's roadmap update, because it's disrespectful and hurts everyone. No one person has the power here to make unilateral decisions; we agreed on that. He's done this once before, and it cost us a lot of users. I'm not about to let that happen again.

Here are the factual pieces of this statement:

- Yara got an email about a roadmap update.
- In the email, it showed that Jay had added features to a product roadmap.
- The roadmap update came without prior consultation with the team.
- Yara has the research to prove these features aren't something that people want as-is.
- Our stakeholders replied with a thumbs-up emoji.
- Jay made a unilateral decision before with negative results.
- Their team agreed to joint decisions.

What remains are conclusions and judgments. Sentences that contain phrases like "power trip," "all-out disaster," and "waste of time," while possibly true, aren't evaluations that a detached observer like a security camera would make.

NOTE **A PATTERN OR ONE-OFF?**

Try asking yourself this question the next time you need to have a hard conversation: "Has anything like this happened before?" If so, try to find three related examples to share. Patterns are incredible in discussions, because they are strong evidence for your case.

One-offs are fine—sometimes that's all you'll get—but one event is almost too easy to explain away and isn't always enough to draw a useful conclusion from. Finding three examples helps you piece things together—it's only when you reach three that you come up with almost undeniable evidence for your conclusions about your issue.

Form Conclusions

Now that you've highlighted the facts from your situation and sifted out the conclusions, you can take a moment to articulate the impact they had, i.e., to form your own conclusions (see Figure 1.6). Taking your time with this step pays dividends in your conversation. There's a helpful way to frame them, too, and from something called nonviolent communication. It helps you talk about what happened in a way that doesn't outright attack the other person. To be clear, the intent with this is not to water down your message or treat the other person with kid gloves. Instead, it helps you fully and effectively articulate what you need to say.

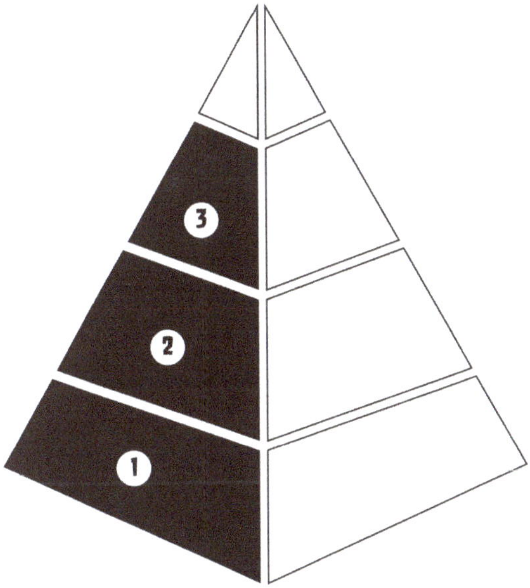

FIGURE 1.6
Step 3: Form conclusions.

Practice Nonviolent Communication

In his book, *Nonviolent Communication: A Language of Life*, Dr. Marshall Rosenberg uses this technique to uncover the heart of any issue. Here is Dr. Rosenberg describing his framework (emphasis added):

> As [nonviolent communication] replaces our old patterns of defending, withdrawing, or attacking in the face of judgment and criticism, we come to perceive ourselves and others, as well as our intentions and relationships, in a new light. Resistance, defensiveness, and violent reactions are minimized. **When we focus on clarifying what is being observed, felt, and needed rather than on diagnosing and judging, we discover the depth of our own compassion.** Through its emphasis on deep listening—to ourselves as well as to others—NVC fosters respect, attentiveness, and empathy and engenders a mutual desire to give from the heart.[3]

3 Marshall Rosenberg, *Nonviolent Communication: A Language of Life*, 3rd ed. (Encinitas, CA: PuddleDancer Press, September 1, 2015).

Using what this book calls *nonviolent statements* gives you a practical way to frame your conclusions by focusing on what you saw, felt, or needed. This approach puts the other person in a space to experience empathy with you by showing them the impact they had on you, which helps them actually hear what's being said.

For conversations at work, focus on forming your conclusions along three dimensions:

- How did this affect you and your work?
- How did this affect your team or company?
- Will this have a large negative impact if left unresolved?

Here's what a nonviolent statement looks like:

> When you [do this] I feel [this way].
>
> Or
>
> When [this] happens, it can have [this] impact.

"When you..." focuses in on the facts that you've established and is free of evaluations, labeling, and judgments. "I feel..." focuses on the impact that fact had on you, the team, or the company.

If you find that someone may be extremely sensitive, and you want to accommodate that, you can remove the "you" from this statement entirely and be more objective. When you tell them that a behavior they exhibited can have a certain impact, it can still help you land your point without judgment. This isn't where you want to start, however, as adults should be able to hear and acknowledge that their actions have impact.

Here are a few examples of what a nonviolent statement looks like:

- When you added those items to the roadmap, it made me feel like my expertise didn't matter, or you didn't trust the team.
- When you make unilateral decisions, it seems like you aren't considering the bigger picture.
- Making a unilateral decision without consulting the whole team can have some negative impact, like lowering morale.
- Something I've learned in previous projects is that if someone makes unilateral decisions, the team cohesion suffers.

This approach works in many scenarios, and it's far preferable to telling someone "This is stupid, you're stupid, everything is stupid" or "We all know you're a big baby."

None of this is judging the other person because you're making an observation and speaking to what you've experienced as true. That's difficult to argue. Despite that, some people will inevitably come back with minimizing remarks, saying you're taking something too seriously, that it was just a joke, to just relax, and so on. We'll cover how to address this in Chapter 8, "Offensive Jokes and Microaggressions."

Next, you'll establish what you want to do with these conclusions by forming clear, actionable goals.

NOTE OUR CONVERSATION: GET IT STRAIGHT

The Facts:

- Yara got an email about a roadmap update.
- In the email, it showed that Jay added features to a product roadmap.
- The roadmap update came without prior consultation with the team.
- Yara has the research to prove these features aren't something people want as-is.
- Our stakeholders replied with a thumbs-up emoji.
- Jay made a unilateral decision before with negative results.
- Their team agreed on joint decisions.

Form Your Own Conclusions:

- Yara thinks Jay doesn't trust the team.
- Yara thinks Jay isn't considering the implications of those actions.

Establish Goals

Yogi Berra, famous baseball player and a person who had a way with words once said, "If you don't know where you're going, you'll end up someplace else." Conversations like the ones this book helps you formulate and have aren't any different. Establishing goals and outcomes let you stay focused on what you need, especially if the conversation gets sidetracked or emotions start to run hot (see Figure 1.7).

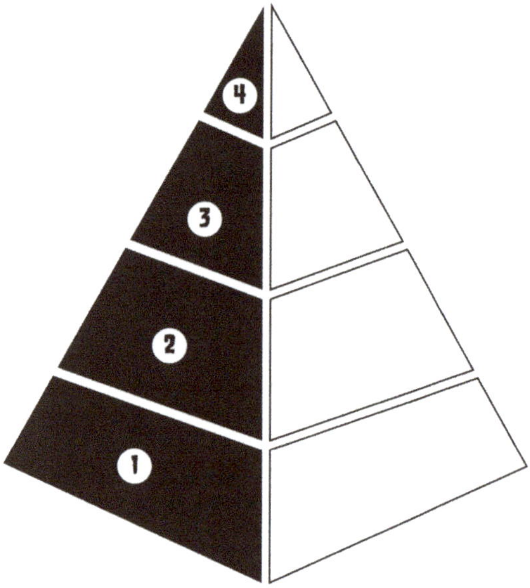

FIGURE 1.7
Step 4: Establish goals.

Define Your Goals and Outcomes

Focusing on outcomes and goals are what make great teams and products, too. Because you know what success looks like, you know how to reroute and adapt when you hit roadblocks. One detour doesn't matter as much if you know where you're headed. And staying true to those goals, especially when things get murky—as they often do—helps get the outcome you're trying to achieve. Here's a template to help focus your thinking:

I want _______________ so that _______________.

Now, apply it to your situation with your coworker. A couple examples could be:

> I want them to consult me before they make a decision that affects the project so that my expertise is respected and my voice heard. Or, I want them to make sure that every product added to the roadmap is validated by research, or we understand the cost of getting it wrong without it.

Clarify Your Goals

It's easy to be so wrapped up in a situation, having processed it from every possible angle, to have the solution be anything other than wildly obvious. People don't live in your head (fortunately or unfortunately), so what's a clear-cut decision to you may still be hazy to others (see Table 1.4). A goal you defined won't ever be fully realized if no one else understands it fully.

TABLE 1.4 UNCLEAR VS. CLEAR GOALS

Unclear	Clear	Meta Goal
I want you to hear me when I speak.	I want you to tell me what you heard me say just now.	Confirm understanding.
I want you to stop being late.	I want you tell me what's getting in the way of you making it in on time so that we can address it.	Demonstrate responsibility and respect.
I want you to be honest with me.	I want you to tell me how you feel about what I did in that meeting and what you'd like me to do differently.	Assess impact.
I want you to show respect for my agency.	I need you to consult me before you make a decision that affects the project.	Honor team interdependence.

When you make requests of people that are too generic and unclear, they won't have much more than a short-term effect. Not only that, but the core of your issue won't be addressed. While it's fair to assume a certain level of self-awareness and maturity in these situations, it's to everyone's benefit to have clear and actionable expectations either way so that there isn't room for misinterpretation. Use your intuition about how specific to get so you don't come off as micromanaging.

If Yara's talking with Jay and has an unclear goal of "stop doing this," it could go one of three ways:

- Jay makes meaningful steps toward involving the team in any decision-related communication, resolving the situation now and into the future.
- Jay fixes the situation at hand and goes back to the behavior.
- Jay doesn't communicate with the stakeholders without the whole team telling him what to say, leading to a worse situation.

A more effective framing of this would be: "I want you to talk with the team before committing to any decision, timeline, or request that affects our roadmap." Requests like this one are clearly actionable and define criteria for success.

NOTE **OUR CONVERSATION: GOALS**

- Jay consults the team before committing to any decision that affects a timeline or a change to the roadmap.
- Jay honors the agreement for no unilateral decisions.

Final Thoughts

Now that you've dug through what you want and you know how you'll get it, you can move on to the next chapter, which focuses on having the conversation. Here are some key takeaways in this chapter.

- Before you begin any conversation, check in with yourself and use Hanlon's razor to ask if you're making a devil out of someone who's just made a mistake.
- Your intentions must be for good. You should never start conversations with the intent of damaging another person or shutting them down.
- Ask yourself what role you may have played in this. You will often find that you may have contributed to the situation, however unintentionally.
- Adopt a discovery mindset. The way you frame the situation shapes the response and success you'll have.
- Put yourself in their shoes. Try a cranky conclusion, which asks how they might pin this on you, or the worst thing they could say.
- Look at the impact chart to see if you even need to have this conversation.
- Separate fact from fiction and learn to see things like a security camera would.
- Writing down your situation and then highlighting the facts helps you be more objective about your situation.
- Form your conclusions in a nonviolent way. Consider saying, "When you ________________, I feel ________________."

CHAPTER 2

Having the Conversation

This chapter guides you through the right side of the pyramid, which focuses on everything to do with having a conversation with the other person (see Figure 2.1). It starts with building psychological safety, leading into sharing your side of the story and managing the back and forth.

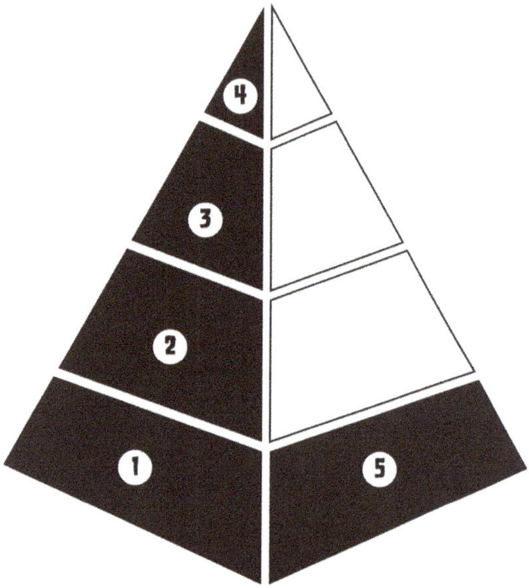

FIGURE 2.1
Step 5: Start with safety.

Each conversation you have, no matter how hard it is or who it's with, has its own nuances you'll need to pay attention to. The structure, thankfully, is the same. This chapter will teach you the concept and demonstrate how to adapt it as you progress.

As you walk through this chapter, you'll continue to build on the example from the previous chapter with Jay and Yara.

Start with Safety

So many companies and teams say they are psychologically safe. They'll say you're free to be yourself at work, that it's safe to fail, or that it's just cool to work for them because a CEO skimmed *The No Asshole Rule*[1] and proclaimed their company was asshole-free. Too few of them really know how to put that into practice beyond

1 Robert I. Sutton, *The No Asshole Rule* (New York: Business Plus, 2007).

saying "We're psychologically safe." It isn't an indictment on those companies, because it's close to becoming just another buzzword like "rockstar" or [cringes] "ninja" that's fast losing its meaning.

Take those notions and set them aside for a moment to focus on what psychological safety means for your conversations. Safety is instrumental, and it's the foundation for any successful, productive outcome. Because of that, you'll want to make sure you start with a solid foundation.

Distilled to its essence, here's what a psychologically safe conversation looks like: psychologically safe conversations respect a person's need to be autonomous, understood as competent, and have a sense of belonging. When these needs are met, someone is able to be honest, experiment, and fail without fear of reprisal.

These needs aren't just something made up for this book. They factor into what's known as *self-determination theory*, which gained legitimacy in the mid-1980s thanks to the work of Edward L. Deci and Richard Ryan, coauthors of *Intrinsic Motivation and Self-Determination in Human Behavior*.[2] According to them, these three needs are universal and must be maintained during social interactions (see Table 2.1).

TABLE 2.1 BASIC PSYCHOLOGICAL NEEDS

Need	How It's Expressed	How You Feel When It's Threatened
Autonomy	Ability to self-govern and have a choice	Coerced, browbeaten, robbed of independence
Competence	Ability to feel equal to the challenge we're facing	Micromanaged, condescended to, or unable to challenge ourselves
Relatedness	Ability to feel like a part of the collective and share in its successes	Ignored, passed over, disrespected, less than

This book works off of Deci and Ryan's research, but it's worth noting that there are other ways that psychologists categorize one's

2 Edward L. Deci and Richard Ryan, *Intrinsic Motivation and Self-Determination in Human Behavior* (New York: Springer, 1985).

basic needs. You may be familiar with Maslow's Hierarchy of Needs, which has some critical flaws; namely, it is possible to reside in multiple layers of this pyramid for different aspects in your life. There is also ERG theory, which Clayton Alderfer proposed after furthering Maslow's research on basic human needs. ERG theory states that humans have existence needs, relatedness needs, and growth needs. There are still others like BICEPS, and SCARF.[3] This book won't cover them, but it's helpful to have an awareness and realize the universal threads that weave through them all.

Regardless of how you choose to categorize them, the following is apparent: everyone has basic needs, and when they are under threat or stifled, situations tend to go sour pretty quickly. To wit, disregard someone's basic needs at your own peril. What follows are strategies that help preserve and honor them as you seek resolution to your conflict.

Ask for a No

If someone asks you "Hey, do you have a second?" or "Can we chat real quick?" you have likely agreed to it regardless of whether it's your direct report, boss, or colleague, despite having a full list of things to do or it not being a good time to have that conversation.

You could say "Not now," or "Can you give me a few minutes?" of course. If you're comfortable doing this, in all sincerity, that's great. Not everyone's like you, though.

Those kinds of questions, especially from people at a higher level than you, don't really give you an easy way out. They often come across as demands and impositions rather than requests. You usually don't go into those conversations prepared, nor are you always truly willing.

Instead, try flipping the question. Instead of asking a question that prompts a (begrudging) "yes," ask them one that prompts them to give you a "no."

There's an entire book on this idea called *Start with No.*[4] The author, Jim Camp, says that asking questions like this give your counterpart "the right to veto." It's an autotomy-preserving tactic that signals the other person does, in fact, have a say in when this conversation happens.

3 BICEPS stands for: belonging, improvement or progress, choice, equality or fairness, predictability, significance. SCARF stands for status, certainty, autonomy, relatedness, fairness.

4 Jim Camp, *Start with No* (New York: Crown Business, 2002).

So, instead of asking "Do you have a second?" try these questions in Table 2.2.

TABLE 2.2 ASKING FOR A CONVERSATION

Try These	Avoid These
Are you busy? We need to talk about a couple of things.	Do you have a minute?
Are you swamped right now? I'd really like a word when you're available.	Could we talk real quick?
Is this a bad time?	Can I bug you for a minute?
Mind if we talk? I could use your input on something.	Can I give you some feedback?

By asking for a no, your conversations are calmer and your counterpart more present because they've actively opted into talking. It's also a great signal that you aren't there to bulldoze them.

TIP WHAT IF YOU DON'T FEEL LIKE THIS IS APPROPRIATE?

This book is filled with tools to help you have hard conversations. However, use your judgment on what's right for your situation. If there's a matter that's really urgent or important, you may need to tell someone "We need to talk" and then go for it, psychological safety be damned. You just need to remember that it may be a tougher time since they're not in a great place.

Show You've Put Yourself in Their Shoes

Another key part to starting with safety is showing that you've tried to be empathetic toward the person or their situation. That might be as simple as acknowledging that the conversation you're about to have may be awkward or difficult. If it's especially high stakes, recall the "Cranky Conclusions" section in Chapter 1, "Before the Conversation," and use one to soften the blow a little.

Consider using a cranky conclusion if you're about to deliver news like the person's getting reassigned, that a project they really cared about isn't going to be greenlit, or if they're going through a particularly rough path. See Table 2.3.

TABLE 2.3 PUTTING YOURSELF IN THEIR SHOES

Acknowledgment	Cranky Conclusion	Avoid These
I know this is important to you, so...	You're going to think I'm a bully for saying this.	Don't freak out, but...
I know this will be awkward,	You're going to think I'm overreacting, but hear me out.	I'm not racist, but...
This is going to be hard to hear.	You're going to say I brought this on myself, but stay with me.	I'm not trying to be sexist, but...

You should never use variants of "I'm not [racist, sexist, etc.], but..." for three reasons:

- This doesn't make you look like a straight shooter or cool insider; you just look like you can't keep someone's confidence.
- If you do this, you're opening up a world of potential hurt for yourself and everyone else should you be spreading something incorrect about another person.
- And a "but" negates everything that comes before it, especially in apologies.

Speaking of apologies, you might also find an apology is in order. You need to make sure that you get this right if so. Good apologies have a formula, believe it or not:

- Get right to the point.
- Acknowledge the mistake.
- Apologize.
- Share what you're doing to be better.

So, should Jay want to apologize for what happened with Yara, it might look like this:

> "Yara, I owe you an explanation and apology. When you saw that email, I'd just come off a call with our stakeholders and was a little flustered. I had some insecurity and wanted to make sure that we put our best foot forward, so I added those items to the backlog. That wasn't what we agreed to, and I'm sorry. I shouldn't have done that and violated your trust. I'll make sure to check with you ahead of time before adding new features to our backlog."

And remember: the best apology is changed behavior.

The Safety Spectrum

Nature doesn't generally deal in absolutes. Instead, things exist on a spectrum. How people react in a tough conversation is no exception. Viewing someone's behavior or responses on a spectrum is incredibly beneficial, as it opens you up to the possibility of nuances.

This book uses a spectrum to chart how people respond in tough conversations, and it's called *the safety spectrum* (see Figure 2.2). In it, people tend to fall somewhere between avoidant (putting their head in the sand) and abrasive (potentially putting someone else's head in the sand). The sweet spot is in the middle, engaged.

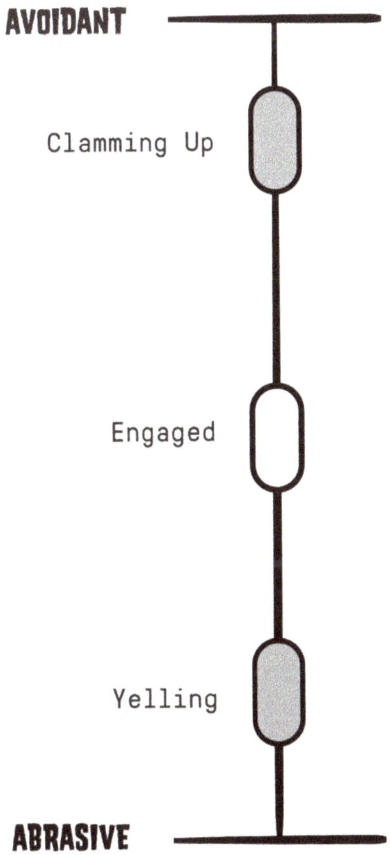

FIGURE 2.2
The safety spectrum is a way to visualize someone's behaviors, organized by avoidant to abrasive.

Knowing where you and the other person fall on this spectrum is key to recentering when the conversation tilts unnecessarily toward one end of the spectrum.

Avoidant

If someone is avoidant, they're trying hard not to have the conversation at all. It's here you'll see people withdraw, give terse responses (e.g., "sure, whatever"), or generally shrink from the conversation (e.g., hunching over, crossing their arms). To wit, this is when someone is cognitively immobilized.

Typically, you'll find that people who are at a lower level than you respond with avoidance and aren't as forthcoming. That's an expected impact when power dynamics are at play.

For those who are more avoidant, you'll have to probe a little and have patience for them to open up. It's entirely possible they won't. It doesn't mean that you won't be able to continue with the conversation—just that they may not be as willing to go along with you.

Abrasive

At the other end of the spectrum are those who have a more abrasive response. Here you might see more defensiveness and intense emotions. This is the opposite of cognitive immobilization: it's a full-scale mobilization of emotion and reaction.

The most common way this presents is yelling, which, in turn, has two types of its own.

The first kind is when someone loses their cool in the moment. That's an understandable, yet still not acceptable, human trait. Your stress and fear responses can trigger some really unexpected, unpleasant responses like that. It still isn't an excuse.

The second type is of more concern: the kind of yelling that's intended to degrade and humiliate. Contrary to the first kind, this isn't acceptable, nor is it okay. This kind of yelling is, without hyperbole, emotional abuse. For decades, researchers have acknowledged that this type of yelling and related aggressions is classified under the umbrella of abuse.

If you've ever wondered what, when, and why to yell at someone, here's a handy, somewhat snarky chart in Table 2.4.

TABLE 2.4 WHEN IS IT OKAY TO YELL?

Valid	Invalid
The person is in danger of mortally harming themself by stepping into oncoming traffic.	They deserve it.
You're trying to communicate across a chasm as big as the Grand Canyon and don't have cell service.	You're under a lot of stress.
They said that's their preferred way of receiving feedback.	The project, team, or business is in danger.

If you're yelling at someone for any reason in the "Invalid" column, apologize and cut it out, full stop. You've likely focused on what you believe someone deserves and are transferring your own stress onto them. That isn't healthy for either one of you.

Instead, focus on doing what's right for the situation, for them, for everyone. There are so many better ways to deal with frustration than yelling.

When you spot abrasive behaviors like this, proceed carefully: while it isn't likely, there is a chance that things may actually become physically unsafe. Chapter 3, "People Losing Control," gets into much more detail.

Engaged

In the middle of the spectrum, you'll find engaged. This is where you want to be.

Being engaged doesn't mean everyone speaks like an emotionless automaton with perfectly organized summaries of their positions. Not at all: that's not what safety is about. Instead, they're authentic, thinking and feeling, and open to discussion. Emotions and thoughts exist in relative harmony and everyone's able to hear opposing or contrasting viewpoints and find a way forward together. Much of what's to come in this book is about keeping someone in the engaged part of the spectrum.

Share Facts

After you've done what you can to get the other person to buy into the conversation by starting with safety, it's time to lay out your facts that you gathered in Chapter 1. As a reminder, here's why you want to start with facts: they're the most objective, powerful, and the least risky thing you can do in a discussion (see Figure 2.3).

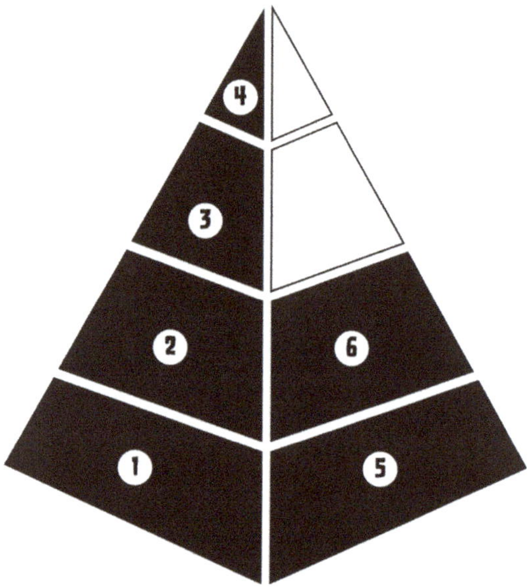

FIGURE 2.3
Step 6: Share facts.

Here are the facts:

- Your friend declined a meeting invitation five minutes before it started.
- Your friend also didn't respond to your previous three messages.

It's entirely possible the other person will come back with facts that you didn't consider. That's fine, because you're in a conversation trying to sort something out with another person, not defending a master's thesis.

Share Conclusions and Goals

Now that you've got the facts out there, it's time to help them see the effects and share your goals (see Figure 2.4). Here, you'll talk about how this made you feel and how it impacted your ability to work. We'll use principles of nonviolent communication to frame your conclusions.

Typically, that involves using phrases like "It makes me feel like," or "It seems like." These phrases signal that you aren't assuming you're correct or have passed judgment. Doing so deters defensiveness because you've led the other person to your conclusion instead of forcing it on them.

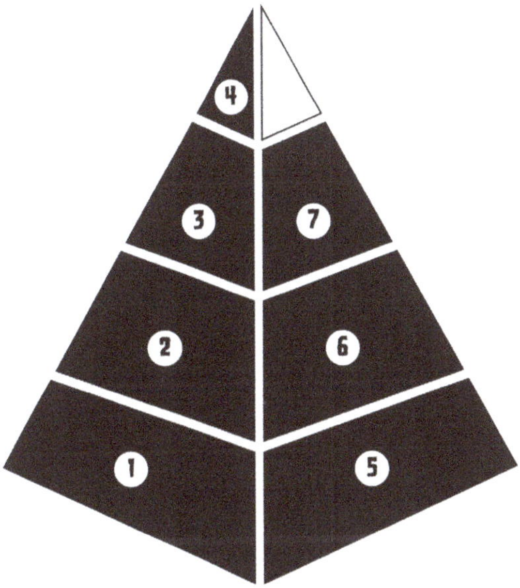

FIGURE 2.4
Step 7: Share conclusions and goals.

Table 2.5 shows a list of things you can say to signal that you haven't reached any firm conclusions. The phrases on the right-hand column are too strong and closed off or too weak and undercutting the argument.

TABLE 2.5 TRY THESE PHRASES

Try These Phrases	Avoid These Phrases
It seems like...	We all know that...
It looks like...	Fact is...
That leads me to think that...	Isn't that the case?
This begs the question of...	Did you take leave of your senses?
I'm feeling like...	I'm probably going off the deep end here, but...
I'm starting to believe that...	You're such a...

TIP **HANG ON A SECOND, THIS SEEMS DISINGENUOUS!**

In one of my workshops, a student asked if using phrases from the table above was disingenuous, manipulative, or inauthentic. It was such an impactful question that I want to address it here. There's nothing wrong with speaking in a way that leaves the door open to discussion. Your goal in situations like these is to strike a balance between your confidence in your conclusions and openness to discussion—speaking tentatively does just this.

Striking the Right Balance

You'll want to state your conclusions confidently and ensure that you don't come on too strong or too weak. Being too strong or too weak harms conversation in different ways by undercutting either you or the other person.

Too Strong

Coming in too strong shuts the other person down because this kind of language doesn't invite conversation. Instead, you're signaling you've already firmed up your conclusion and have passed judgment. This approach harms the safety of the conversation as well as pre-empting deeper discussion. It might sound like this:

> "You didn't reply to my last three messages and canceled our last meeting five minutes beforehand. Everyone knows you're bitter, so cut the crap and say what you mean."

While it would undoubtedly feel incredible to say—it might well be true, too—this reduces the recipient to a label. By doing this, you've dehumanized them and cut off everything except their fight, flight, or freeze responses.

Too Weak

Coming in too weak hurts your message. This self-deprecating talk is a disservice to you, your message, and the other person. Too weak sounds like this:

> "You didn't reply to my last three messages and canceled our last meeting five minutes beforehand. I'm probably being oversensitive here, but I don't think you are enjoying working with me."

This may seem like a gentle approach, but it goes too far and only undermines your own credibility. Statements like this signal that you don't really believe what you're saying. And if you don't believe it, why should they?

You've had your entire life so far to understand your feelings. Don't do that lived experience a disservice. Own what you believe and be willing to be shown where you're wrong.

Well-Balanced

Being well-balanced ties it all together nicely. You're sharing your conclusion based on what you've learned, stated so clearly and confidently, and now you can let them take the next step of opening it up to them.

> "You didn't reply to my last three messages and canceled our last meeting five minutes beforehand. I'm starting to think our relationship is in trouble. Can we talk about it?"

Open It Up

You can't have a conversation without dialog. Otherwise, it's just bulldozing monologue. Now that you've laid out your facts and talked about the impact they had, you open it up to them so everyone can get to the bottom of this (see Figure 2.5).

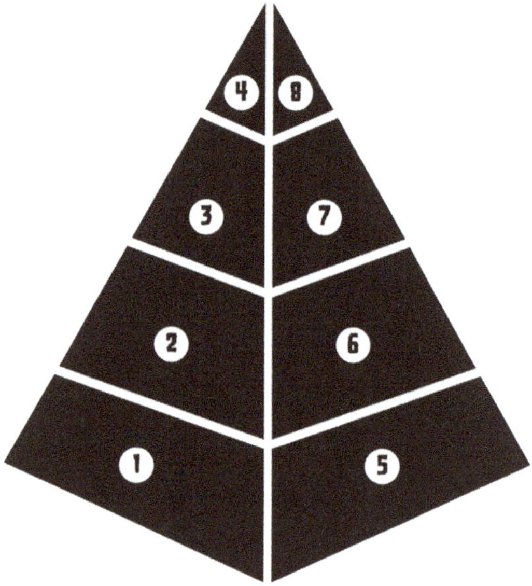

FIGURE 2.5
Step 8: Open it up.

Open-Ended Questions vs. Closed Questions

You should always prefer open-ended questions. Always. They invite more conversation and understanding. They're what draw out avoidant people and calm down abrasive responses. If your question starts with words like "what," or "how," you're off to a good start.

In contrast, closed questions invite confirmation and stifle discussion. Both have their place, as closed questions can be helpful (more on that in a moment), but the one you'll want to employ most here is the open-ended question.

You probably noticed that "why" didn't make the list. Here's the reasoning: it's a defensive trigger. "Why" implies judgment, that you've reached conclusions, and that they need to be justified and defended. Putting the other person on the defensive is usually the last thing you want to do. Questions starting with "what" and "how" get you far more insight than a simple "why"—and without the hassle.

Still curious about how that works? Which of these two questions would make you feel more comfortable answering:

1. Why were you late again today?
2. What caused you to miss our meeting today?

If you're like more readers, you'd choose the "what" question. The "why" question makes you wonder if your explanation is good enough and up to the other person's standards. "What," by contrast, is a nonjudgmental question that seeks understanding.

Closed questions have their place and are useful in confirming facts (if someone was in a certain meeting). They can also be misused to browbeat or trap someone in a conversation.

One such abuse is what this book calls a "yes chain." That's a series of questions where the obvious and expected answer is yes. After a few rounds of "yes" questions, the asker arrives at their point. And because you've agreed with the previous questions, they argue, you must agree with their conclusion. That's a bad faith argument that you shouldn't ever pull on someone.

To bring it back around, let's look at the questions you should consider asking the other person shown in Table 2.6.

TABLE 2.6 OPEN-ENDED VS. CLOSED QUESTIONS

Try These Questions (Open-Ended)	Avoid These Questions (Closed)
How do you see it?	Isn't that the case?
What are your thoughts?	Am I wrong?
Can you help me understand?	Does that make sense?
What am I missing here?	Why did you do this?

Managing the Back and Forth

Now comes the easy part. Really. You've already done the hard part, which was starting the conversation in the first place. The rest is far easier in comparison.

Here's where the deeper insights and paths forward begin to emerge. There's still work to be done, though. Picture this like an archaeological dig, where coaxing a buried object to the surface requires a delicate, practiced hand. That's what you're going to learn how to do next.

Here, you'll rely on actively listening, being honest, and calling back to your shared goals. What you learn next helps you uncover a mutually beneficial path forward.

Reflecting

Active listening is helpful and shows you're involved in the conversation. But meaning can get lost from what one person thinks, to what they say, to what you hear. Remember, your brain often works so quickly that you've arrived at a conclusion without realizing it.

To counter that, you can use reflecting to make sure that you're both truly understanding each other. It's important not to do this all the time, because it will make you sound like a robot. Used authentically and sparingly, reflecting builds a shared understanding and signals that you're really hearing the other person (and not just planning your next response), as you're often using their own words in your responses to them. It can also be used to deflect or defuse anger. It takes three forms: echoing, labeling, and summarizing (see Table 2.7).

TABLE 2.7 REFLECTING

Type of Reflection	Echo	Label	Summarizing
How They Work	Repeat certain words or phrases verbatim in a neutral tone.	Tentatively assign an emotion to what they're saying.	Repeat back the main points, asking for clarification or if there's something they want to add.
Example	Stabbed you in the back?	"Oh man, it seems like I really kicked up some dust here."	"Okay, there's a lot to unpack here. Let me put it back to you so I know I'm getting everything (summarize it). What am I missing?"

If you choose to echo, give the conversation a beat before saying anything else. This frees you from becoming defensive or exerting effort in crafting a reply and leaves space for the other person to contribute. Echoes are a targeted approach to get them to explain the emotions and driving forces behind what they're saying. If you're feeling antagonized, this is also a perfect tool to use because you're redirecting the other person's energy back onto them. It's like verbal kung fu.

You can also use a label. As discussed earlier, it's best to speak tentatively here—no one wants to be told how they feel in a conversation like this. This can also achieve the goal of showing that you're listening and give the other person a chance to correct any misinterpretations.

Lastly, reflecting can take the form of summarizing what they said. Make sure that while you're doing this, you're listening to them. Like, really listening. Not the kind of listening where you're just nodding along and patronizing them, all the while planning your next response. This is the kind of listening that pays full attention to the other person. After all, you're only able to resolve the problem once you fully understand it. You can't do that if you aren't listening to the other person.

Putting It All Together

Here's how the conversation could go:

Our Conversation

> Yara: Hey, Jay, are you busy? I want to talk about the roadmap updates I saw last night. I told you in a previous meeting that we shouldn't add them right now, because our research showed users don't want them. We also agreed no one can make a unilateral decision because those decisions have a huge impact on the product.
>
> Jay: Okay . . .
>
> Yara: It seems like you don't trust me and the team, or you aren't considering the implications of their requests. What am I missing here? Can you help me understand?
>
> Jay: Well, they're in charge, right? We gotta do what they say and make them happy.
>
> Yara: Make them happy?
>
> Jay: Yeah, they want to succeed. They say it, we do it.
>
> Yara: Okay, that's my job, too. Success, not happiness. Just adding them to a roadmap makes it hard for me, you, and them to succeed. We need to see how what they want maps to what our users want. If we don't evaluate them, we'll waste time and money, which will be much worse in the long run. Did you evaluate them?
>
> Jay: Oof, I didn't. I'm sorry, I was moving too fast and got stuck on doing what they said.
>
> Yara: Okay. We need to make sure we're setting ourselves set up for success, so how can we figure this out?
>
> Jay: They didn't say I had to add them; I just did it without thinking. I'll go talk to them, tell them about the research you did, that I was

moving too fast, and need to make sure that we're doing what's best for the app and our users. I'm sorry, I panicked. I'll make sure you're included on these things beforehand. I didn't intend any harm.

Yara: Thanks.

Final Thoughts

If you're lucky, this is where you both realize that you fully understand the issue at hand and know what to do going forward. If you're luckier, you understood what got you to that spot in the first place.

It isn't always that easy, as what follows can take so many different forms. Maybe your goals were at odds, maybe you couldn't agree, or maybe they just lost control. The remainder of this book focuses on all of those varied and unusual scenarios. You can rest assured, though, that what you learned in these chapters is what you need to navigate what comes next, no matter what form it takes. Here is a recap:

- Start with safety and get the other person to buy into the conversation. You can use questions that prompt them to reply with a "no."
- It's important to demonstrate empathy at the outset. Leading off with a cranky conclusion can be helpful as it shows you've put yourself in their shoes.
- Consider their reactions and body language in terms of the safety spectrum. If they're avoidant, you may need to draw them out. If they're abrasive, you may need to calm them down.
- After everyone's ready for the conversation, lead off with your facts. Facts are the basis of all your conclusions, and you want to start with them. Facts are objective, powerful, and the least risky things about a conversation.
- Share your conclusions and goals by speaking tentatively about how you're seeing the situation, but don't water yourself down, especially around your goals. Strike the right balance between confidence and openness to discussion.
- Use open-ended questions to invite discussions, avoiding questions that prompt defensiveness (such as those that begin with "why").
- During your conversation, manage the back and forth with reflecting. You can echo what they said, label it, or summarize it to continue to dig deeper.

CHAPTER 3

People Losing Control

You're going to find yourself in situations where someone has lost control. It's not great, but it happens, and you're going to need some practical advice. Whether they're yelling, throwing things, or pounding fists, this chapter will give you what you need to navigate the situation or safely remove yourself from it.

Before continuing, just be aware that the tactics that follow may not seem natural, normal, or even fair. Liken them, if you will, to the advice you get for bear encounters when going camping in the wilderness. Common advice for that situation includes not running away from the bear, or rushing it, or talking to it in low tones (which indicates you are prey). It's weird not to run and counter to your instincts, but those are proven methods to keep you safe. The tactics you learn here are written in that same spirit.

It is also monstrously unfair that you, the target of someone's aggression, bear the burden in this situation. That said, while you live in an unfair world, you can still find ways to protect yourself.

The Problem

The problem began when Jeff, an Agile consultant, was brought in to assist Guillermo's team. "They were a large financial institution, and the company was struggling with planning the work of 10 development teams for the next six months." He continued, "It was really tough, Guillermo managed 10 teams, which is a lot of dependencies to consider."

Guillermo was under pressure from his partners, too. He felt that he'd lose credibility, and ultimately his job, if bringing in Jeff failed.

The problems began when Jeff and Guillermo discussed their priorities. The conversation went like this:

> **Jeff:** "Okay, let's talk about these priorities we have for the next six months and rank them."
>
> **Guillermo:** "You can't rank them, because everything is high priority and has to get done within this time frame. We agreed on this with our business partner."
>
> **Jeff:** "Of course, but the engineering team can't work on everything at once. There are too many dependencies that prevent that from being possible, so we have to prioritize their work so that we manage those dependencies and tackle the priorities appropriately."

Jeff said in his interview for this book: "That didn't work, so I took another tack." After careful, thoughtful research and interviews with the engineering team, he crafted a plan that balanced both the engineering team's dependencies and the leadership's priorities for the next six months.

"I was pretty proud of it, given that it was such a large, complex problem." Jeff put those priorities up on a board, and the team felt relieved at having a clear view of what they needed to do.

It was a short-lived victory.

Shortly after posting the plan, Guillermo stormed in while Jeff was talking with the team. He tore the board down and got in Jeff's face, screaming at him in front of the group.

He said, "This is *not* our priority list! You can't just move things around like this. Everything is the same priority!" He went on to say, "We're going to get annihilated by our partners if they see this because that's not what we talked to leadership about! It's *all* important and has to be done at the same time!"

The Solution

The goal for any conversation where yelling is involved is deceptively simple: *slow it down.* You want to slow the conversation down because, at this point, someone's emotions have taken over and reason goes out the window. And without reason, you can't have a dialog. And without dialog, you can't have a resolution.

Luckily, you can build muscle memory that helps you in situations like these.

Understand Why People Lose Control

First, it's important to understand what happened. Most people lose control and yell because they feel disrespected, misunderstood, or are scared of losing control of a situation, so these yellers resort to emotional violence to get their way. Or as behavioral science expert Susan Weinschenk put it in an interview: "insecurity." This insecurity destroys any psychological safety for anyone else in the conversation.

Weinschenk went on to say, "Whatever the reason is that the person feels insecure, it will make the conflict much worse for them because they're going to get very defensive."

In situations where yelling is involved, the amygdala perceives this as an existential threat and jumps into action. This is called an *amygdala hijack,* a term coined by Daniel Goleman in his book *Emotional Intelligence: Why It Can Matter More Than IQ*.[1]

NOTE AMYGDALA HIJACK

> An amygdala hijack is an emotional response that is immediate, overwhelming, and out of measure with the actual stimulus because it has triggered a much more significant emotional threat.

In an amygdala hijack, the amygdala redirects blood flow from the neocortex to the mammalian and reptilian parts of your brain, so it's much harder to think straight or to resist your fight/flight/freeze urge. Better put, it cuts off blood to the part of your brain that reasons.

Weinschenk said, "For some people, when they come up against conflict, it's going to set up what in psychology we would call 'arousal,' and that doesn't mean sexual arousal, it just means paying attention. That's not necessarily a bad thing." She went on to say that some people may perceive some kinds of conflict pleasurably, but it's downright scary for others.

Re-Center

When something is off-balance, you need to steady it so that it can come back to center. When it comes to tough conversations, you'll find that a little clarification is in order.

The first way Jeff could re-center was forcing a breather. That could mean a change in environment or a forced pause. Since the team was still present for this confrontation, Jeff had the chance to dismiss them and said, "Whoa, whoa, whoa, hang on. Let's just the two of us talk and let the team get back to work. [Then after the team leaves] Okay, what am I missing here?"

Having that moment (the breather) would give Jeff time to collect himself. It might also take a little oxygen from Guillermo's fiery power trip. Jeff's move also served to short-circuit any attempt by Guillermo at going on said fiery power trip, as he had taken the team out of the equation.

---

1 Daniel Goleman, *Emotional Intelligence: Why It Can Matter More Than IQ* (New York: Bantam Books, 1996).

Another way Jeff could reply is by using nonviolent "I statements." (See Chapter 1, "Before the Conversation.") This approach helps communicate needs while reducing the chance that someone gets even more offensive.

You will also want to avoid labels. If Guillermo is screaming or yelling, the situation can backfire on Jeff, if he uses labels like "yell" or "scream." Here's why: when you label behaviors, your counterpart may get even more defensive. That's because you're telling them about the surface-level behavior (yelling) and not what they're doing (defending something important that justifies their actions).

Use Refocusing Statements

You'll find that occasionally the other person gets tripped up in a misunderstanding. Given that the blood flow to the neocortex is suspended, it isn't a surprise.

Refocusing statements are the ideal tool to use for this situation. They comprise a statement that addresses the misinterpretation and reestablishes the focus of your goal. They might look like this:

> I'm not saying ______________; I'm saying ______________.
> Or, if necessary, add: What am I not seeing?

For Jeff, it could be:

- "I'm not saying everything isn't important; I'm saying that the team can only work on one thing at a time. Am I missing something?"
- "I'm not saying your priorities don't matter; I'm saying this is the order in which they can happen based on what your team's capable of. Where are we missing each other?"

It's a subtle but effective shift that acknowledges the misunderstanding and moves toward clarity.

Establish a Shared Vision

There's some peace in the idea that, when you step back far enough, most people want the same thing. It's difficult to see that notion when you're in the thick of it. So, a shared vision statement can help you here. A shared vision statement focuses on common goals to identify a shared definition of success, and it illuminates how individual actions affect the greater whole. A shared vision is usually present in a situation, but it can get obscured.

Asking questions like these can help you realize the shared vision together:

- What's the core issue here?
- How does this fit into your objective?
- What's the end goal that you're trying to accomplish?
- You're doing *x*, which prevents me from doing *y*. What are you hoping to achieve?

With Jeff, "I asked him what his real issue was here? Was it that he was looking bad in front of others?" He said it was, and the fact that I assigned numbers to the items indicated that some things were more important than others. That was certainly not how my brain worked, because I considered them to be an indicator of which order to approach them. We just revisualized it on a timeline and kept it mostly as-is."

Look Out For...

Here are the main ways that situations like these can go sideways and how to address them. If you aren't careful, things can escalate, and you'll find yourself sucked into the toxic soup of cortisol and survival instincts.

Escalations

There's always a chance that someone who is yelling will escalate. After all, they've already demonstrated their volatility by yelling in the first place. Guillermo's already shown that he can get physical, as evidenced by his tearing down the board. Caution is warranted.

If you decide to stay in the conversation, focus on the following:

- **Tone of voice:** The louder you get, the louder they will get. Try staying at a neutral level.
- **Body language:** Try to keep your arms down and avoid crossing them. Avoid sharp gestures.
- **Pace of speech:** Try to speak slowly.

Each of these responses to potential escalations signals calmness, and that you're unbothered or nonchalant. You can also use statements like the following:

- Whoa, where's this coming from? We're on the same team!
- I get that this is hard, but we can't fix it if we're talking like this.

There's always a chance you won't feel comfortable staying in a conversation like this. It may not be worth your time or effort. If you want to gauge that, Weinschenk mentioned there are five levels of attachment that people can have for an idea. Depending on the level, where you are will affect how, or if, you're going to have any success in staying. One is the lowest level and five is the highest.

"If you're at level five," Weinschenk said, "that's really out there. The more attached you are to what you believe, the harder it is going to be for anyone to interact with you."

If you feel someone is at a five, or they're crossing a boundary for you, have statements like this ready to go. And be ready to follow through:

- "I can't be in a conversation like this. We'll talk later when things cool off."
- "When you raise your voice, I can't think straight."
- "You don't get to talk to me like that."

Here's how it went with Jeff and Guillermo:

> Guillermo: "This is *not* our priority list! You can't just move things around like this. Everything is the same priority! We're going to get annihilated by our partners if they see this because that's not what we talked to leadership about! It's *all* important and has to be done at the same time!"
>
> Guillermo: "You damned consultants, you think you can come in here knowing everything and change whatever you want. It doesn't work that way, asshole!"
>
> Jeff: "We can talk when you lower your voice. I'm going to step out for a few minutes and come back." (Then he left the room.)

Getting Sucked In

You aren't going to be any good here if you get caught up in the situation. A little mindfulness always helps, and it's important to make sure that you're aware of your breathing, which can both prevent you from going over the edge and take you back from it. There's a breathing technique the U.S. Navy SEALs use called *box breathing*, which is a tremendous help in tense times. Box breathing calms your stress hormones and lowers your heart rate just by breathing on a 1:1:1:1 cadence. The U.S. Navy SEALs use it to reduce stress and increase focus. If it can work for them in ultra-high-stakes situations, it can help your conflicts in the office.

Figure 3.1 shows how it works: inhale for the count of 3, hold it for 3, exhale for 3, wait for 3, and begin again.

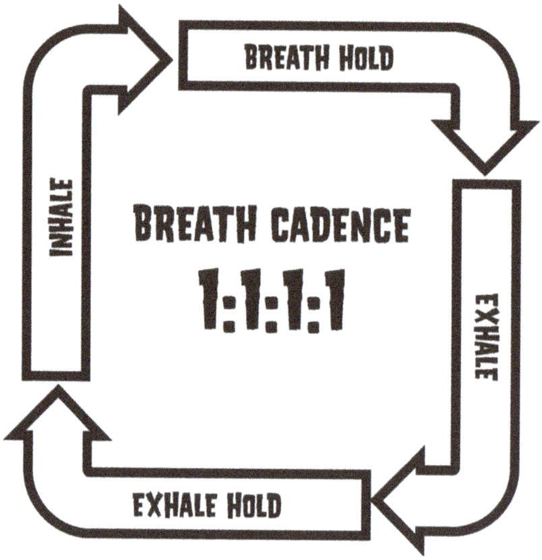

FIGURE 3.1
Box breathing is helpful at keeping you grounded in your body, especially in high stress situations.

This is a perfect thing to do when someone else is yelling. Focus on your breath and figure out how you're going to slow this situation down. It's also the first thing you should do when you step away from the situation, in order to let the other person cool down (as well as yourself) before going back into the room.

Further, it's awful to be yelled at and stuck in experiences like this. But if you yell back, no matter how much they deserve it, the situation is going to spiral out of control. It's best to pull out in moments like these.

Final Thoughts

These conversations can go any number of ways, including escalating beyond your comfort level. Always listen to your gut and know that it's okay to leave at any time—there's no reason why you should feel obligated to stay in a situation like this. Here are some ways you can handle an unexpected situation:

- Slow it down. Speak slowly and calmly.
- Ask questions to pull someone out of their anger spiral. Remember to start questions with "what" and "how" to keep things neutral.
- Try refocusing. "I'm not saying *x*, I'm saying *y*."
- Remind people that you're on the same team. Try to establish a shared vision.
- Have some statements prepared in advance if you need to get out of a situation. This advance preparation will come in handy if you find yourself surprised by someone yelling at you.
- It doesn't matter what someone deserves, do the right thing and don't yell back.

CHAPTER 4

Lying and Gaslighting

Dealing with someone who is lying can be a tricky business. Obviously, a lot of emotion, doubt, and work goes into figuring out how to address the lies. It gets worse when you add another form of manipulation to the mix: gaslighting, which is a type of deflection and manipulation where someone tries to convince you that you don't know what you are doing or are otherwise incompetent.

If the term *gaslighting* isn't familiar to you, it comes from a 1938 stage play called *Gas Light* by Patrick Hamilton, which he later adapted into a film in 1944, starring Ingrid Bergman. In the film, Bergman's character is convinced by her husband that she's mentally ill so that he can steal her jewelry and money. (It's also beautifully shot, by the way.) The term has gained popularity since the 1980s and has made its way into the workplace and dictionary.

To continue the metaphor, this chapter will help you create your own sort of gas mask that protects you against the noxious fumes that are coming from someone who is lying and gaslighting. You'll learn how to neutralize their tactics, in order to have the conversation you need and the outcome you want. The focus of this chapter has a sizable self-defense aspect to it because the strategies employed by people who gaslight are multipronged and dizzyingly confusing.

The Problem

Nancy was a senior design director at a tech company who worked with Freddy, her manager.

She said, "We had regular, biweekly one-on-ones. But they were just us, no records, no notes that I ever saw. I regularly asked for feedback on how I could improve, because I knew that no one was perfect."

She asked that question several times over the course of a year, and the response was always the same from Freddy: "Everything's great, you're great. You're doing a good job. I have no feedback."

So, when Freddy and someone from HR asked to have a conversation with her about her performance issues, she was understandably shocked. The chat went like this:

> **HR Person:** "Hi, Nancy. We're here to talk about your performance issues and create a performance improvement plan to help you."
>
> **Nancy:** "Wait, what?"

HR: "Freddy shared that you have performance issues around delivering your work on time, and we want to work on fixing this."

Nancy: "Freddy, this is the first you've ever mentioned any performance issues with me."

Freddy: "No, in all of our one-on-ones, we've talked through these issues."

Nancy: "Oh no, that's not true. I have repeatedly asked for feedback. You always said I was doing great, and you had no feedback. You have never led me to believe that there was room to improve anything, or that there was anything you wanted to see me do differently."

Nancy ultimately kept her job but was reassigned to another manager. The HR person later confided in Nancy that Freddy had a pattern of making things up and denying the other person's viewpoint. Further, the HR person said that this situation wasn't going to affect Nancy's future with the company. While it didn't solve the problem for the others whom Freddy might undermine, Nancy was off the hook.

This situation still came at a cost, particularly around career growth. Nancy felt that her career was stagnant when she could have grown it during the time with Freddy. To find out that her boss said she was "failing" despite never having received any negative feedback was destabilizing and made her question herself.

The rest of this chapter focuses on what the conversation could have looked like had Nancy pursued the matter further. But before you have any conversation like this, recognize that truth, like everything else, exists on a spectrum. To understand it, "The Truth Spectrum" in Table 4.1 will help guide your conversations.

NOTE **REMEMBER: KEEP IT HUMAN**

Don't make the mistake of reducing someone to a label, such as a liar, an idiot, or anything else that strips them of their humanity. It dehumanizes the person and complicates the situation unnecessarily. Instead, view them as someone who is not telling the truth and is not being transparent, or whose behavior is out of bounds. This way, you'll deal with the situation and the person differently because you're still letting them retain their humanity. When you take that away, you're doing to them what they did to you.

TABLE 4.1 THE TRUTH SPECTRUM

	Truth	Miscommunication	Omission	Lie	Gaslighting
Description	Both people tell each other what they know.	One or both has incomplete or incorrect information.	One has information that they are withholding from the other.	One knows the truth but is deliberately telling the other person something different to harm them.	Both have the same information, but one is convincing the other that they don't know what they're talking about.
Outcome	Ideal.	Less ideal. No harm, no foul.	Less ideal. Can be a requirement for the job or can be unethical.	Shady. Unethical. Lying is personal and subjective.	Emotional abuse.

When you consider where your situation is on the truth spectrum, it will help you proceed accordingly. If it's a miscommunication, the remedy can be as simple as saying "Okay, I'm hearing two different things here. You're saying *x*, but I'm hearing *y*. Let's find out what's missing." If it's more serious, then read on.

The Solution

When truth and reality are in conflict, you need to shift your mindset and responses. Other parts of this book will encourage you to give someone the benefit of the doubt and assume a positive intent. Never forget that it is entirely possible you're dealing with a good person who made an honest mistake or an omission to save face. What follows can still help you in those situations.

Assuming positive intent becomes less effective when dealing with more serious deceptions—those that are harmful or catastrophic to a team, business, individual, or overarching goals. When gaslighting is also present, its harmful impact prevents positive intent from being a viable approach. The toxic nature of gaslighting undermines any benefit from assuming that the other party has good intentions.

People who lie and gaslight rely on your limited store of willpower and powers of recollection. So, the worst thing you can do with someone who is actively manipulating the truth is to go in unprepared. Gaslighting, in particular, requires a strong approach, because the primary strategy is to pit you against yourself while the other person tries to get their way. This means that you need to go in and speak from a place of strength and facts, and to stay focused.

Highlight the Lie

In conversation with Nancy, Freddy said something that wasn't true, and it was going to cause problems for Nancy if she didn't address it directly and immediately.

> Freddy: "Why haven't you delivered the product roadmap? You said you'd do it by yesterday."

How Nancy (and you) should reply to someone who is lying depends on how they reply. Here are some solutions that might work:

- **Call their bluff.** Call it every single time by pointing out the contradictions. When you make them do the work of answering these, they construct a house of cards. What they're saying will stop matching reality, and when held up to scrutiny, no part of it will stand up to the weight of truth. So, you're letting them trap themselves.
- **Respond with silence.** If what they say sounds like an obvious lie, simply say nothing. Look off into the distance as if you're processing what they said, or stare directly into their eyes and remain silent. If someone is lying, they won't be able to stand it and will often walk back or retract their lie.
- **Reflect and repeat it back to them.** Remember that reflecting techniques are powerful tools here. By repeating their lie back to them and then leaving silence in the air, you make them answer their own lie.

Here's what Nancy could say:

- "I didn't say that. You said that you'd finalize and deliver the roadmap. You said, 'Don't worry about that, I've got it handled.'"
- "I said I'd do it by yesterday?" [stays silent]
- "I didn't. I would remember saying that, because it's such a big deal for us."

Let's say that Freddy dug in further. He could deny that he ever said that, and the two most effective ways of tackling defiant liars are these:

- **Stick to your experience.** "That's what I heard."
- **Call back to the record, if one exists.** "It's in our previous email and Slack channels."

Document It

Speaking of records, if you have a recording or a transcript of what the other person said, it can help you in moments when they are denying the truth. Getting a written record of a conversation isn't as tricky (or underhanded) as it may seem. Most devices have a built-in live transcription tool, but online services exist, too. By using a recording, you've got an easy way of pulling up the conversation to call out the differences in both stories.

NOTE RECORDING CONVERSATIONS SAFELY

Always try to record with consent. Recording someone without their consent could be illegal. Laws vary from state to state and country to country. It's best to make sure that you aren't going to do something that could land you in hot water, or at least be aware of the risks.

The best approach here is to simply make it a matter of fact or procedure for your conversation. For example:

> "Hey, I'm trying a new way of taking notes that helps me stay focused on the conversation. I've got an app to take meeting notes for us by getting a transcript of our conversation. Is that okay with you?"

or:

> "Mind if I try something? I have this neat app that takes notes for me by transcribing our audio and helps me stay focused on what's important. I can send you the notes when we're done, too."

This way, should you find yourself in a situation where someone is giving you contradictory information in the moment or retracts it later, you can refer back to your notes pretty quickly and discuss the discrepancy.

Nancy could also make a habit of sending a follow-up message that covers the key points of conversation and what each person agreed to do. If there's ever any difference between reality and what the other person says, you've got something to refer to.

Consistency is key here. The more you document via email and make it the norm, the more you avoid getting snared in a trap. It's as simple as this:

> "Here's what we covered in our meeting today. Let me know if any of this isn't right, otherwise we'll assume it's correct.
>
> - Thing One
> - Thing Two"

There's a chance the other person will ignore the email, but now you've got something on your side that they don't have, which is evidence. Hard evidence is a heck of a lot harder to refute than the "I-said-you-said" conversation. By doing this, you're making a case for yourself while hardly putting in any effort at all.

Similarly, be as public as you can about what you're doing day-to-day. The more people who see what you're doing, the less chance that anyone will be able to do you any harm. You'll become a less interesting and vulnerable target because what you said and did are a matter of public record. That doesn't mean it will go away entirely, but it does reduce the target that's on your back.

Change the Format

Lies thrive in the dark and wither in the face of evidence. If you change the game, it's harder for those who lie and gaslight you to win. So, why not employ a few variations on standard meeting types that can work to your advantage?

Stand-Ups and Retrospectives

You might have heard of a stand-up. If not, it's a quick, usually daily, 15-minute meeting that teams who practice Agile software delivery do. It's intended to minimize unnecessary work, lengthy meetings, and promote visibility into what's happening. Each member on the team tells what they're working on and what they need help with. Adding or publicizing the results from these meetings can help you position yourself in a safe place.

There's also a retrospective, which is a look back at what happened recently. It typically happens every week or two. In it, a team discusses what went well and what could have gone better.

These practices help in two ways: they produce evidence and force a time limit. There's an added bonus that many companies (as of this writing, at least) practice these procedures, so it's likely to be accepted more easily.

Here's how the stand-up format can go. Each person can fill something in individually and discuss it with the group at large.

Person	I'm working on...	I feel good about...	I need feedback on...	You need me to know...
Nancy				
Freddy				

If your company uses Slack, there's even a nice Slackbot automation that can send this out on the regular channel for you. The important thing here is that you're giving structure to the conversation and making it more difficult for the person to go off-script. Yes, they could ignore it, but don't give up and gently redirect them if that's the case.

As for retrospectives, meetings could look like this for you:

Person	I felt good about...	I wondered about...	I feel like I could have done better about...
Nancy			
Freddy			

Make sure to ask everyone who attends to come prepared to discuss these topics. Giving them a little homework helps you here. Also, be sure that you send follow-ups via email. When you get the results of this, you'll have evidence that can be used if the person is lying or gaslighting.

Look Out For . . .

The tactics others employ here are focused on confusing you or killing something by a thousand cuts. Sometimes, in the worst cases, there will be outright provocations. When challenged, someone who is lying or gaslighting will likely try to change things up on you. They may throw more information at you, try to confuse you even more, or use a host of other tools. With the tactics and tools that come next, you'll be prepared and ready to address whatever happens.

Deflecting

Deflecting can look like someone picking apart every little part of your reality, critiquing your approach, or using a cycle of positive and negative emotions to manipulate you (see Table 4.2). The adversary can even change the pace or density of information to further confuse you.

TABLE 4.2 DEFLECTIONS

Type of Deflection	Description
Death by a thousand cuts	Picking apart specific examples one by one.
Tone policing	Making the problem they caused to be about your reaction or approach rather than addressing the core issue.
Changes in demeanor or information density	Going faster or giving too much information in order to confuse or frustrate you.
Praising and provoking	Using compliments or insults to shock you into submission.

Death by a Thousand Cuts

Earlier in this book, you learned how powerful both patterns and examples are when having a hard conversation. But that's another thing that goes out the window if gaslighting is in play. Being gaslit is an attempt to whittle away at your understanding and the basis for having the conversation.

Someone who is gaslighting you may try to single out each little event and dismantle it. It may sound like:

- "Give me one clear example."
- "Tell me when this happened. Maybe it can be easily explained."

Be careful not to play this game, because the actual intent is to shred your argument into ribbons. Instead, try this:

- "This isn't about one isolated incident but a pattern of behavior that is concerning."
- "This is about a consistent pattern, not just one example. Focusing on isolated incidents misses the bigger picture of what I'm trying to express."

- "I'm expressing how I feel because I want to resolve this, not debate the validity of my feelings."
- "I've given you examples in the past, and we've gone over this. What's important now is addressing how we move forward."
- "It's not just about specific events, it's about how these actions make me feel repeatedly. I need us to look at the overall impact, not just the details."
- "My point isn't to argue over details but to discuss how these patterns are affecting our relationship."
- "I'm not going to relitigate the past. We need to focus on how we can change things going forward."

Tone Policing

Tone policing is a particularly nefarious tactic, and it occurs when someone else takes issue with your approach or response to the problem they created. There's a logical fallacy associated with this one—the appeal to hypocrisy. And because it's a fallacy, you know not to buy into it.

It is impossible for someone to have a perfect approach all the time. Even the most cool-headed among us are prone to snapping from time to time.

The fortunate part of this tactic is that it is fairly easy to spot and therefore equally easy to redirect. Hypothetically, should Freddy say something that prompts Nancy's emotions to get the better of her instead of addressing the issue she brought to him, Nancy could say:

- "My approach is secondary to the problem we're having. Let's take the energy that we're spending on that approach and refocus it on the problem at hand."
- "If you were as considerate about the situation as you are to my approach, would we even be here?"

If Nancy is successful in getting Freddy to focus on the core issue, there's a chance at a good resolution for their problem. But there's also the chance that her, or your, approach wasn't ever going to be good enough, and the other person never meant to fix the issue.

Freddy could also choose to deflect and focus on another tangent that's loosely related, in an effort to sidestep the issue that Nancy brought to him. This could take the form of changing the subject or hiding the deflection by saying there were other more important issues to discuss. Remember: no one gets to tell you what is or isn't important to discuss in situations like this. You get to decide this. You and no one else.

When deflecting comes into play, rely on your reflecting technique:

- "I'm not talking about that issue; I'm talking about this one."
- "That's not the issue we're discussing right now."
- "We can put a pin in that and come back to it, but I need for us to focus on this issue now."

Changes in Demeanor or Information Density

Make sure to look out for someone's changing demeanor, tone, or verbosity. When you see changes in these areas, it's a hint that they may be lying. People who lie often change tack when they are losing control of the narrative in an effort to reclaim dominance.

They may resort to:

- Gaslighting you to convince you that you're wrong.
- Saying it's complicated to convince you that you don't fully understand the situation.
- Throwing a lot more information at you (also known as *browbeating* or *steamrolling*) to exhaust your mental processing power.
- Feigning anger that you question their integrity to make you feel like you're disrespecting them.
- Turning it around on you and making you the problem in order to confuse you.

That's fairly easy to counter once you spot it. To spin up and maintain a false reality and narrative is a cognitively and emotionally intensive undertaking. Rightly so—because they are likely keeping multiple sets of facts in their mind. The counter here is simple: make them keep going.

Forcing someone to expand or rehash parts of their story in a different order highlights the holes and gaps in their stories. It could look as simple as "Wait, what happened before this? I'm having a little trouble keeping up." Here are some other things you could ask:

- "Wait, what came before [specific detail about their story]?"
- "Okay, let's walk through this backward."

- Intentionally recount something incorrectly to see if they get tripped up.
- "How am I supposed to square [this information] with what you just told me?"

If you find that the other person gets tripped up, the details change, or they get frustrated that you're slowing them down, you may have spotted a lie. You can also switch to using the reflecting techniques covered in Chapter 2, "Having the Conversation," to help you here or ask them to confirm which is true.

The Praise/Provoke Cycle

Another tactic employed by gaslighters involves giving praise or compliments to you and then abruptly provoking you once you've dropped your guard. They may start by complimenting your outfit, your work, or general pleasantries. Then when you've softened a little, they can lay into you with criticism and critique.

The *praise* part of this cycle is easy enough to spot: they're laying it on thick. They are giving effusive or lofty compliments such as, "Your work has never been better!" or "I have never seen anyone do anything better than you, ever." Don't trust those false comments, because they are meant to soften you up.

The *provoke* part of the cycle can be a manipulative tactic used to undermine your confidence and make you feel like it was you who was out to get someone from the beginning. For instance, if you get a transcript of a conversation, the other person may claim you were out to create confusion intentionally, when in fact, you were simply seeking clarity.

They may also belittle you. It's crucial to speak from a place of strength when they do. If they say, "You're imagining things," counter with, "I don't imagine facts. I know what's true." Similarly, if they claim there's no reason to be upset, assert your right to your feelings: "I get to decide my feelings. Not you."

Emphasize that your feelings aren't up for debate and that their attempts to deflect are transparent. By maintaining focus on the core issue and speaking from a position of confidence, you can effectively counter their manipulative tactics.

Lastly, they may try to tell you that you're being too sensitive. To that, you can say "Yeah, I am sensitive. But that isn't the issue. Your behavior is." Or "That may be, but that's beside the point."

Stay Grounded

When a gaslighter picks you out, they try to pick you off so they can have a better chance of getting what they want. In this kind of situation, you need more eyes and more people who can shine a light on the truth. When it's just you and the gaslighter, you have no power. They will take whatever tack they can, including victimhood, so they come out ahead. When someone tries to confuse you about what the truth is, having other people who also hold the truth helps you regain your center.

You could ask questions like:

- Does what they're saying sound like something I would do or say?
- Does what they're saying sound like my character?
- How likely is it that they are projecting something onto me?

There's a small chance that, yes, this does sound like you. Most likely, it doesn't. So, disregard whatever is coming from the gaslighter and get some outside help. Here's how this could look:

- Nancy asks her friend if she seems likely to forget a big deadline. It doesn't feel like her to do this, but Freddy throws so much information at her that it's impossible to catch everything.
- Nancy's friend said no, she cares too much about the success of the business to let something like this slip. She calls to mind another scenario where Nancy worked overtime to get something over to their client because she cared.
- Nancy realizes that Freddy isn't telling the truth and is trying to pin a failure on her.

Final Thoughts

It isn't easy to have these conversations. In fact, most people shy away from them because conversations with people who lie and gaslight trip up their sense of security or equilibrium. If you can use the techniques laid out here, you're going to have the best chance of resolving the situation:

- Those who lie and gaslight rely on your limited store of willpower. Use tools that will give you a recording, notes, or a transcription.
- You can't handle gaslighting by yourself. You need more eyes and more people who can shine a light on the truth.
- Changing the format of your meetings can work to your advantage. Consider the stand-up and retrospective format.
- If you want to trip someone up who is lying, make them repeat themselves and ask questions about various parts of what they're saying. Intentionally get it wrong to see what they say.
- If you see someone complicating the issue, changing their tone, or getting more verbose, you may have spotted a lie.
- Direct confrontation is the least effective and most difficult part of this technique. It only works if you need to wash your hands of something, or you give the other person a reason to come clean.

CHAPTER 5

Conflict with Your Boss

This chapter covers what is, hands down, the riskiest conversation you'll have at work.

Meet Ellen. She's a senior manager who's navigating a post-acquisition situation at her company. Dallas, the CEO, is overseeing the transition; he's staying on in a new role. As part of the acquisition, Dallas reassured Ellen's team that absolutely nothing would change for six months because he and the new owners wanted to see how the company ran before making any changes.

Cut to day two: the big changes start rolling in. The first change requires them to shift a fundamental part of their email marketing business, which would break their entire workflow. The second change would be that her team won't be able to double in size as originally planned; in fact, they can't hire anyone at all. Tensions are always high in these situations, but after this decision, Ellen's managers are ready to walk.

Dallas is a visionary CEO. His ideas are sometimes outlandish but are usually right. As a result, he's highly skilled at building narratives in his head and seeing them through. He's still running the company after the acquisition. He's been known to steamroll or give orders and not have them questioned.

> **Ellen:** "The acquisition isn't going well. We were told there would be no changes at all for six months. Now we are being forced off our main system, and we can't hire anyone. My leaders are telling me they aren't being heard, and they feel like they aren't being listened to. Frankly, I have several people ready to walk."
>
> **Dallas:** "Look, this is just the new culture. You gotta get on board. End of story."

While there's a little bit of back and forth afterward about other tactical issues, Dallas effectively shuts the conversation down with that statement and moves on to other things. Deflated, Ellen leaves.

The Problem

You and everyone else know on a deep level that conflict with your boss is hard. It's interesting, however, to understand why our brains resist it.

For millennia, humans have followed leaders and are trained from an early age to submit to authority. There are also steep penalties for stepping out of line, including things like fines, citations, firing, and even corporal punishment. So, it's safe to say that going against your boss isn't something your brain (or at least most people's) is used to or is likely to be comfortable with.

Some cultures have an added hurdle of a larger power distance, meaning the social costs for going against your boss may be so great as to be considered taboo. Chapter 10, "Understanding Cultural Dynamics," goes into more detail on this subject.

However, if you can get past the discomfort of initiating this conversation and focus on conveying the impacts/costs of what's happening to your boss, this will put your mind in the right place and ease your stress level.

Add to that—the costs are real. One interviewee wondered: "Will having this conversation jeopardize my future?" It's a wise question, because you might make a "career-limiting move" by having this conversation. Another one told their boss they disagreed with a decision and were told, quite flatly, "Well, you don't need to work here then. You're fired."

However real the costs may be, this chapter will give you the best possible guidance for having hard conversations with your boss.

The Solution

For these conversations to be successful, you need to understand that there are things you can control, things you can influence, and things that are beyond your grasp. Realizing what you can and can't control is liberating, especially if you're talking to your boss.

What Can You Control?

People whose job is taming chaos are primed to struggle in differentiating between things they can control and things they can influence. While you have varying degrees of influence in many things, there's a key thing to remember: there's a zero percent chance you can control everything (see Table 5.1). When you let this sink in, you'll remove an immense amount of stress around the conversation and can make decisions with a clear head.

TABLE 5.1 WHAT CAN YOU CONTROL?

What You Control	What You Influence	What You Don't Control
Your emotions	Other people's decisions, provided you have a relationship	Anyone's decisions you don't have a relationship with
Your responses		Global events
What people below your level do		Market forces
What your job description empowers you to do		

When it comes to your boss, you're in influence territory, so your goal here is make your case and leave the rest to your boss.

Not controlling outcomes doesn't mean giving up. Quite the opposite: it frees you to push as hard as you want because the decision is on someone else. So, you can tell your boss about the impact on you, the team, or anyone else and leave knowing you've done your best.

Influence Takes Time

Sometimes people, especially visionary leaders, need time to process an idea that runs counter to their narrative. Even if you're rejected or shut down in the moment, you may still hit a nerve or spark a thought in your boss. Ellen knew this and tried the following the next day:

> **Ellen:** "Okay, I don't think I did a great job articulating this yesterday, so I want to try again. Here's where things are going poorly. And here's what needs to happen in order for some of this to change. We need you to give us goals and outcomes. Let us figure them out and include us in conversations rather than making decisions for us. We know our business. We know the things it can do. We need to slow down on some of these things that we're being told are non-negotiable. Like moving off our email system for one."
>
> **Dallas:** "Yeah, but it's not negotiable. This is what the new owners want."
>
> **Ellen:** "It has to be negotiable. We're going to lose all my leadership if we don't fix this. It's not going to go well if I tell them this has to change right now."

Dallas: "Okay, I hear you. I didn't realize everyone was on the verge of leaving. I'll talk to the owners to see if we can slow things down. I'll get back to you."

Afterward, Dallas agreed to have a conversation with the new owners about slowing things down. The time to reflect gave him a chance to push past his reactionary instincts, and he realized that "tough love" might get them through the situation, but the cost for this would be too high.

There may be situations in which more time is necessary and more data. Other situations require that you just tell someone this will sting or hurt and then let them work through it themselves.

Get a Buddy/Be Pragmatic

While it's certainly possible to talk to your boss directly, you may feel a little less safe making that move on your own. Here are a couple options if that's true: get a buddy or see if there are other ways to get this information to your boss without directly involving you.

If you're concerned that you may take too much heat talking to your boss one-on-one, rely on the tried-and-true buddy system and get someone to go in with you.

There's nothing wrong with a little theater here, either. The two of you could "serendipitously" walk by the boss's office casually or write them a message requesting a quick chat because the two of you were "just discussing something and wanted their input on the matter." It's unlikely you'll get fired, and even less likely that there will be two firings or retaliations. You've also boosted your chances of getting a positive reception by having someone else echo what you're saying.

NOTE A NOTE TO ALLIES

If you count yourself as an ally, this is the perfect spot to put it into practice. This will look different for everyone you support, so start by asking your teammate what you can do. Then do just that and only that.

You don't have to solve the problem for your boss. What you do could be as simple as giving them the space to work through ideas on their own or help them clarify their thinking. This way, you're validating their perspective and experience, as well as getting information on which suggestions might be most effective.

In fact, it's worth going further here: don't join that meeting with their boss or try to solve it for them. In doing this, you're sending a signal that they can't do it on their own and that they need you to save them. People don't need to be saved; they just need something to balance themselves and regain their footing.

You could also see if there are ways to get this information to your boss without directly involving the two of you. Maybe it's a possibility to bring something up in a staff meeting or a public chat channel. Maybe consider getting someone who has a little more clout to bring it up.

Look Out For . . .

There are three main things you'll want to look out for in these conversations, the first of which is what it may cost you to either defer or not have the conversation. Next, you'll learn to look for signs that your boss might be feeling threatened. And, finally, what should you do in the unlikely event they give you the axe?

Talking Yourself Out of the Conversation

Humans love flexibility, but they avoid making irreversible decisions. And having a hard conversation with your boss certainly qualifies as one of those; after all, you can't take back what you say to them and don't want to be labeled as difficult or getting in their way. So, you avoid the conversation or defer it for an unspecified later date, hoping to never revisit the idea.

This line of thinking is dangerous because it doesn't consider the cost of *not* having the conversation (see Table 5.2).

Think about a rubber band. If you pull it back a little and let it snap on you, it'll sting a bit. But if you pull it back until just before it breaks and let it go, it's going to hurt a lot worse. The same thing applies to talking yourself out of difficult conversations.

Consider the following: What happens if the business fails because you didn't bring something up? What if people get hurt because your team failed to consider a safety issue you avoided?

Now, what do you think happens if your boss comes to you asking why you didn't say something? That conversation will, at best, go poorly for you and your reputation. By not speaking up, you let problems fester.

TABLE 5.2 THE COSTS OF CONVERSATIONS

Real Costs of Not Having It	Potential Costs of Having It
Losing your funding	Getting labeled as difficult
Losing your job	Getting yelled at
Losing your credibility	
Having a worse outcome because you didn't act	

Having a hard conversation with your boss isn't easy. It requires courage and a commitment to truth and reality, and the willingness to absorb a little damage. Now that you can see that the costs for not having that conversation are significantly more impactful than having it, it should be a little easier to have it.

That said, stop thinking of reasons to avoid a conversation; think of the cost of not having it.

At-Risk Safety

Bosses aren't always easy to talk to. While some bosses welcome dissenting opinions and hard conversations, it (sadly) isn't the case with everyone. Other bosses can be combative, dismissive, or abrasive. Dealing with the latter is the focus here.

When you see bosses react poorly, your best bet is to pull back and focus on the decisions or impact a course of action has, not the person behind it. You can also establish a shared vision. Here's more from Ellen:

> Dallas: "Look, this is just the new culture. You gotta get on board. End of story."
>
> Ellen: "Dallas, hang on a second. We want the same thing, which is that our acquisition goes well, and my leadership team doesn't skip town. But we're moving too fast, and the costs of doing it this way are way too high. If your goal is to see this company grow like we laid out in our planning, you've got to work with me to get there. If not we're going to lose the people who keep this place together."
>
> Dallas: "Ellen, you hang on a second. Nothing about this company would be here if it weren't for me. Why can't you just make it happen and stop complaining? Everyone's conspiring against me here, and I'm being ganged up on by you and your leadership."

Just as with your teammates, you'll want to establish a shared vision with your boss. Hopefully, you understand what your boss is looking for in terms of success and what metrics are important to them. If not, you'll want to start by learning what's important to your boss. By understanding those metrics, you're going to make the conversation more relatable for them and, by extension, easier to participate.

Be direct about the impact the situation will have on you, the team, or whomever else is involved. Being clear and aligning your shared vision will make or break a conversation.

Here are some responses Ellen could use:

- "Let's step back for a second. One, you're in charge here. Two, I'm only showing you what I and the leadership team are seeing as potential impacts. You call the shots. I'm just telling you where we think they'll land."
- "I fully appreciate that this isn't an easy conversation, and I recognize that you're the one in charge. I hope I'm making it clear that I only want what's best for the company here. I'm just concerned about losing the team and the effect it will have on our merger."

"You're Fired!"

Being fired is what everyone dreads the most about conflicts with their boss. After all, who wants to threaten their paycheck or career trajectory, even just a little? There's good news here—because most of these fears are irrational. While this claim may seem absolutely ludicrous on the surface, please do read on before tossing this book across the room, letting your pet destroy it, or using it as kindling for a campfire.

First, it's important to remember that you know what's best for you. There are likely solid reasons why you may not feel you're in a position to have a conversation. You may really need the paycheck, or you may feel that you're going to get shut down because you don't enjoy the same privileged position that others in your company do. By all means, do what you need to do to stay safe and secure.

Second, it's important to remember the following two pieces of information:

- People get fired for any reason or no reason at all, regardless of what the law may say.
- What would you do if your boss came in and suddenly laid everyone off tomorrow? You'd go find a new job.

Third, go through the following questions in Table 5.3 to challenge those (potentially irrational) notions.

TABLE 5.3 GROUNDING YOUR FEARS

Question	Your Answer
What substantial evidence exists to support this fear? Has it happened before?	
What evidence exists that runs contrary to this fear?	
Might I be jumping to conclusions?	
What would I advise a friend to do?	
What do I or the team stand to gain by having this conversation?	
If the worst happens, will this matter in a year? How about five years?	

After finishing those questions, you may come to the conclusion that your fears do, in fact, have solid grounding. However, there's a decent chance you realize you're fretting over nothing. The five minutes it took you to go through this exercise has potentially saved you several sleepless nights. Now you can stop borrowing trouble because you're free to have the conversation without the worry that you're going to get canned.

If you do get fired, here are a few things to consider so you aren't surprised and can prepare in advance:

- Security may escort you out immediately.
- You may not have an opportunity to get any of your things or say goodbye to anyone. Most times, your things will be mailed to you.
- You may immediately be locked out of all your company's software.
- Even though you may know this is a possibility, you're probably still going to be surprised, hurt, or steamed about it for a week or so.

Final Thoughts

In closing, if you're the boss and this sounds a little like something you've done in the past, it's good that you've read this far. There are a few things you'll want to keep in mind: you're the one who sets the tone for how feedback is given and received. If you respond to your team in a way that shuts them down, you'll make it tougher for them to give you and each other honest feedback in the future.

If you haven't been gracious about receiving hard feedback in the past, it's never too late to change tack. Your team only wants what's best for the company. Remember they've got a different perspective than you, so they're privy to things you might miss. That's especially true if you're operating at a highly strategic level. So, remember these points:

- If you're a leader, know that you can't do everything your team wants all the time. Tell them so and commit to being transparent with your reasoning.
- Conflict with your boss isn't easy, and it's hands-down the riskiest conversation you'll have at work.
- Your brain isn't used to going against authority and will be very good at talking you out of having the conversation. Some cultures have an added hurdle where it's taboo to go against your boss. (Refer to Chapter 10 for more guidance.)
- The key to these conversations is knowing what you can control, what you can influence, and what's completely outside of your grasp.
- Shift from thinking of reasons to avoid a conversation to the costs of not having it.
- If you feel safety is at risk when talking to your boss, pull the conversation back to focus on the decisions or impact a course of action has, not the person behind it.
- Relatedly, it may help to remind your boss that they are in charge, and you're doing your best to help them make the most informed decision.

CHAPTER 6

Conflict on Remote Teams

Here's a question: What seems like a run-of-the-mill, tough conversation but actually isn't a run-of-the-mill, tough conversation? Answer: One you don't have in person.

Why? Having conflict remotely causes you to lose "high-fidelity conversation," leaving everyone at a disadvantage. A high-fidelity conversation is one in which all participants have access to the full range of a human's communication, including tone of voice, nonverbal cues (such as body language), and being able to make eye contact.

The absence of this information leaves you in the dark about what someone truly means when they speak. That's why those Zoom calls or emails have a tinge of dread or angst to them.

Understanding why this is so difficult in the first place helps frame an appropriate response. To start, there are several different levels of conversational fidelity you can have:

- **In person**, which gives you the full range of verbal and nonverbal cues such as body language, tone and full range of everyone's voice
- **Video**, which loses most body language due to cropping parts of everyone's bodies out of the frame and fidelity of their voice (video chat apps often compress audio)
- **Phone**, which loses out on all nonverbal cues
- **Text**, which loses out on all nonverbal cues and tone of voice
- **Email**, which loses out on everything else, including the synchronous communication (read: Slack and SMS) and leaves you only with the transcript of what everyone says

The goal for these tough conversations is to have them in as high a fidelity as you can. While email and Slack have dramatically reduced the friction for communication, they come at the expense of clarity and thoughtfulness.

Remember the last email you got that was a forwarded email with just "thoughts?" It's too easy to send a half-baked email that leaves too much open to interpretation; plus, you're at the mercy of the reader's mood, state of mind, or distractions they experience, which could contribute to them missing key parts of your message. (The next time you're tempted to send an email like this, imagine someone saying "Thoughts? No thanks, I'm trying to cut back.")

When you lose conversational fidelity, your brain's survival circuits activate. They fill in all the gaps in communication with negative assumptions, leaving you prone to misinterpreting someone's message.

Or conversely, someone who isn't great at communicating over text may complicate matters by a poor choice of words. Survival circuits were certainly helpful before civilization began, as they could alert you to perceived dangers like tigers coming to eat you or strangers stealing your food, but they are counterproductive in the day-to-day work communications and situations you experience today.

The Problem

Take the following situation, for instance. Danny and Jack worked at an agency. Danny was on the management side, and Jack was in sales. Danny's direct report, Wendy, was caught in the middle of some chaos from Jack's end.

There was confusion throughout the sales process, leading to Jack abruptly telling Wendy she needed to do something differently than what the client and Danny had asked her to do. Plus, he wanted her to make sure that he was involved in every conversation she had with Danny.

"It was pretty stressful for her," Danny said. "She didn't have a clear idea of what to do or whom to listen to. Not to mention this also stressed out the client, who saw the chaos and wondered if they'd hired the right people."

Danny tried to talk with Jack, but it didn't go well:

> Danny: "Jack, I need you to let Wendy do her work uninterrupted and keep all project-based communication going through me. This confusion is stalling her work on the project because she's hearing conflicting directions from each of us. If we can get on the same page before talking to her, she can focus, and everything can go smoothly."
>
> Jack: "You aren't going to cut me out of this process. It's my client, and I'm calling the shots here. I need to be in every meeting and manage this project. I'm not asking. I'm telling."

The team was remote so much of this was left up to interpretation.

The Solution

Situations like Danny's require a delicate touch. That's especially true when you aren't having high-fidelity conversations. Fortunately, there are options.

Increase the Fidelity

When you don't see someone directly in person, it's easy to see them as less than the human they are. And because both Danny and Jack were working at a fast-paced company, demands for time and attention were always high.

Instead of continuing a conversation over email or text, starting with a phone call gives everyone the benefit that the tone of voice provides. Even better would be a video call, because seeing and hearing people in real time humanizes them.

"I asked him something like 'hey, mind if I give you a quick call? I think some of our meaning is getting lost in text and this is a lot to type.'" Jack agreed." Danny mentioned how helpful it was to do this, partly because he didn't want to type all day when a call would do.

Once you're on a phone call with people, you can follow the usual steps of laying out facts, sharing the conclusions you drew, and opening it up to them.

Push for Clarity

If you aren't able to get on the phone, you need to take extra efforts here because you're working at a lower fidelity. The lower the fidelity, the higher the effort required for safety.

For email and text-based communication, you're going to need to make your aims extremely clear. It's very easy to have this look like a demand, which shuts down collaboration and only makes for more problems. Make sure to include the following information:

- Your intentions and goals (which will help establish shared vision)
- What you aren't saying, if misunderstanding exists (refocusing)
- An option for high-fidelity communication, i.e., to make yourself available by phone
- Reassure people that you both want the same thing (safety)

NOTE **IF WRITING IS YOUR ONLY OPTION**

If you have to write something, try writing and then reading your message aloud to see how it sounds. If you would be comfortable receiving the email you just read, there's a decent chance it will be well received by the other person.

For these next conversations, assume that Jack is upset and says, "You aren't going to cut me out of this process."

If Danny wanted to focus on a shared vision, the conversation could look like this:

> Danny: "I hear you and that's not my intention. What if we set up time each afternoon to discuss what's happening? That way you can stay in the loop and Wendy can do her work uninterrupted."

If Jack misinterpreted Danny, he could say something to the effect of:

> Danny: "I'm not saying you can't have input on this project and that I'm cutting you out. I'm saying we need to get aligned before giving Wendy potentially conflicting information."

Lastly, this helps Jack know that Danny is listening because Danny just summarized Jack's main points.

> Danny: "Okay, it sounds like you're feeling out of the loop and need some more input on this. Am I getting that right? Anything you want to add?
>
> Jack: Nah, that about sums it up.

Use Emojis (Yes, Seriously)

Back in 1982, Carnegie Mellon's bulletin board system was a forum for staff and students to talk about nearly anything. Jokes often prompted misunderstandings. Enter Carnegie Mellon computer scientist Scott Fahlman, who first proposed using :-) as something to denote a joke. Since then, emoticons and emojis have proliferated.

And, as luck would have it, people's brains "readily and accurately perceived :-) as a smiling face by its users," according to one study.

So, it seems pretty safe to conclude that if you use emojis and emoticons, it will help get your message across. That said, try not to pepper in too many; if you do use too many of them, you may lose credibility or come off as insincere.

Look Out For...

When you're remote, people are prone to misinterpret what you say, do a monologue or talk over you, bulldoze you, or fall quiet as things suddenly go silent.

Monologuing and Talking over You

It's tempting to believe someone is trying to dominate a conversation when they talk on at great length or talk over you. Yes, you do need to contribute to the conversation, but don't jump to the conclusion that they're being pushy just yet.

Your first go-to is Hanlon's razor. It's possible that someone is bullying you, but the most likely reason is an internet connection issue that leaves delays between when they stop speaking and you start. It's certainly annoying, but out of your control. Casually bring up that there's a delay, since bringing awareness to the issue can often resolve it.

It's also true that not every situation has a succinct summation, nor are participants great at distilling a situation down with absolute clarity. There may simply be too much to discuss, especially in highly complex and stressful situations.

And you may also be working an issue out with someone who just can't help themselves. Some people who are neurodivergent tend to "infodump." *Infodumping* presents as someone who is excitedly sharing lots of information that seems excessive to other people. This process is a normal and completely valid method of communicating for people with ADHD (attention deficit hyperactivity disorder) and some forms of autism.

Your author is one such individual, who owes his infodumping tendencies to struggles with ADHD. This can still present issues that stop the bidirectional flow of conversation, but there is peace that comes from knowing some people can't always help it and are trying to work on it.

Your best bet in any of these situations is an old standby: getting their attention. Two common ways are to raise your hand or start to speak. Most chat apps today allow for some form of notification to the speaker that you are raising your hand. It's a time-tested signal that you need to get a word in.

Danny said, "It got pretty tense when Jack talked for about nine minutes straight. It may not have been that exactly, but I think it was pretty close." Not only was it difficult to get a word in, but it was also entirely too much to ask someone to process that information in one go.

Danny let him finish, but if you find yourself in that spot, try something like this: "Hey Jack, hang on a sec. There's a lot to unpack there, and I want to make sure I got it all."

Using a phrase like that is a perfect way to slow down the conversation so that you have a chance to speak and work in some reflecting techniques.

You'll also want to talk a little more slowly when you take your turn speaking. Speaking more slowly engages the mirror neurons in your brain, so your slower speech is a calming cue to the other person that they aren't in any danger. It also keeps most people from rambling. You'll still find some people are eager to get back in and reclaim dominance, but that's where the next section comes into play.

You'll also encounter another kind of bulldozer in these conversations: people who just can't help themselves.

This condition can present as hyperactivity and excitement about matters at hand, which makes regulating interruptions something of a struggle. Of course, this doesn't excuse the behavior of the interruption, not by any means. There is peace, however, that comes from knowing some people can't help it and are trying to work on it.

Bulldozing

There are some people who don't fit into any of the aforementioned categories and like to utilize bluster as a way to show dominance or wear your brain out. This quality presents as the other person dismissing what you're saying. Here's a situation where you'll need a little more assertiveness.

People who really want to force their opinion on someone will use every opportunity to take up more airtime. They will cut you off and talk down to you. They'll dismiss your statements out of hand, or they'll ignore you.

In that case, interrupt and tell them something like the following:

> "I wasn't finished."
>
> "Hey, it seems like you really want this. But you need to consider the other side. Let me finish, and we'll figure it out."

Some people are known bulldozers. When talking with them, you'll want to get ahead of it by saying something like this:

> "I've got a few points I need to make, so hang on."
>
> "There's a lot to this, so I'll let you know when I'm done."

Going Silent

The typing indicator in text or an email is in the top three most anxiety and anger-inducing inventions in messaging. If you're going back and forth over text, a quick check-in can go a long way toward establishing safety. Make sure, however, that you don't robotically check in every two minutes or so with the other person, lest you come off as pushy.

If you don't hear from the other person after what seems like a normal amount of time to you, send them a message saying, "I'm just checking in. Are you still with me?"

For Danny, it may look like this:

> Jack: [types a message but stops, deactivating the typing indicator]
>
> Danny: "Hey, I'm just checking in here. Haven't heard from you in a few minutes."
>
> Jack: "I'm still here; just working out my thoughts."
>
> Danny: "That's fine, take your time. If it's easier, I have time for a quick call."

When someone types, but seems to stop, you only have that one bit of information to go on. They were typing, and now they're not. Your brain does its thing and fills in that gap with a negative thought. It thinks "Why did they do this? Did they snub me? Are they too mad to type? Or am I going to drown in a wall of incomprehensible text?"

NOTE SEND AUDIO MESSAGES

> An audio message is a great way to increase fidelity without both people being in real time. It also gives you the added benefit of tone of voice. So, if you need to slow it down or reinforce a calm tone, this is your ticket. All major chat apps as of this writing allow you to do this.

There's another law that's helpful to remember here: Parkinson's Law. It states that "work expands so as to fill the time available for its completion." For example, if you give yourself an hour to have this conversation, it will most likely take an hour. If you set no time limits or endpoints, then it's likely to go on much longer than anyone would like.

So, consider adding a time limit to force attention. Here's what Danny could say:

> Danny: "Hey Jack, I know this is important to resolve. I have another important thing coming up and wonder if we can focus on this for the next half hour. I'll give you my undivided attention."

This option can help you get to the resolution you want quicker, as you both know the time and attention available to address an issue. If you find that this time isn't sufficient, you may opt to sideline it or find a more suitable time to discuss it.

Final Thoughts

Before wrapping up, consider the best remedy for remote conflict: prevention. If you can have smaller, more frequent rounds of feedback and positive experiences, it makes the harder conversations much easier to navigate because everyone has already built rapport and knows you're coming from a good place. So, try this: start small and ask someone "What's one thing I could have done better here?" If you keep doing this, harder conversations aren't half as painful.

Danny and Jack ultimately figured it out, but it required another round of conversations. Jack was struggling to meet his quotas, and it was manifesting in strange ways. "We got to a good place, at least where that project's concerned. Wendy got to do what she needed. We kept in close contact but let her do what she needed without bothering her."

Lastly, if you were wondering what the other two worst inventions in text messaging were: read receipts, which shows if a message has been seen by the recipient, leaving the writer wondering things like "Why didn't someone reply yet? Do they hate me?" The second is ducking autocorrect.

Some key takeaways in this chapter:

- Aim for high-fidelity conversation at every turn. The lower the fidelity, the higher the need for safety.
- Our brains interpret gaps in information as negative, which is why things like the typing indicator can feel like a snub.
- Don't be afraid to use emojis. A smiley is perceived the exact same way as an actual smiling face.
- You may need to step back and establish a shared vision to understand what each person needs to succeed.
- If the other person goes on at length, slow it down. This approach helps you redirect the conversation and gives you time to speak.
- If you're going back and forth over text, try to send an audio message, which is a great way to boost fidelity without the need for someone to get on the phone.
- Check in on the quiet ones. If you see they're taking a while to reply over text, a gentle check-in can help them know you're still interested in talking and moving forward.

CHAPTER 7

Bad Blood

Much of this book focuses on how to have conversations in the heat of the moment or soon thereafter. But what about times when your relationship with someone is so rotten and gnarled from some past event that you wonder if it's even salvageable?

When a wound goes untreated, all manner of ailments can crop up. And the longer it goes without attention, the worse it gets and the harder the remedy can be on you. Relationship issues are the same way: if you don't attend to the problem, it's going to get worse and infect other parts of your work life (maybe your personal life as well).

The Problem

Here to illustrate this point is Jim, a sales professional in the bicycle industry. He serves clients focused on achieving specific metrics, such as reaching a mile within a set time or improving biometric data. Jim acknowledges his tendency to argue, saying, "I have a history of also being a little gruff or crass and initiating conflicts that don't need to be there." As an expert in his field, Jim is frequently called upon to assist his team in closing deals.

In this instance, Jim was called in to help close Selena's deal. He barely knew Selena, having only met her once at a company event. They had "no appreciable footing," he said.

Selena's clients, in contrast to Jim's, don't care as much about data. They really want to focus on more holistic goals, such as getting in shape for mountain biking. Selena is so close to closing a deal, she can just see her client signing the paperwork if she closes her eyes.

The collaboration became challenging when Jim began discussing e-bikes and their biometric data tracking capabilities. Lacking context for the customer's needs, Jim viewed the conversation through his own clients' preferences and not those of Selena's clients. This led him to advise against the e-bikes, mistakenly believing they wouldn't meet Selena's client's needs. They backed out, and Selena lost the deal.

Then came the group text with Jim and his boss.

> **Selena:** "This guy doesn't know what the hell he's doing or what he's talking about. He's out here killing deals and saying things that don't support my process."

Jim's director messages him on the side, saying not to worry about this, he'd look into it. Jim, as you've learned, doesn't shy away from a tough conversation. So, he ignores his director completely and calls Selena, ready for a fight. Here's part of their conversation:

> Jim: "Selena, what you just did wasn't cool. I expect you to act with integrity and not challenge my competence in front of my boss. Don't suggest that I don't know what I'm doing. If you've got issues, call me, and I'm going to make sure that the bosses stay out of it from here forward. This is our conflict to resolve and ours alone."
>
> Selena: "So you're accusing me of not having integrity now? You, the guy who doesn't know what he's talking about?"

The call ended shortly thereafter with both of them pretty steamed and was followed by a few months of silence. Then Jim found out that they were both going to be at a corporate event together where customers would be in attendance. He didn't want to go into this event with a cloud hanging over the two of them. So, what could he do?

The Solution

Common wisdom dictates that you have a conversation like this because it's better for you both. While that's mostly true, it's a colossal and dangerous oversimplification that can lead to wasted effort. A book that offers such advice belongs in a dollar store bargain bin right next to the *Chicken Soup for the Soul* books. And you didn't buy this book for bargain bin wisdom, you bought this book for actionable advice. So that's what you'll get.

The remainder of this chapter lays out two paths for you to cure bad blood. One where you have the conversation with the other person, and one where you don't. Neither of these end with bad blood... on your end at least. First, let's talk about a loaded term: forgiveness.

Forgiveness

This chapter would be incomplete without a discussion on forgiveness. Let's define forgiveness in specific terms (see Table 7.1).

TABLE 7.1 FORGIVENESS

What It Is	What It Isn't
Something that is designed to benefit just you	Obligatory
Choosing to overcome pain	Forgetting
Releasing shame, bitterness, and fear	Endorsing the other person or what they did
Choosing compassion, even though the other person isn't owed anything of the sort	Saying it's OK, but still being bitter and holding a grudge
Recognizing and taking your power back in a situation	

According to *Forgiveness Therapy: An Empirical Guide for Resolving Anger and Restoring Hope,*[1] a widely cited, evidence-based source on the matter of forgiveness, there are massive benefits to be had from choosing forgiveness: for example, reductions in depression, bitterness, and rumination.

Forgiveness can sometimes be a deep, dark, and scary cavern to explore. So much so that it may require the aid of a trained therapist or other professional. Assuming that you don't need those people, there are a few questions you can ask yourself.

There's one additional myth to debunk here: the idea that forgiving and forgetting go hand in hand. Some people may be able to forget past hurts. Lucky you if that's the case—but most people can't. It's better that way, in fact. If you forgot what hurt you, physically or emotionally, there would be a lot fewer humans on Earth today. Learning and avoiding harm was, is, and always will be key to humanity's survival. So, don't sweat it if you can't forget a past hurt, because it's entirely human.

Forgiveness is one part of the solution. Next, you need to decide how to proceed. It's important to weigh your options. In keeping with the injury metaphor, the best time to treat a wound is immediately after it happens. The second-best time is right now. So, ask yourself: Is the

1 R. D. Enright and R. P. Fitzgibbons, *Forgiveness Therapy: An Empirical Guide for Resolving Anger and Restoring Hope*, 2nd ed. (Washington, DC: American Psychological Association, 2024).

pain of staying with things as they are worse than the pain of having the necessary conversation and its potential upsides? See Table 7.2.

TABLE 7.2 WORKSHEET: SHOULD I FORGIVE THEM?

Potential Question	Answers
What do I stand to gain by forgiving them emotionally?	
What do I stand to gain by forgiving them socially?	
What does the team stand to gain?	
Will I try to forgive them?	

Option 1: Don't Have the Conversation

If you decide that it's best not to have the conversation (or to forgive them), you'll still have some work to do. Here, your focus is on releasing bitterness and setting boundaries.

Release Bitterness

When it comes to bitterness, here's the key thing to remember: it does not serve you to hold onto bitterness; in fact, it actively harms you. Consider this quote from Nelson Mandela, who had, to put it mildly, a lot of experience in dealing with bad blood. He said, "Resentment is like drinking poison and then hoping it will kill your enemies." When you hold onto bitterness, here's what happens:

- You can't fully contribute, because your anger has coagulated into bitterness.
- You open the door to more cynicism and negativity.
- You spend unnecessary energy and effort on something that happened in the past.

One way to release your bitterness is by writing a burn letter. If you're unfamiliar with the concept, it goes like this: you write this person the nastiest, meanest, most honest letter you can regarding them, the situation, and how you've been hurt, making sure that you pull no punches. What's in this letter doesn't have to make perfect, coherent sense; it just has to get the feelings out of your head and onto the paper. Once you've written it down, look it over and tell yourself you're releasing this bitterness.

And then burn it. Yes, literally.

A match or fire will do just fine. But for a little extra flair, try a brûlée torch. And maybe enjoy a good glass of wine as it goes up in smoke. After that, consider yourself freed from the tyranny of those thoughts and hurts.

Focus on Boundaries

Next up, you'll focus on boundaries. Even if you opt not to have this conversation or forgive them, you'll probably have to interact with them in some capacity. It's wise in those cases to set up boundaries. Ask yourself these questions:

- What's one reasonable way I can protect myself? Not being in the same meetings? Moving teams?
- How can I still contribute without working closely with them?
- Can I limit my time with them or minimize input from them?

While you ultimately know what's best for you, and perhaps not having the conversation is the right move, hopefully you'll at least give option two a read before deciding.

Option 2: Have the Conversation

If you want to talk to the other person, here's how to do it. As Jim said, "This notion of swallowing my ego, of being the first one to say that maybe I'm wrong, has been... difficult. I'm just as proud, stubborn, and aggressive as a lot of people who've had some success."

If you feel ready to have the conversation, feel free to skip to the end of this chapter. If you'd prefer a little more preparation, read on.

Get Context

Look for other people who were involved with or work closely with the other person to try and uncover that person's motivation. Keep in mind that these are other people's views, which also lack the complete picture. That's fine, you're simply using this approach to pick up on likely patterns.

In this case, since Jim's director was involved, that's the perfect place to start. Luckily, that's exactly what Jim did.

> **Director:** "Look, this is a tense situation. You don't understand what she was dealing with. So let me try to fill you in."
>
> **Jim:** "Okay."
>
> **Director:** "I don't want you to be in the dark, and I don't want you to feel attacked. Both of you are really good at what you do."
>
> **Jim:** "Alright, go ahead."
>
> **Director:** "Selena has been working at this deal for nine months, and she's had a hard time showing her client what the best offering for them would be. She's been through a lot with them—she's been diligent and patient, but they've given her mixed signals. There's a lot of stress on Selena's plate, and this felt like a huge setback for her. She felt like it came from someone who wasn't on her team."

Get in Their Heads

Much too often, people don't consider the other person's needs or wants, which leads to rough situations like the one you're in right now. Maybe it was you, maybe it was them. Most likely it's a little of both, and neither of you meant for it to come to this. So, do spend some time trying to understand their needs, motivations, and what they might have gone through.

Jim sums things up perfectly here: "I can't go on assuming it's all about me. But there are two people here, each coming with different stories, contexts, and motivations. If I don't know those things, I don't even know what the conflict is about."

Ask yourself these questions:

- Could we both have been right and just gotten in each other's way?
- What might have been going on for the other person at the time?
- How might they have felt after I did what I did?
- What negative outcomes did I (unintentionally) cause?
- What needs did I trample? Autonomy, competence, or relatedness? (Refer back to Chapter 2, "Having the Conversation.")

This is also a perfect time for "Cranky Conclusions" (discussed in Chapter 1, "Before the Conversation"). In this situation, you'll ask questions like:

- How would they say I contributed to this?
- Fill in the rest of this sentence: "You blew this because…"

In Jim's case, Selena would say that Jim's contribution to this situation was coming in without all the context. He didn't know what Selena had said, nor what the full goals were. Jim came in focused solely on his own area of expertise without asking how he could help.

Now, by asking yourself these questions, you've primed your brain for empathy, which will be the key to curing the bad blood between you both. Without understanding where everyone's coming from, any attempt at solving this problem is like running with scissors in a forest at night—you're going to trip and hurt someone.

Ask Them for a Conversation

Much like in Chapter 6, "Conflict on Remote Teams," you'll want to have this conversation in as high fidelity as you can and reduce the chance of additional misinterpretation and harm. There's a different tack that you might want to take here: ask for permission over text. Here are some options you can try:

- "Would you be open to talking about how to work better together? I could use some pointers. I really want both of us to succeed."
- "I don't feel great about how things ended, and I wonder if you'd be open to patching things up."
- "Could we talk? I really want to support you as best as possible. Maybe you could help me understand how to do that."
- "I really blew things up with us. I'm sorry for what I did. What can we do to make it work between us? We could do a lot of good together."

Don't be surprised if you don't get a reply. Some people will still avoid conflict at any cost or are still sore from their own bitterness, but all you can do is try. And maybe try again—gentle persistence almost always pays off.

Here's a text that Jim sent:

> **Jim:** "Last quarter, what I said got in the way of what you'd worked on for a long time. I just want to talk and understand what happened from your perspective. I want to look at how I

can help you in the future. I know I'm going to be back out with you in a couple of weeks, and I don't want us to be seething and having problems working with each other. If we end up just not liking each other, that's fine. But I really want to know what we can do to make this work professionally."

[Selena calls Jim]

Selena: "Hey Jim. Saw your text. Whatcha got?"

Jim: "A lot of questions. Starting with: what was it about what I said that hurt your deal? What could I have said differently to help the client understand what I was talking about and how it wasn't in opposition to you?"

Note here that Jim's message had all the following notes, which are essential in giving the right signals for a conversation like this:

- He set aside his ego.
- He asked for a conversation.
- He focused on positive outcomes for both of them.
- He asked to hear more of where she was coming from.

Setting aside your ego and asking for a conversation on how you both can win sends the right signals to the other party. It shows that you really want to try and work it out with them and that your intentions are in the right place.

When having this conversation, here are some additional questions to ask:

- What does support look like to you?
- Going back, if you can, what would the ideal situation have looked like for you?

The last question in the list above could backfire and lead to more problems if you aren't careful. The next section covers how to address any problems that arise from asking it.

Look Out For . . .

The conversation you're having can easily go sideways if you aren't careful. You may find that one or both of you ends up arguing again about past hurts, or you may find yourselves getting too emotionally triggered to think straight.

Relitigation

When there's bad blood involved, issues can (and will, sorry to say) flare up without warning. It's important that you don't end up arguing again in the present about what happened in the past. Instead, listen quietly to where the other person is coming from. It may take some time, as you're essentially releasing pressure from a valve. Don't stem it and don't shut it down—let the other person talk it out. And if you caused this hurt, ensure that you give a genuine apology, even if you've already done so. There's little sense in constantly apologizing, but it doesn't hurt to apologize a second time—apologies sometimes get lost or forgotten when someone is hurt.

When you have an opening, your focus should be to deploy reflecting statements (covered in Chapter 2). This approach ensures that you don't spend more time rehashing the same old argument. Here's how:

- "I really blew this for you, I'm sorry it happened. It sounds like I got in the way of [this specific goal]. Would doing [this specific thing] give you what you need?"
- "Oof, now that I hear it again, that was really inconsiderate. I'm sorry. Can you tell me explicitly what support looks like for you so that we don't go through that again?"

If it happened to you:

- "Look, that really hurt, but it's in the past. What I'm hoping to do is figure out what we both need to succeed so that neither one of us gets to a place like this again."

If you're still hitting a wall with each other, try involving your bosses:

- "Okay, it sounds like we're both doing exactly what we should, but we're still getting in each other's way. Would you be opposed to taking this to leadership and getting their input on how to change things, so we aren't set up in opposition to each other?"

Getting Triggered

If they're getting triggered, call back to shared purpose. Imagine if Selena said something like this:

> Selena: "This just proves my point that you don't know what you're doing. You took money from me when you tanked that deal. Actual. Money. I have a MORTGAGE and KIDS, man. Do you know how stressful this is?"

The first thing Jim could do is pull back and try to work out a shared purpose.

> Jim: "Whoa, I didn't mean to put us back in that space again. Can we pull back and figure out what to do so that this doesn't happen again?"

Jim could also try a reflecting statement:

> Jim: "I'm not saying I didn't tank this, because I clearly did. What I'm saying is I want us to be able to work together so the company can win. Is there anything you'd be willing to try?"

If the conversation gets worse, or you want more information on what to do when people lose control, see Chapter 3, "People Losing Control." There are also some tips in case you find yourself getting triggered, such as box breathing.

Lastly, you may see that things are going so poorly that there is no chance anything can happen. In those cases, gracefully exit. You can leave the door open to future conversations if you like. Try these:

- "Okay. I think this conversation may be making things worse. I really want to figure this out, so maybe we can talk again later."
- "Looks like we're at an impasse and can't figure this out together. I'm going to ask someone else to get involved so that we can resolve this."

Note that if you get anyone else involved, you're likely tanking your relationship with them. Sometimes that's necessary for your, their, or even the company's own good.

Final Thoughts

Here's one final quote from Jim that sums things up perfectly when it comes to bad blood: "I can't go assuming it's all about me. There are two people here, each coming with different stories, contexts, and motivations. If I don't know those things, I don't even know what our conflicts are about."

Finally, remember that bad blood, just like an infection, may require a couple of rounds of treatment to get out of your system. Here are some key takeaways:

- The cure to bad blood is to focus on forgiveness and forge a path ahead with the other person.
- Forgiveness isn't forgetting or endorsing what the other person did to hurt you; rather, it's a powerful affirmation of your strength that releases the bitterness and hurt to let you heal.
- You don't *have* to have a conversation with the other person. There are many ways to maximize your impact while minimizing contact with them, but the best outcomes happen when you do have a conversation.
- Watch out for getting pulled back into the same argument. If you sense that's where you're headed, use reflections to redirect the conversation.

CHAPTER 8

Offensive Jokes and Microaggressions

NOTE **AUTHOR'S NOTE**

> A heads-up: The advice here has been created in consultation with BIPOC (Black, Indigenous, and people of color) and other diversity, equity, and inclusion experts.

How many times have you heard a variant of this statement after you called someone out after an offensive joke, meme, or comment: "Oh, come on, you can't be seriously offended by this. We're just having a good time. Relax." Odds are it's a lot.

What's more annoying is that these types of comments (and the reaction people on the receiving end of the joke have) are exacerbated by Slack, Twitter/X, and their ilk. In the past, there was an upper limit of how many offensive jokes you could hear, but social media and its services have eradicated such limits.

The Problem

In Chapter 1, "Before the Conversation," you learned about Hanlon's razor, which invites you to consider that others may not realize the harm they're causing with these jokes. It doesn't mean that those jokes are okay, or that they don't hurt. It does mean that most of those terrible comments come from a place of ignorance. For clarity, "ignorance" is intended in the purest sense of the definition: when someone just doesn't know any better. That's different from willful offenders, who are a different sort entirely. You'll learn to deal with both here.

To illustrate how you can approach these situations, meet Adelaide and Rose.

Adelaide is a product manager at a startup. She also happens to be Black. Every quarter, the company announces profit-sharing bonuses. It's a big moment for the team to celebrate. It's not uncommon to hear people say what they're going to do with this extra cash. Some go on vacation, while others pay off debt.

Rose is a newcomer, and this is her first quarter receiving this bonus. She was hand-picked by the CEO to join the team because her family and the CEO's are very close. It's obvious to everyone that Rose is well-heeled, owing partly to Rose being very open about it.

When Adelaide speaks up to her friends about what she's going to do, she talks about getting a new car to replace her current, problematic one. Rose, however, has some thoughts.

> Rose: "Oh no, you should get a washer and dryer. People like you should spend your money on that."

Adelaide didn't respond immediately. She was stunned, feeling like she'd been sucker punched. Rose likely didn't mean anything by it—most people don't—but Adelaide still felt the sting. It's as if someone accidentally steps on your foot while running past you: they may not have meant it, but it still hurts just the same.

At the time—closer to ten years ago—Adelaide didn't have the vocabulary to name what just happened to her when Rose lumped her in with comments such as "people like you." Today, there is a term for that: *microaggressions.*

Understanding Microaggressions

Microaggressions are subtle forms of discrimination that use assumptions or value judgments against someone who belongs to a particular group (e.g., racial, cultural, gender, or religion). *Racial Microaggressions in Everyday Life,*[1] written by Derald Wing Sue et. al, has a wonderful chart worth reading in full. See Tables 8.1 and 8.2.

Here are a few examples that people experience in the workplace:

If what you're saying sexualizes, dehumanizes, or stereotypes someone, these are signs you should reconsider your phrasing. Read on for how to handle anything from a microaggression to a full-tilt horrible joke.

1 D. W. Sue et al., "Racial Microaggressions in Everyday Life: Implications for Clinical Practice," *American Psychologist* 62, no. 4 (2007): 271–286, https://doi.org/10.1037/0003-066X.62.4.271

TABLE 8.1 MICROAGGRESSIONS BASED ON GENDER, RACE, AND/OR IDENTITY

Theme	Description
Alien in own land	Assuming a person is a foreigner.
Ascription of intelligence	Assigning intelligence to a person based on race, gender or (perceived) abilities.
Intrinsic skills and personality types	Using stereotypes of race, gender, and sexual orientation to assume an individual's interests and talents.
Color blindness	Refusing to acknowledge race or sexual orientation.
Denial of individual prejudice	Statements denying those with social privilege have that privilege or any oppressive thinking.
Myth of meritocracy	Statements which assert that race, class, gender, abilities, or sexual orientation do not play a role in life success.

Examples	Implicit Message
"You speak good English; you don't even speak with an accent." (when said to a person of color)	You are not American.
"Your people are good at math, right? Can you figure out this Excel sheet equation?" (when said to an Asian American)	Asians are naturally gifted in the sciences and math; they do not work hard for it.
"Oh, you are a bio major? Are you studying to be a nurse?" (when said to a woman)	Women are not smart enough to be doctors—men would rarely, if ever, be asked this question.
"You're gay? You have to give me some decorating tips!"	All gay men are interested and talented in interior design and decorating.
"Women in power lead by emotion and are too sensitive!"	Women are "genetically" emotional and sensitive. They are not intelligent, rational and impartial.
"When I look at you, I don't see color."	Denying a person of color's racial or ethnic experiences.
"America is a melting pot."	Assimilate to the dominant culture.
"I don't support gay rights because they are 'special rights'—everyone is equal!"	Denying that queer people are treated differently in our society.
"I can't be racist. My friend is Puerto Rican...I voted for Obama...My girlfriend is Asian, etc."	I am immune to racism because I have had positive associations or relationships with people of color.
"As a woman, I know what you go through as a racial minority."	Your racial oppression is no different than my gender oppression. All forms of discrimination are equal.
"I am not homophobic - I have gay friends, and I love *Project Runway*!"	I am immune to homophobia because I have LGBT friends, and I associate with mainstream stereotypes of queerness.
"We all know she got hired because she is a woman!" (often said in a male-dominated field)	Women are not as qualified as male candidates; gender was "used" as a way to get ahead.
"I believe that the smartest and most qualified students should be admitted. The most qualified person should get the job."	People of color are given extra unfair benefits because of their race.

TABLE 8.2 OFFENSIVE PHRASES

Offensive Phrase	Who It Affects	Why It's Bad	What to Consider
"I'm going to open the kimono."	Women from Japanese culture	Sexualized, misogynist	"To be fully transparent..."
"You're so articulate."	Any	It assumes everyone else who looks like them isn't or that it's somehow unique	Be more specific. "I really appreciate how you said that."
"You're a compliment to your people."	Any BIPOC	It assumes everyone else who looks like them isn't good	Focus on them as an individual, not as a part of a bigger group. "You're really nailing this."

The Solution

As mentioned in Chapter 3, "People Losing Control," it's deeply unfair that you have to do anything at all in situations such as these. The primary (and ideal) solution here would be that the other person should educate themself and stop making those jokes. The practical approach to this would be to manage your response in such a way as to shut this down.

Make Them Explain It

The primary approach Adelaide (or you, should you be witnessing something) could take is to feign ignorance and let them explain themselves. Karen Catlin (author of *Better Allies*[2]) has a few tried-and-true methods for handling these kinds of jokes or comments: tell them you don't get it and ask them to explain how that comment is funny. She says this "forces them to confront their biases and realize that something is offensive. And chances are, they're going to say 'it's not worth it' and let it go."

2 Karen Catlin, *Better Allies: Everyday Actions to Create Inclusive, Engaging Workplaces*, 2nd ed. (San Mateo, CA: Better Allies Press, 2021).

Here are a few things you can say in moments like this:

- I don't get it.
- How's that funny?
- Where's the joke?
- I'm having trouble seeing how that isn't offensive.

NOTE **REMINDER: USE WHAT AND HOW**

It's best to avoid using "why" questions in situations like this, as this is a defensive trigger. Focus on other open-ended questions that keep the logical part of their brain engaged. For more on open-ended questions, see Chapter 2, "Having the Conversation."

Another helpful way of getting someone to explain is to use a reflecting technique (see Chapter 2). Some of the things that she could say are:

- You people?
- A washer and dryer?
- You people? It sounds like you're trying to lump everyone who looks like me in the same group.
- You people? That's pretty offensive. Is that the vibe you want to give off?

Then follow it by a beat or two of silence, letting your comment sink in. This will underscore that the other person should consider their words more carefully.

Call Them In, Not Out

Most people's default method of thinking is to call someone out in the middle of the room. You may, however, do well to consider a gentler approach, aptly titled "calling them in." Karen explains that "the mindset you want to have is not blaming or shaming them. Instead, bring them along on the journey that you might be on yourself to be more inclusive of people. It's also going to go over better in private, especially if you sense the other person didn't mean it."

Here's another example from Adelaide. This time, she's being told how articulate she is. While it may be a well-meaning comment, she says Black women get this a lot, and the underlying assumption is that all other Black people aren't intelligent and articulate.

> **Rose:** So, how is it that you're working with content?
>
> **Adelaide:** My background's in marketing, journalism, and writing.
>
> **Rose:** Oh, you're so articulate.

If you want to call someone out, you might have a solid idea of what that looks like. You may even have a few perfect lines that will properly roast the offender. However, going back to what you learned in Chapter 2, remember there are three basic psychological needs to consider when dealing with others: autonomy, competence, and relatedness. In this case, relatedness is the need most at risk if you call someone out. That may result in two people being harmed, which isn't ideal.

If Adelaide (or you) wants to call Rose in, here's how that could look:

- "I made a joke like that once and quickly learned that comments like that are considered offensive. I'm sure that isn't your intention, but you should be aware."
- "Heads up. I found out that you shouldn't say things like that, because it's degrading to [the affected group]."
- "Yikes, that's pretty rough. Is that the vibe you want to give off?"
- "I used to think this was hilarious, but then I learned that it's pretty offensive."

By taking this approach, you're bringing someone along on your journey and not needling them with shame or ridicule.

There's another approach that's related. If Adelaide sees that the other person wants to learn, she will draw their attention to what was offensive in the conversation, and hopefully they won't make the same mistake twice. She doesn't want to take on educating someone as to why something was offensive (nor should she have to), but this approach is often enough to set someone on the right path with minimal effort on her part.

The Head-On Approach

After Rose's comment, Adelaide was (understandably) upset. Here's how she replied, though she says now that she regretted it. Rose was well-connected with the CEO and received preferential treatment, getting the best projects for herself. Adelaide blowing up would put her in a tricky spot. But she'd had enough. Here's what she said:

> Adelaide: "Wait, what? You people?"
>
> Rose: "You know, single parents. It must be hard for you with your kids to always have to go back and forth to the laundromat."
>
> Adelaide: "First of all, I have one kid, and I have a washer and dryer that I own. Second of all, what do you mean by 'you people?'"
>
> Rose: "Nothing, sorry. I didn't mean any offense by it."

This approach has a few benefits, namely that you're dealing directly with the issue at hand. It's possible that this could backfire on you and land you in a worse situation; everything depends on your rapport and standing with both the other person and your company.

Here are some other things Adelaide could say:

- "Okay, stop right there. Not every person who looks like me is the same. Making assumptions like this can come off as racist."
- "Saying 'you people' is offensive. I'm sure you aren't intentionally doing that, but that's where we are."
- "That's not okay."

And finally, just saying "ouch" can go a long way in helping someone remember there's a human on the receiving end of those degrading comments. When you do it, just like you do with the reflecting techniques you learned about in Chapter 2, give a few beats of silence afterward. Most self-aware people will catch onto this and apologize. If that's not the case, head to the next section.

Look Out For...

There are two big things to look out for here. One is bad faith arguments, which are designed to be annoying and frustrating. The other is playing into whatever stereotype may be in their heads about you or the group they are joking about.

Bad Faith Arguments

Bad faith arguments are (somewhat infuriating) tactics that are meant to trip you up by introducing bogus arguments and whatabouts. Here's the thing to know about them: you can't win here. These tactics are designed to give your argument death by a thousand cuts. The only way out is not to play the game. To get out, try using a reflection tool or refocus on your goals for this.

Table 8.3 shows a few common types of these arguments and how you can respond.

TABLE 8.3 BAD FAITH ARGUMENTS

Type of Bad Faith Argument	Description	Refocusing Statement to Use
Strawman	Presenting an extreme version of an argument that you never made in order to distort your position.	No one's saying *y*. We're talking about *x*.
Slippery slope	Related to strawman, saying if you do one thing, you open the door to other, worse things.	No one's saying *y* will happen, we're only talking about *x*.
Ad hominem	An attack on a person or group's character instead of the issue at hand. Designed to poison the source.	Yes, they may have done some bad things, but that doesn't change the core argument.
Cherry-picking	Choosing only data or sources that support your opinion.	That doesn't take all of the facts into account. We're talking about *x* specifically.
Bandwagon	Arguing that because it's widespread or common means that it isn't harmful.	Regardless, it's hurting me.

Because these types of arguments can take many forms, it isn't going to be possible to list them all out in a neat and tidy table. But regardless of the form it takes, if you find yourself getting confused or flustered, refocus and call back to your goals.

Playing into Their Hand

In more antagonistic situations, you'll experience people baiting you in hopes of riling you to prove their point. This is an an extension of the ad hominem argument, and it merits its own section. Adelaide's been there, and she knows this territory all too well. If someone can discredit her, they can discredit her argument.

Adelaide, being a Black woman, has to manage the "angry Black woman" trope. If she responds with a snarky comment or raises her voice, she almost automatically loses and gets branded as one. She's learned the hard way to find other paths to make her point. There are other, similar costs for people in other groups who speak up. Most women, for example, can be labeled as "difficult" or "bossy," which is a code word for "bitch."

Use Silence

Silence is powerful. Simply not responding and leaving an empty space in the conversation can be a great tool to show how someone has overstepped your boundaries or offended you.

Often, in group settings, you find that others will step in or move on quickly. Hopefully, someone in the group is a good ally who will speak up in the moment or find the person afterward to help them understand where they went wrong.

Either way, here's how Adelaide deals with it. "I'll let somebody say something and just let it hang in the air. Because the longer it hangs, especially if there are other people on a call, the better it works out for me." This is because she's not reacting. The last thing people hear isn't Adelaide's voice; rather, it's what the other person said.

Final Thoughts

If you find that you're the one making these jokes, it's great that you read this far—you're taking the best piece of advice on offer here: being open to learning. Make sure that the learning you do doesn't require the person who is affected to educate you. The second-best bit of advice is to learn to make genuine apologies when you offend someone. (Genuine apologies don't contain "but" or start like "I'm sorry you feel that way.")

- One of the best ways to call attention to a bad joke or microaggression is to feign ignorance and ask someone to explain themselves. Say you don't get it.
- Silence is powerful. If you find that someone's making an offensive joke, go silent and let them realize why you might not be responding.
- Try to call them in, not call them out. Bringing them along on your journey is the best way to help someone learn and shut down an offensive comment.
- Watch out for bad faith arguments. Use refocusing statements and call back to your goals.

CHAPTER 9

Disrespecting Boundaries

When writing this book, it became uncomfortably clear that people have issues with boundaries—some with setting them, others with respecting them. The stories ranged from the mildly annoying texts on the weekends to the overtly awful ones about being touched or hugged against their will.

This chapter covers four types of boundaries: social, digital, physical, and emotional (which covers social media and your devices) and how to deal when someone breaks them. It also helps you set healthy boundaries, which will reduce the likelihood of any weird boundary busters. You'll hear two stories that cover all four of the boundary types.

The Problem

Meet Dani and Maja, who both work at a consultancy. Dani is a product designer who deals with anxiety and needs to set clear boundaries to manage her anxiety. She works with Maja, a project manager at their company. Maja expects everyone on her teams to be fully available to the team whenever something arises. It isn't uncommon to see Maja replying to emails on a Saturday evening, and only in the most dire of circumstances would Dani do this.

Maja's lack of tact often causes some mess and friction. It's currently hindering her performance and relationships at work. Dani's boundaries and perceived unavailability have been off-putting for some members of the team.

Social and Digital

Dani said the tension hit almost immediately after starting work with Maja. "Right as we kicked off a project for a large financial company, Maja asked everyone to send their phone numbers so we could text each other." In the past, Dani had had people abuse this privilege by calling and texting her during off-hours, even though she had said not to for unnecessary and nonemergency reasons.

It made Dani anxious, and she felt she couldn't really get any time off from work. Her doctor advised her to set some hard boundaries, so she did. In this case with Maja, she said, "In the spirit of collaboration, I wanted to offer my phone number with some conditions."

Those conditions were:

- No texting and all communication should take place at work over their company chat app.
- Only call her number for emergencies.

Maja agreed to these conditions up front. But less than 30 minutes later, guess who emailed? And texted. Then called. Yep, Maja.

> Dani: "Hey Maja, what's up? Everything okay?"
>
> Maja: "I wanted to go over logistics and plan for our next meeting. I don't see you in the office."
>
> Dani: "I was very clear that I didn't want to use the phone unless this was an emergency. This doesn't sound like an emergency."
>
> Maja: "My mistake. Can you still talk?"

Dani found herself more and more anxious and avoiding her phone at all costs, even when friends would reach out. In this case, Maja broke Dani's social and digital boundaries.

More on this story in a moment. First, the other two types of boundaries.

Physical and Emotional

For this chapter, it was necessary to narrow the definition of physical boundaries to exclude inappropriate touching and worse. It's a gigantic field that makes it impossible to cover in a section of a chapter, or even a set of chapters.

Emotional boundaries include how you interact and what you discuss with one another; this could include things like political or religious beliefs, or things that might trigger anxiety or discomfort.

Consider the story that Justine, a designer, shared about her relationship with Elizabeth, a newer, more junior designer. Elizabeth, who came on to help with their company's design system, is young in her career and has a lot she wants to prove.

Here's some context: the team is in a meeting with their director to discuss a project update. The room has stadium seating, so anyone who stands up now towers over the person in front of them.

> **Director:** Okay, so how's the new registration flow coming? Any updates from our last round of research?
>
> **Justine:** Yeah, we found out from user testing that for every required field we add to the sign-up process, abandonment increases by 7%. At present, if we add shipping and billing up front, we're looking at 28% abandonment. It'd be better to add these when people are checking out so that—
>
> **Elizabeth:** (standing up behind Justine and interrupting loudly) Oh my godddd, Justine, the registration is fine. You know the design system needs to be the top priority, so stop screwing around!

Justine got angry because Elizabeth interrupted her, stood over her, and pointed fingers at her. She fired back that she was still talking. Before she knew it, Justine said, the conversation escalated, and Elizabeth was in her face, literally pointing fingers. She doesn't remember the specifics then, mostly because her amygdala dumped a ton of cortisol into her blood and her stress response took over. She only remembers walking out. There's a lot to learn from this situation.

First, you may be wondering why the director didn't do anything. You may also wonder what prompted Elizabeth to do this (Justine certainly did). Perhaps her director was just as shocked as Justine. Maybe Elizabeth had too many coffees. Either way, it wasn't great for Justine.

This experience left Justine feeling deeply uncomfortable and unsafe because Elizabeth invaded her physical and mental space, and no one stopped it.

So, what to do about Justine's problem with someone invading her personal and emotional space? Or Dani's problem with digital and social boundaries? The solutions to both aren't so different.

The Solution

First, the best way to prevent boundaries from being broken is to articulate them. To do this, you'll learn about working agreements and how they can help. The second-best way is to reinforce them. And you'll use working agreements and nonviolent communication to do so.

Create Working Agreements

A working agreement is a way of codifying your team's norms and preventing overstepping. It's a collaborative exercise that your team does together when it is formed, so it can establish a few basic rules. The agreements usually cover a few things, like the following:

- How meetings go
- Where to look for "sources of truth"
- Which channels communication happens on
- How decisions get made and conflicts are resolved
- And more, depending on your team's needs

NOTE WORKING AGREEMENTS

> Working agreements aren't a substitute for a basic code of conduct. No one should have to spell out basics like "don't yell at me" or "don't objectify me." The intent behind a working agreement is to augment your relationships, not serve as the baseline for acceptable behavior.

You can create a whiteboard exercise that allows each person to contribute to this, and then you can discuss and finalize it as a group. It's best to let people do this on their own so that each person has a chance to contribute equally and fairly. See Table 9.1.

It's worth revisiting your working agreements when someone new joins the team and periodically as a team's needs or directions change.

TABLE 9.1 WORKING AGREEMENT CONSIDERATIONS

Events	Considerations	Types of Boundaries	Examples
Meetings	Will meetings be timeboxed? Will start and stop times be enforced?	Social	Default to 30 minutes, hard starts and stops.
	Will invites include agendas and meeting links?	Social	All meeting invites include expected outcomes and Zoom links. Meetings without will be declined.
	How can we allow people who are quieter to contribute?	Social	We will do round-robins so that everyone gets a chance to speak.
	How can we accommodate those who are remote?	Social	If one of us is remote, all of us will join from our own computers.
Communication	What's the primary source of our communications? Email, Slack, etc.?	Social, Digital	Slack.
	What happens in emergencies? How will we know it's an emergency?	Social	Emails go out with "urgent" in subject line.
	What is everyone's preferred contact method in emergencies? Call? Text?	Social, Digital	Varies by person.
	How do we handle memes, jokes, and humor?	Social, Digital, Emotional	They're okay in public channels unless they're political or social issue related. Those types of humor stay in DMs between individuals, as long as it doesn't violate company policy.

TABLE 9.1 WORKING AGREEMENT CONSIDERATIONS

Events	Considerations	Types of Boundaries	Examples
Availability	What are the expectations if someone's communicating during nonstandard hours?	Social, Digital	Start messages with "Ignore until Monday."
	Do we want to establish core working hours?	Social, Emotional	Core hours from 10 a.m. PT - 2 p.m. PT.
	How do we know if someone's not available or shouldn't be interrupted?	Social, Emotional, Digital	They appear offline, have headphones on, or have focus time on their calendar.
Decision-making and conflict resolution	Who has the final call on which areas?	Social, Emotional	Varies by team or by area of responsibility.
	What assumptions do we make (e.g., good person, bad circumstances)?	Social, Emotional	Assume positive intent, but don't overlook the impact.
	How do we deal with out-of-bounds behavior?	Social, Emotional, Physical	Call out the behavior and remind them of their agreement.
Feedback	How does each person prefer to receive feedback? Immediately, publicly? Later, privately?	Social, Emotional	Varies by person.
Physical interaction	How does each person feel about high fives, fist bumps, or hugs?	Physical	Varies by person.
	How does each person feel about social distancing?	Physical	Varies by person.

Codify How to Address Out-of-Bounds Behavior

If you see someone violating boundaries, it's best to start by assuming positive intent and that they didn't mean any harm. As described earlier, *remember that intent is only part of the equation and doesn't apply to repeat violators*—you also need to deal with the impact, whether it's intended or not. Not dealing with this impact will continue enabling bad and harmful behavior.

One part of the working agreement that's helpful is a consistent, clear way of addressing this kind of behavior. It's helpful for four reasons:

- Everyone knows how to highlight it, so it's easier to start those conversations.
- Everyone knows how to receive and deal with it, so it's easier to resolve.
- Everyone is aware of the consequences of violating them.
- It's much less likely to turn personal because this is about them not honoring the team's agreements, rather than simply annoying you.

Table 9.2 can also be personalized to your company or team's culture. But it should contain two parts: components and examples.

TABLE 9.2 ADDRESSING OUT-OF-BOUNDS BEHAVIOR

Component	Examples
A callout that's unique to the team.	An emoji (e.g.,)
	A code word (e.g., "red flag")
A response that thanks them for calling it out and an inquiry about what it is.	If you agree and understand: "I hear you, I'm aware and trying to work on that. Thanks for calling it out."
	If you don't agree or don't understand: "Thanks. I'm not sure what I said. Do you want to talk now or later?"
	If you actively disagree and understand: "Thanks. That's not a viewpoint I share, but I'd like to hear where you're coming from. Can we talk later?"

You don't have to do this in the moment; it's up to you to decide when it's best. Maybe you'd prefer to call it out on the spot or perhaps it's a one-on-one conversation afterward. Look for how you think it would be best received and take that route.

To make this intervention even easier, you could set up automated Slackbot responses if someone says something out of bounds. It's much easier to receive because it comes from a bot, rather than directly from a human. So, all you need to do is type a command and Slack will do the rest.

Additionally, the conversation is much simpler if Dani's team has a working agreement. Here are two ways that a conversation could look:

- "According to our team working agreements about communication, this is out of bounds."
- "Hang on, this doesn't align with what our team agreements state. Are they out-of-date?"

Of course, rigid adherence to a process or working agreement will always lead to more friction and failure, but you know best when to flex and when to stand your ground.

Look Out For . . .

The worst scenarios occur either when there aren't any boundaries, or when there are, but people repeatedly flout them. It's much the same as putting tissue paper over a leak: if you're going to have boundaries, they need to be sturdy and reinforced.

Not Having Defined Boundaries

All of what you have read up until now has been about how to set boundaries. But what if there aren't any working agreements or healthy norms? You can still call out boundary-crossing behavior with the technique you just learned. Here's how that could look:

- Raise your hand in the moment or find that person afterward.
- Tell them, in a nonviolent way, that what happened made you uncomfortable because it crossed a specific boundary for you.
- Add safety by telling them you don't believe they meant any harm by what they did.
- If it's reasonable, try to find another way so that you can both get what you need.

Repeat Offenders

If you're continually experiencing problems, your best move is to start by documenting everything. This approach is the best process for those who forget (or "forget") your boundaries. After that, you can be pragmatic about how you approach it.

Document

In Dani's case, the calls and texts kept coming. Sometimes, she got three to four per day. She wanted to be clear about the issue and its impact. She also wanted to document what she needed via email. Here's what she said:

> "Hi Maja, you've called a few times for things that didn't seem like emergencies, and it looks like we should talk about the impact of this. When you call me while I'm working, it negatively impacts my ability to deliver good work. The more of these interruptions I get, the less focused, deep work I'm capable of. Our clients deserve the best, and I want to be able to give it to them.
>
> That said, I need you to only call me if it's an emergency. I define an emergency as when the client is angry, and I need to take immediate action to fix the problem.
>
> If you need more consistent connection, I'd be glad to set up a time for us to sync daily, so nothing gets dropped."

In doing this, Dani frames this in terms of the impact of Maja's behavior. She also establishes a paper trail, clarifies her boundaries, and offers a way forward so that both can get what they want. Because she frames this in terms of how it impacts their clients, she's more likely to get agreement from Maja. Justine did something similar by letting her manager know that Elizabeth was continuing with this behavior.

Be Pragmatic

It's possible for Dani to push back and say that texting her isn't acceptable. And she'd be well within her rights to do so, especially if it's her personal device and she has trouble dealing with anxiety.

Being different from everyone else on the team, however, can be its own problem. So, it's worth considering a pragmatic approach. Is there a way that Maja could communicate in a way that's natural for her without it causing Dani any additional anxiety? (Hint: Given that this book is about how to find ways for both people to get what they need, the answer is yes.)

In this case, Dani could try a virtual number (aka a burner). Burner numbers are incredibly helpful in situations where you may get spammed by sales folks, or you're meeting someone new and don't want to compromise your personal safety or privacy. These can prevent abuse, so why not employ them while at work?

By using a burner number, folks at work can text or call without giving away Dani's real number. Dani can also route it through Slack or most any chat app a team uses so that it never bothers her on her personal device unless she wants it to. And the team will never know it's a burner, either. They just communicate in a way that's natural to them, and Dani gets to keep her boundaries. These aren't very expensive—most are around $5/mo. It's a small price to pay for peace of mind and not having the label of "difficult" attached to your reputation.

Unfortunately for Dani, Maja never stopped, and Dani wasn't aware of burners at the time. So, she ended up blocking Maja's number on her phone and said she would only communicate via Slack or in person.

Final Thoughts

There are other boundaries that you shouldn't bother talking to the other person about. Some of these things need to go directly to human resources or someone you trust, and you can forget any kind of negotiation or direct communication. You don't even have to make a report; telling a savvy HR person that a certain type of behavior needs to be prohibited will clue them into what needs to happen, and they can deal with it at the employee handbook level.

This case was especially true for Justine, as Elizabeth's behavior worsened. Extremely so. "She came up to one of our tables just as we were breaking up a meeting. She asked what the meeting was about." She didn't recall the specifics, only that Elizabeth started joking about "bringing a shotgun to work." It's an extreme example, but Elizabeth was out after that. You should take a similar approach with other kinds of abuse, threats, or harassment.

- The best thing you can do is be clear about your boundaries.
- If no boundaries exist, consider creating a working agreement with your team.
- When you codify how to address out-of-bounds behavior, it's easier for everyone.
- If someone's a repeat offender, start documenting.
- Be pragmatic about how you approach the situation, look for a way for both of you to get what you need.
- Direct communication about boundary issues isn't always necessary. Sometimes you need to go directly to leadership or HR for a resolution.

CHAPTER 10

Understanding Cultural Dynamics

In this chapter, you'll learn how to approach hard conversations and conflict with people from different cultures. Its aim is to make something very clear: no book can tell you exactly how to act when you're working with anyone from any culture—everyone is unique. You must learn to recognize people as individuals, not just as a part of a larger population.

First, a seemingly odd segue. It will make sense later, so stick with it. Think for a moment about a game you likely played growing up: checkers. You're probably familiar with the rules about how the pieces move. But checkers has different playing styles across the world, even though the pieces and board look the same. That's the case with American and Italian checkers. While regular checker pieces can capture kings in American checkers, that isn't permitted in Italian checkers. So, before you really dive into playing, you need to learn which version of the game you're playing. You might say you need to... check(ers) your assumptions.

The Problem

Now, to make this metaphor real, meet Enid. She's the newest intern at a startup incubator, and she's from India. She's working with Doug, her American counterpart. Doug doesn't manage Enid but has been there longer than she has.

Growing up in an Indian culture, Enid says, "It's always been really ingrained that we listen to people in authority and power. As an Indian, my parents ingrained a fear of not listening to your teachers or your principal." Naturally, her relationship to authority at work would follow a similar pattern.

She says that when she started her internship, she said yes to everything. "I found it really hard to push back or have boundaries. I didn't want it to look bad, nor did I want to ruin any opportunity for full time." Doing this was overtaxing her. "Sometimes that meant I was working way beyond my mental capacity and the things that I could handle."

So, when an ambitious Doug said in a meeting on behalf of both him and Enid that they could update a tome of long out-of-date documentation in a week, Enid internally panicked. She thought there's no way she could do this without sacrificing sleep.

Doug wasn't her manager, but he'd been there longer. Enid assumed that meant he had more power than she did, so she didn't speak up. "I thought he'd think I'm not taking it seriously or he'd have a negative perception of me that impacts my role. Maybe I'd get fired," Enid said.

Doug, used to direct feedback, expected Enid to speak up if that decision didn't work for her. So, why didn't Enid just speak up? And how could this have been avoided? The answer lies in understanding the dimensions of culture and how they shape people's personalities.

The Solution

Humans view others through the lens of their own lived experience. And they aren't always aware they're doing it, which leads to conflict when a situation doesn't match their expectations.

There's a term for this: *ethnocentrism*. In short, it's the evaluation of other cultures according to preconceptions originating in the standards and customs of your own culture. While not bad in and of itself, ethnocentrism is associated with enabling some truly rotten attitudes, such as racism and xenophobia.

Once you gain curiosity and learn how to understand others' cultures, you mitigate the negative effects of ethnocentrism, and by extension, many conflicts at work. The brain loves to take shortcuts to save energy—ethnocentrism is certainly one of them—so getting away from these ways of thinking requires a bit of effort. It won't be as hard as you think, though.

Understand Dimensions of Identity

When it comes to the dimensions that make up someone's identity, you need to be mindful of a few things:

- Some aspects present stronger than others.
- The aspects that present stronger can change based on the situation or over time.

In 1950, an IBM engineer named Geert Hofstede came up with the dimensions that shape culture and, by extension, a person's identity. Hofstede's research contains six dimensions; however, this book only considers these three: power distance, individualism vs. collectivism, and assertive vs. collaborative.

To lead you through this section, here's the story of Korean Air Flight 801 and its crash into a mountain. It perfectly exemplifies the issues at play with dimensions of identity. In 1998, Don Phillips, writing for the *Washington Post*, summarized the crash:[1]

> The crew of Korean Air Flight 801 grew nervous as the Boeing 747 approached Agana, Guam, on a rainy night in August. Something didn't feel right.
>
> The plane, being flown by autopilot, was descending steeply. The crew talked about the altitude, and someone said several times that the airport "is not in sight." But investigative sources said neither the copilot nor the flight engineer spoke out boldly, as trained, to alert the captain or even to urge breaking off the landing.
>
> Alarms suddenly sounded in the cockpit. After an excruciating pause of several seconds, the captain finally cut off the autopilot and prepared to pull up. At almost that moment, the crew of another plane perhaps 50 miles away saw the clouds ahead glow bright red. The red glow was the Korean Air jet slamming into the top of Nimitz Hill, killing 228 of the 254 people on board. The moments of hesitation may have made the difference because the jumbo jet would have cleared the hill if it had been just a few feet higher.

Power Distance

Power distance is the extent to which the less powerful members of a group expect and accept an uneven power distribution (see Table 10.1). This value affects how likely someone is to speak up to their leadership when there's a problem, much like the one Enid faced with Doug and the flight crew faced with their captain.

In high-power distance cultures, people are much less likely to contradict or speak out against leaders when faced with a difficult situation. What's interesting here is Geerts' research indicates that Koreans live in a higher power distance culture, whereas their flight training was created with American norms in mind. America is a lower power distance culture.

Paul J. Sherman, Robert L. Helmreich, and Ashleigh C. Merritt of the University of Texas psychology department indicated in a study that national culture greatly contributes to the determination of whether

---

1 Don Phillips, "Is Culture a Factor in Air Crashes? Guam Probe May Raise Touchy Issue," *The Washington Post*, March 17, 1998.

a pilot relies on automation. There were 5,879 pilots from 12 nations in the study and every single Korean pilot responded "yes" to preferring automation and whether the effective pilot "always" used automation. They concluded that pilots from more hierarchical national cultures, such as South Korea, may be more inclined to follow flight management software's authority without question. Certainly not every single South Korean Air pilot will always follow automation. Each situation and person involved contains more nuance than a single study can convey, but such a high number does indicate a pattern worth keeping in mind.

TABLE 10.1 POWER DISTANCE

Low-Power Distance	High-Power Distance
You can disagree openly with those in power.	You don't disagree or dissent at all with those in power.
You follow most of what your boss says but call out any problems you see.	You follow everything your boss says, even if you see a problem with it.
You expect to be consulted on matters that affect you.	You expect to be told what to do in all situations, even those that affect you.
Power is less centralized, and teams self-organize.	Power is centralized and tasks are delegated.

To gauge how someone falls on this spectrum, ask these questions:

- When was the last time you disagreed with your boss? How did it go?
- Do you typically ask questions about your tasks, or do you just do them?
- Do you typically collaborate with your boss on new initiatives, or are they generally handed down?

What this means for you is that some people may have a stronger deference to authority and advocate for doing things the way it's always been done. Some people from higher power distance cultures may find it more difficult to deviate from their standard operating procedure unless a leader explicitly says that is expected. This is easier for smaller power distance cultures to address, as it's expected for people to speak their mind.

Enid, who had been aware of this cultural difference on some level, said, "I remember the first time where I said to my manager, 'You want this project done, and I'm keen to do it, but I can't do it by this Friday. It's gonna take at least three weeks.'" How did Doug take it? He said that's cool, and thanked Enid for telling him.

Individualism vs. Collectivism

This spectrum looks at the degree of interdependence a society maintains among its members. It addresses things like whether harmony should always be maintained and direct confrontation avoided or if it's acceptable to speak one's mind. Essentially, do they think in terms of "I" or "we?" See Table 10.2.

TABLE 10.2 INDIVIDUALISM VS. COLLECTIVISM

Individualist	Collectivist
It's about me.	It's about us.
You may receive feedback directly from your boss.	Receiving feedback directly from your boss may be an embarrassment, and it is usually delivered indirectly.
Business relationships are transactional, you can get fired for performance issues.	Business relationships are more familial, you're less likely to get fired for performance issues.
Task over relationship.	Relationship over task.
Rewards come from individual performance and are distributed unequally.	Rewards come from group performance, distributed equally.

To gauge how someone falls on this spectrum, ask these questions:

- Do you typically receive feedback directly from your boss, like in an annual performance review?
- Do you typically say "I" or "we" more when referring to the company or team?

Once you understand whether someone is more individualist or collectivist, you can change your tack to show what the individual will gain vs. what the group will gain. Their particular leanings may be different than the rest of the team, and that's not so bad. It's healthy tension, and it pushes you to recall that not everyone thinks the same way.

For Doug and Enid, there's also a clash. According to Hofstede's model, the U.S. ranks strongly more individualist than collectivist. After all, "liberty" is what it's all about in the States. People in the States are generally expected to take the initiative and responsibility for their lives, work, and success. It's not that way everywhere, though.

South Korea and Enid, on the other hand, lean more toward the collectivist. People who align more as collectivists tend to place a higher value on loyalty to their group or organization, to the extent that it may be prioritized over other rules and regulations.

Assertive vs. Collaborative

With this dimension, it's all about how aggressively issues and tasks are addressed. The more assertive end of this spectrum has people being much more direct. Assertive can be associated with being a "Type-A" personality, "my way or the highway" mentality, or sometimes a bully who will do anything to "win." The collaborative side, on the other hand, is more considerate of the individual and everyone's needs. They want everyone to win. See Table 10.3 for examples.

TABLE 10.3 ASSERTIVE VS. COLLABORATIVE

Assertive	Collaborative
Decisive, aggressive, and competitive.	Intuitive and driven to consensus.
Live to work.	Work to live.
With conflict, the strongest or pushiest win.	With conflict, compromise and negotiation win.
When done poorly, comes across as coercive or manipulative.	When done poorly, comes across as inept and indecisive.

If you find that someone is more collaborative, you'll want to consult them more on decisions to make sure they're getting what they need. It's the viewpoint of this book that the workplace needs more of a collaborative approach. You may also want to keep in mind that these folks may be less inclined to speak up for themselves.

NOTE **ASSERTIVE VS. COLLABORATIVE**

> Hofstede's research calls this value *masculine vs. feminine*. This book appreciates the research that underpins the ideas but rejects such framing in favor of a more equitable, less arbitrary label.

To gauge how someone falls on this spectrum, ask these questions:

- The last time you had a conflict, did you have to push your way to a victory? Or did you take another route?
- The last time you had a bad time at work, did you grit your teeth and get through it or talk about how the situation impacted you?

For Doug and Enid, they are both from nearly opposite ends of every spectrum. Doug is used to being low-power distance, individualist, and assertive (but he does find himself a little more collaborative than he used to be). That's also the culture of their team. Enid, on the other hand, is used to higher power distances, has more collectivist tendencies, and is more collaborative. Both have a little learning to do on how to work together.

And again, Enid knew that she needed a bit more assertiveness. She said, "It took me a really long time to emphasize boundaries and say things like 'that's really late for me,' or 'I don't have time for this or things like that.'" But once she did, she had a much easier time.

Be Curious

Darren Hood, an expert in the field of emotional intelligence, has much to say on this topic. First, and most important: "I cannot expect everybody to be me." But often people do exactly that.

The solution, as obvious as it may seem, is to understand the perspectives of other people. "When I come in contact with someone, I have to make it my business to educate myself about their perspectives. I need to understand what's important to them. I need to understand what may or may not be taboo for them." Using the dimensions of identity from earlier in this chapter can help get this process started.

He also made another solid point: "We make the world go round because of our awareness and willingness to humble ourselves to that other person's perspectives. Make it important to understand what that person deems important and valuable. It just... makes everything work."

So, what could Doug do? He can take the time to educate himself on Enid's culture, what her values are, and what she cares about. By doing this, he can take the best tack with Enid and create an environment where she can contribute as fully as possible.

Here are a few practical ways Doug (or you) can try this out:

- What's their favorite candy or treat? Then order some and share it around if you can.
- What's their favorite holiday to celebrate? Then search the web and ask them what their favorite part is. (Thanks to Dalia Ahmed for this idea.)
- How do they prefer to receive feedback? In public or private? In conversation or email? Immediately or later? This can tell you much about how they prefer to contribute.

Look Out For...

There are two main things to look out for: stereotyping and shortcuts. Both are pernicious and require extra attention so that your message comes across clearly and is as well received as it possibly could be.

Stereotyping

President Barack Obama, running a few minutes late to speak at his final White House Correspondents Dinner, said "I know I was a little late tonight. I was running on C.P.T. Which stands for jokes that White people should not make." C.P.T, if you're unfamiliar, means "Colored People Time." It refers to the stereotype that Black people aren't ever on time.

Some people joke that stereotypes exist for a reason, but that's just a logical fallacy at work—namely, confirmation bias. In short, the more you look for something, the more you see evidence that confirms your belief. Sure, Black people may be late to things sometimes, but no more than anyone else would be. Singling out a particular group isn't fair because everyone does it.

Here's the thing: stereotypes lie to you. They make others seem less-than. And it's your job when working out a conflict with someone else of another culture to avoid these stereotypes.

When you use a stereotype, you make the other person feel very much like an "other" and not one of you. You've unfairly grouped them with another group and reduced their identity to a label. It's likely you didn't mean to do so, but these actions and words still have impact, which you'll want to mitigate by apologizing and educating yourself.

Stereotypes typically affect the following areas and can be both positive and negative:

- Social
- Gender
- Religion
- Culture
- Race
- Financial

Really, though, you can stereotype anyone who identifies with a certain group. It could be engineers, designers, stakeholders, or even customers. Table 10.4 shows a few ways that these stereotypes could play out at work.

TABLE 10.4 STEREOTYPES AT WORK

Area	Example
Engineers	[This person] certainly doesn't look like an engineer. Engineers from [this country] are the best because they're good at math.
Designers	Designers [of this gender] have to have everything just right. Designers from [this culture] are so argumentative.
Managers and stakeholders	They don't care about anything but meeting deadlines. [This gender] is so bossy. They're from [this financial background] so all they care about is making money. They just swoop in and ruin things, they have no idea what's going on.
Customers and users	People from [this culture] really need help with finances. People from [this part of the country] are so entitled.

Shortcuts

There are many, many lists or tips for what people from other cultures expect. And while they are sometimes helpful, they're far too often reductive, simplistic, and encourage stereotyping. You know by now that brains love shortcuts. That's what gives ideas like ethnocentrism and pernicious stereotypes more weight than necessary. It's also what makes more problems for you than necessary.

There is no substitute for listening and looking. Yes, it requires a little more work but is truly the key to unlocking paths forward when you're from a different culture. Darren Hood has solid advice: "I make it personal. It's one person at a time." When you stop thinking about generalizations, you resist the urge to use shortcuts and be, as Darren says, "cognitively lazy."

NOTE ARE YOU USING A SHORTCUT?

> If you hear "Americans prefer" or "Japanese expect," consider that to be a red flag unless it's from (respectively) an American or Japanese person.

Here's how you counter it: learn about the culture that the other person is from. Understand what body language means to them. Look for authoritative sources, such as people who are actually from that place. Darren summed it up: "Everyone is made up of their upbringing, what they've been exposed to, and experiences they've had." We need to understand and honor those when we interact with someone. That's the key to figuring things out with them.

Final Thoughts

While entire books and courses have been dedicated to this chapter's topic, you've saved yourself loads of time by reading this chapter. Now, you understand the core tenets of how to engage in a better conflict with someone from another culture—namely, being curious, educating yourself, and listening.

This chapter closes with some fairly blunt, yet perfect advice from Darren: "We are too much in a hurry." And it's true. So, take the time to slow down and get to know someone—it will cover many of your unintentional missteps.

Remember three key dimensions that define someone's identity:

- Power distance is how likely someone is to defer or speak to authority.
- Individualism vs. collectivism is how much someone cares about the group versus themselves.
- Assertive vs. collaborative is how dominant someone may want to be in a situation.

There's no substitution for curiosity and suspending your stereotypes.

CHAPTER 11

Unmet Expectations

How do you talk to someone who's not measuring up or failing to meet their obligations? Sure, you could be brief and blunt, but in doing that, you risk destroying their (or worse, your team's) motivation. You also risk not uncovering the underlying issues, preventing a clear understanding of the problem and ideal outcomes.

The Problem

We'll explore this issue through the story of Lee and Marcus. Lee is Marcus's director, both of them work in a consultancy. Marcus isn't doing well, and is underperforming by not delivering work that meets the bar, nor is he doing it a timely manner. To complicate matters, Marcus isn't great with getting feedback.

While this chapter focuses on someone who is underperforming, its lessons are applicable in many other situations you find yourself in at work. A few of them being the following:

- Being late
- Missing deadlines
- Missing quarterly or yearly targets
- Slacking or not pulling their weight
- Having a negative attitude
- Having poor hygiene

Lee says that "Marcus interviewed well. But when he started, we noticed he was going a little slower than we expected. Marcus spent a disproportionate amount of time working on wireframes." Marcus's behavior was in direct conflict with Lee's client's expectations.

The Solution

Before you jump into action, take a beat. Listen and understand the situation. Doing this gives you clarity on the problem and ensures that you can get to the bottom of things. Once you do, you can focus on a plan of action.

Listen and Explore Before Solving

Too often, people start at the end by jumping to conclusions. It's just what minds are trained to do, but you can't let it happen here. The more you listen, the more insights you gain, and the more doors you open for better outcomes.

Luckily, Marcus had a standing weekly working session with Lee to ensure that he settled in well. That also carried another benefit: the ability to spot and correct any missteps before they became problems.

The first thing Lee did was talk to Marcus to see what was going on with his work.

> Lee: "So, you've been at this for a couple weeks. I'm noticing you're still on the sketch phase. We typically prefer to be further along here. Can you tell me what's happening?"
>
> Marcus: "Yeah, I'm still trying to understand the team, and I think better when I'm sketching wireframes. I'll try to move faster."

Lee highlighted something crucial that every manager should do: call attention to the problem and let them try to solve it first. It's important because you don't want to chip away at someone's autonomy the first time you talk to them. If you jump to solving, you put a basic psychological need at risk (see Chapter 2, "Having the Conversation"). Plus, you risk having learned helplessness, which will hinder both of you going forward. In most cases, you'll want to approach problems like this:

1. Highlight the problem, probe for causes and solutions, but let them take the lead on addressing it. This is the solution most of the time.
2. Revisit the problem, but be much more direct about what needs to happen next. Define clear outcomes and what needs to happen to get there.
3. If it's still an issue, and especially if you're in leadership, ask yourself if you've been clear enough. Then take appropriate action.

When you're probing, use lots of open-ended questions (see Chapter 2). These questions will help you get to the bottom of things.

NOTE ONE WORD TO AVOID

Remember: try to avoid "why," since this is a defensive trigger word. You can get better answers with questions that start with "what" and "how."

If you're having the conversation a second time, it's worth being more direct about your expected outcomes—they may have misinterpreted something.

The second time Lee talked with Marcus, it was a bit more direct:

> **Lee:** "Okay, I understand that you think best in wireframes. I get that. I want to get a good balance that allows you to do that while also being able to deliver work quickly. What I'd propose is that you sketch in wireframes, but only show the team the more polished mockups. I'd like you to try that for next week's presentation. Is that workable?"

After checking in with the team, it was apparent that this conversation didn't resolve Marcus's performance and delivery issue.

Lee faced a choice on which issue to deal with first: Marcus's performance or his morale-sinking attitude. Lee chose to focus on the work first: "Mostly because that was the most tangible way to see improvement, and the team was falling behind. But I wonder what would have happened if I had talked about his attitude issue first."

So, before discussing more about how Lee handled things related to Marcus's work, it's worth talking about what Lee didn't deal with: the secondhand information about Marcus's attitude.

Deal with Secondhand Information

There will be times when you need to talk to someone without all the facts. Often, that's how leadership finds out about issues—through hearsay. Maybe someone like Marcus is toxic to their team or perhaps they're constantly coming late to client meetings.

Whatever the case, you've got a little more work ahead of you when there's hearsay: untangling everyone else's conclusions and observations about what's going on. Why? Because everyone else looks at the world through their own lens, which distorts things a bit.

NOTE HEADS UP, BOSSES

> If you're the boss, you have even more work to do. The intensity of a situation is magnified just by the simple fact that you're intervening. You have to work extra hard to be neutral and suspend judgment early on. People won't always tell you the whole (or true) story. So, focus on gathering all the facts before forming your own conclusions.

When Lee heard from multiple sources that Marcus wasn't performing well, nor was he taking critiques as well as he should, it was concerning. Lee said, "I heard he told other people how much he hated what we're doing; how it felt like someone was always looking over his shoulder. He was being defensive when receiving feedback, too, even though it was based on user feedback." Lee heard this from people at every level, too, not just his team.

The impact of Marcus's defensiveness and negative comments had an understandably negative effect on the team's morale. Why shouldn't it? The team couldn't trust their teammate, he wasn't great to work with, and his attitude held things up unnecessarily.

Should Lee have opted to discuss this, he would have needed to maintain a bit more tact so things didn't get worse. Here's how it could have gone:

> Lee: "Marcus, I don't like to work with secondhand information because everything tends to get distorted. I've heard that you've said a few things about how we work, specifically issues you have with how we collaborate. So, instead of putting all the pieces together myself and potentially missing something, I thought I'd come to you directly and hear what's going on. I haven't formed any conclusions yet, so tell me: what's happening there?"

If you find yourself in a situation like that, Table 11.1 illuminates how to navigate such a situation.

TABLE 11.1 DEALING WITH SECONDHAND INFORMATION

Step	Example
Address secondhand info and its failures.	I don't like to work with secondhand information, because everything tends to get distorted. I've heard [this issue] and instead of putting all the pieces together myself I thought I'd come to you directly and hear what's going on.
Ask open-ended questions to gather facts.	Can you tell me how ______________ is going?
Form your conclusions.	Okay, it sounds like ______________.
Open it up to them.	What do you think should happen next?
Form a plan to address it.	This can be co-created, or dictated based on the situation or your relationship with them.

Only after you have listened and gathered all the facts can you start sharing your conclusions and forming next steps. What happens next will depend on your relationship to them. (For example, do you manage them, or are they a vendor?)

Establish Outcomes and Accountability

After you've gotten the proper context about your situation, it's time to move toward a solution. The ideal solutions involve establishing measurable outcomes and accountability.

> **NOTE** **REMEMBER: KEEP IT ABOUT THE WORK, NOT THEM**
>
> It's rare that someone intends to put another person in a bad position, so when talking, state how what's happening affects you or your team. Remember to do this in a nonviolent way (see Chapter 1, "Before the Conversation").

Leaders must pay special attention here: if that's you, ensure that you aren't setting your team up for more shortcomings like the one in front of you. Solving this issue doesn't mean that you've solved the underlying cause(s). Lucky for Lee, the team had an existing standing critique, making it easy to ask Marcus to present something each week.

Here are the things to work through when establishing outcomes and accountability:

- What's the problem and how did you get here?
- What are the stakes if the problem isn't resolved?
- What's the expected outcome?
- What's the remedy or expected outcome?
- How do you measure accountability and progress?

Find Clarity

When it comes to defining outcomes and measuring accountability, clarity must be your prime consideration. Err on the side of being too clear, as you're rarely as concise in your requests as you may think. If what you ask isn't clear, you risk misinterpretation and not getting the results you need (see Chapter 1 for more on setting clear goals).

Write It Down

It's also important to write these things down for three reasons:

- You're forced to articulate your goals more clearly than if you were just talking or thinking to yourself.
- You've got a helpful reference point for the other person to measure their progress.
- You've got a concrete record should you need to reassign or terminate them.

Don't just write it and send it, though: email is best for documentation, not communication. And make sure that you're following whatever protocols your HR department requires. Yes, you could just put this in a message to them and be done with it, although that's a little cold. It's best if you personalize and humanize it a bit with a conversation.

Maybe say something like this:

> Lee: "So, I need to be direct here. I'm still not seeing the level of progress I need to see, and the work I see is not meeting the bar for what we expect here. Specifically, you're still on wireframes, and we've discussed twice that you need to deliver higher fidelity work faster. In the interest of no surprises, I want to tell you what I expect. I need you to have delivered high-fidelity versions of this work to the team by next week. No more presenting wireframes. I also need you to have progress that you show in our weekly design critiques. If any of this isn't clear, or I'm missing something big here, please let me know."

The following techniques help you get a clear shared understanding of the problem and how to move forward together. Table 11.2 shows how that could look for Lee and Marcus.

TABLE 11.2 OUTCOMES AND ACCOUNTABILITY

Problem	Delivering lower-fidelity work that doesn't meet the bar for quality. Not considering accessibility in design. Not taking feedback well.
Stakes	This jeopardizes the team's ability to deliver the project, their morale, and your position in the company.
Expected outcome	Deliver work that meets our clearly defined standards.
Remedy	Other designers will spend time mentoring. Feedback from users will be incorporated.
Accountability	Show something weekly at design critiques.

Also worth noting here is that remedies can take many forms, all of which will vary based on your relationship to the other person and the severity of the situation. Here's when you may want to change your tack, as shown in Table 11.3.

TABLE 11.3 REMEDIES BASED ON RELATIONSHIP

At your level	Tracking systems for visibility Daily or weekly syncs
Below your level	Tracking Systems for Visibility Performance improvement plans Termination or reassignment Extra training or coaching Daily or weekly syncs
Outside of your hierarchy (e.g., vendors)	Freebies to sweeten the deal or regain trust Renegotiation of rates Reassignment of a particular representative

Look Out For...

Any time you have a conversation like this, you're at risk of people getting defensive or emotional. It's possible that they might turn things around on you with personal attacks, but you can counter those attacks by adjusting the tone you take when speaking to them, as well as how much you engage with them—sometimes you just have to deliver bad news.

Turning It Around

A common (and very effective) deflection tactic that signals things aren't going well is when someone flips the script on you. It's in almost every argument: "Yeah, well what about the thing *you* did?" In short, most of these are types of ad hominem attacks. The most common is trying to paint you as a hypocrite or someone who's also guilty, but there are several other ways that people can turn things around on you, including the following, shown in Table 11.4.

TABLE 11.4 TYPES OF AD HOMINEM ARGUMENTS

Type of Argument	Example of Argument
Questioning your motives	I think you're really just out for yourself and your friends. You don't have my best interests at heart.
Doubting your expertise	You aren't an expert in this, so why should I listen to you?
Policing your tone (avoiding the argument to focus on how you framed it)	You're too emotional about this. Calm down.
Painting you as a hypocrite	You didn't set me up for success, so why should I be blamed?

Despite the amount of nuances these arguments contain, there are a number of valid ways to address them. You'll know best which one to use. Your first line of defense here is cranky conclusions (see Chapter 1) because it takes the steam out of their train at the outset of your conversation. Here are four other great options:

- Remember that patterns are your strongest ally. Single instances are easy to blow off, while patterns are much more difficult. Share your patterns and then make them do the work of squaring the pattern with their defense.
- Use reflecting techniques and open-ended questions. Some people reflexively get defensive, so this technique helps re-center them and the conversation.
- If they bury you in verbal garbage or steamroll you, acknowledge their thought but decline to address it and call back to your goals.
- Use refocusing statements to deflect arguments that are irrelevant or paint you as a hypocrite. You can choose to address them directly if they affect the outcome or your credibility.

For example, say Lee talked with Marcus about his lack of progress and he got defensive.

> Lee: "I'm sorry to say, Marcus, this just isn't up to par. There doesn't seem to be any accessibility consideration, nor a consistent method for laying out the app."

Marcus: "Well, you didn't exactly do a good job of showing me what "par" is. How can I meet this if I don't know what it is? Nothing about my onboarding was clear. I don't know how you expect me to succeed if you don't clearly lay out what your expectations are."

Here, Marcus is distracting from the point.

Lee: "Okay, let's talk about what I can do differently in a moment. Right now, we need to focus on upping the quality here. You need to spend time reading through Apple's "Human Interface Guidelines" and making sure the app you're designing looks like an app. You also need to understand how what you're designing will be used by people with disabilities, specifically with regard to vision. I'll see if I can make that any more clear in our documentation. But for now, what questions can I answer to make sure it's clear what you need to do right now?"

Marcus could also go on at length to defend himself, or call in any number of tangential arguments. While it doesn't bear writing out here, you'll know them when you hear them because they won't match up with the core of what you need them to do. If you feel yourself getting too far off the mark from the original goal, all you need to do is get the other person to refocus:

Lee: "I'm not saying those aren't valid issues, I agree we should look into them. However, I still need for you to focus on the actions we just outlined."

Tone

Lee could also opt to go a little stronger if it's warranted. Generally, raising the spectre of someone's job being in jeopardy largely decimates any sense of safety someone has. It also doesn't look good for you. Lee is cautious about such directness; being more direct has "the stigma of being labeled as difficult or a bitch boss." So tread carefully.

NOTE **DON'T FORGET ABOUT KINDNESS**

While you should never sugarcoat a situation, kindness is always important. Remember everyone is doing the best they can, given their skills and knowledge at the time. Never belittle or berate someone, because this is one of the most sensitive conversations you could have.

This is, however, helpful if you're in a situation where a vendor or service provider isn't meeting your bar. Ultimately, you will know what's best in your situation. Here's a stronger version as an example:

> Lee: "Marcus, the work I'm seeing isn't meeting the bar [name specific instances of issues and how he's been told before]. It's jeopardizing your position here in the company. No one wants that outcome, least of all me, but you deserve to know the stakes. Let's work together on a plan to make this right."

Then Lee could go on to mention the concrete expectations set out in the previous statement. Marcus, having heard the first statement, said he'd get it together.

Delivering Bad News

It shouldn't be a surprise that you may end up having to cut ties with this person. Maybe one of you gets reassigned. Maybe you let someone go. These situations are painful, but there are still ways to address them with kindness and directness.

One day, Lee knew Marcus wasn't going to be able to do what he needed him to do. "In a team review session, the work he showed was the exact thing he'd received feedback on a month ago, nearly untouched. I knew then he wasn't going to make it."

It wasn't an easy choice. "I felt accountable for this. For him. For what it did to the team," Lee said. Ultimately, Lee realized, "The pain of admitting it wasn't working and making a quick change was the best thing to do. It was hard." Next, Lee said, "I informed our leadership and people team so they could put all the machinery in place. After we did all the necessary steps, I calmly showed him the door."

There are books that focus specifically on the topic of ending someone's employment, and your company likely has policies in place that you should follow, but these are the guiding principles:

- This isn't a negotiation. You've already made the call and are informing them of the decision.
- Be direct. Tell them in the first sentence or two that you're letting them go. Then specify the reasons.
- Tell them what happens next with benefits, final pay, etc.

The above may not apply to your situation. So, imagine for a moment that Lee and Marcus were teammates instead of manager and employee. In this case, Marcus had a pattern of committing Lee to attend meetings when Lee was busy working with another client or taking lunch. Lee talked with Marcus twice before about the need to check with him before booking time. The conversation could look like this:

> **Lee:** "I've talked to you twice about needing to check with me before scheduling meetings. I have other clients that I work with and what happened last week caused me a lot of headaches. So, if I get another meeting request without you checking in beforehand, or it conflicts with something, I'm going to decline it."

In this case, you don't need to do much else other than end the conversation.

Final Thoughts

One final note: these are hard conversations. People can, and do, become emotional and cry. Don't stigmatize them or make them feel ashamed because of it. People can be entirely clear-headed when crying, and crying isn't an emotional defect.

Instead, it's a sign that this person cares deeply about the situation. Validate that this type of conversation can be hard (without patronizing), and ask them if they need a minute or if they're okay to continue. Then honor what they need and remember these points:

- Make sure that you start with listening. Be truly present in the conversation. You never know what you'll uncover.
- If you're faced with secondhand information, go directly to the source. Assume that the person telling you unintentionally missed something and form your own conclusions.
- If you establish clear outcomes and accountability, you're going to get the results you want. Vague goals result in ineffective resolutions.
- If you're delivering bad news, be direct and get to the point quickly.
- Look out for ad hominem attacks. They represent the primary way that people turn arguments around. Remember highlighting patterns and using reflecting techniques will help you here.

CHAPTER 12

Staying Strong When People Are Being Pushy

When engaging in conflict, the phrase "when push comes to shove" might come to mind, along with the instinct to push back and defend what's yours. This chapter offers a more fitting metaphor: to envision yourself as a deeply rooted tree. These trees stand tall and firm, remaining unmoved even in the strongest winds. The approach here isn't about pushing back, but staying grounded. It's about maintaining balance and finding equanimity without the need to overpower anyone.

The Problem

It wasn't the first time Elisa told Fabrizio that she wouldn't be able to help out on his project. "It was, in fact, the fourth time I'd said so," she said. Helping Fabrizio, her colleague and teammate who lived across the country and worked in another of their company's offices, would require a week's worth of travel for a sales event. This event didn't align with her, nor the company's, priorities. It was also uninteresting and impractical to uproot herself from her life on such short notice, mostly because she could do her work from home.

But, Elisa said, "He kept coming back to me because no one else wanted to help him out. We were on a team, but each of us had different responsibilities. I did have the skills required for that event, so it was technically possible for me to help out, but it wasn't in the cards that time."

She added, "Fabrizio was a force of chaos who had a reputation for wearing people down until they gave in to what he wanted. He burned a few bridges at the company that way." While what unfolded between Elisa and Fabrizio wasn't unique, it was certainly weird. And weird situations bear much fruit when it comes to learning.

The rest of the chapter explores several ways in which their conversations could have played out so that Elisa and Fabrizio both got what they needed. It also, through uncovering Fabrizio's motivations, teaches you how to understand what makes pushy people tick. Finally, you'll learn how to choose the right response for you and your situation—whether it's side-stepping, directly countering, or even negotiating with them.

The Solution

The first thing to understand here is why people get pushy, and whether they're actually being pushy or gently reminding you of something you agreed to previously. Afterward, you can adapt your approach to find common paths forward or reinforce your boundaries.

Why People Get Pushy

In situations such as this, you have to wonder what's behind someone's pushiness. Is it ego? Is it desperation? Plain old not getting the hint? Or maybe it's because of something you did or didn't do? The reasons why people cross the line with their pushiness are numerous, but there are several that recur consistently. Knowing each of these reasons helps you chart a path forward for whatever action you decide to take.

What may initially come across as a power trip or power play will likely, upon closer inspection, be something else. Before you deduce it's a power trip, step back and see if it might be ignorance or fear-based. See Table 12.1 for more information.

TABLE 12.1 WHY PEOPLE GET PUSHY

Reason	How to Spot It	What's Behind It	How to Get Around It
To remind you of responsibilities	Check in with yourself: Was this something you agreed to?	An objective way to remind you of commitments without an overt attack.	If you agreed to something, do what you agreed to do. If not, or you no longer can do it, renegotiate.
Not knowing better	Too many assumptions or too few questions. Annoyance.	Ignorance on your boundaries or priorities. Lack of knowledge about the culture or situation. Inexperience.	Educate them on your boundaries, competing priorities, or any possibly unwritten rules.
Fear	Visible panic, angst, stress, or worry. Hyper focus on everything being perfect.	Previous trauma or failure. Thinking a loss of respect, standing, or a job is at stake.	Get a clear signal on their goals and intentions and highlight where conflicts exist. Point out gaps in thinking.
Power trips	Pushing despite being told no. Excessive talking, guilt tripping, or steamrolling. You're with them or against them.	Sense of inadequacy or desire to feel more important/ dominate. Others are a pawn in their game.	Win by choosing not to play. Use the "gray rock" tactic (mentioned on page 150). Fall back on data, be objective.

Elisa shared some additional context about the situation that made it clear which of the above options it was, but you'll find that out later.

Is It Worth It?

Set aside for a moment any feelings of wanting to dig in your heels (or just giving in) and ask yourself: will it be worth it if you do it? This is different than asking yourself if you give in, will they go away. You're not letting yourself be a passive victim either way; instead, you're actively weighing and choosing what you do. Try this experiment and ask yourself:

- What's the short-term impact on you?
- What will you gain if you do it in the short term? How about the long term?
- Consider both tangible and intangible benefits such as goodwill, contacts, or experience to help you move up.
- Is what you gain greater than the impact it will have on you to do it?

It's possible that you will decide that you have something to gain from this. In that case, you've just made a thoughtful, calculated decision to benefit from what someone may be trying to foist on you.

You may also decide you will gain nothing, in which case you've dodged a metaphorical bullet.

For Elisa, she knew she might gain some goodwill, but given her hard work over her time at the company, she felt she had had enough. The impact was high, because it was difficult to get out of some other commitments she'd made, which stopped her from achieving other more valuable goals.

Know, State, and Reinforce Boundaries

People assume that you are in agreement with whatever's going on unless you speak up. This addresses those people who don't know any better. It applies to both your personal boundaries and infractions on the team or company culture.

If you're finding yourself frustrated, consider which of your basic psychological needs might be under stress. Is it one of the following instances?

- **Autonomy:** Where you have control over your actions?
- **Relatedness:** Where you feel like you're a part of the team?
- **Competence:** Where you're feeling like others wonder if you can do your job?

Chapter 9, "Disrespecting Boundaries," goes into greater detail on this.

Situations in which someone doesn't know better are a great opportunity to understand if the other person is violating any unwritten rules about how things are done in your company. These rules exist in nearly every company, regardless of how complete the policies seem. If so, bring them up to speed on what's happening and how this violates a rule.

NOTE A WORD OF CAUTION

> Some people use this to their advantage. If you find yourself on the receiving end of a conversation like this, the old adage of "trust, but verify" applies here. It's never a bad idea to casually bring it up with another teammate to get more context. You're going to either get more context or find out the other person may not be entirely truthful.

If you're the type who prefers to keep it blunt, you could follow E. B. White, American writer of *Charlotte's Web.* When invited to serve on a public committee, he had this blunt, yet not unkind, response:[1]

> Dear Mr. Adams:
>
> Thanks for your letter inviting me to join the committee of the Arts and Sciences for Eisenhower.
>
> I must decline, for secret reasons.
>
> Sincerely,
>
> E. B. White

1 Source: https://twitter.com/lettersofnote/status/397354825915985921?lang=en

If you prefer an even more blunt approach, there's always also the story of "Bartleby, the Scrivener: A Story of Wall Street," a short story by the American writer Herman Melville. While you would be well advised to avoid using Bartleby as a model for your work ethic, his five-word reply is an eternal classic: "I would prefer not to." A few other options are shown in Table 12.2.

TABLE 12.2 DECLINING AND REJECTING PUSHINESS

Angle	Sample Response
Deflect	"I've got to focus on *x*, so I can't help. Have you tried asking *y*?" "My priority right now is *x*, which needs my full attention. Another time, perhaps."
Reject	"No, thanks." "That question's a little too personal." "It looks like you didn't like my answer, I'm not going to change my mind though." "I've said this already, the answer was and will continue to be no."

There's nothing wrong with saying no and ignoring questions after that, either. And you'd be well within your rights to do so. It is, however, much more instructive (not to mention fun) to game out what other options you or Elisa may have if faced with a similar situation.

A blank stare, while incredibly bold, will make the other person feel as if they've crossed a line and stop their pushing—all while you sat back and said nothing. If you want to attempt this, give it a try in some lower stakes situation with a willing partner. You'll need the practice so you can build up that muscle.

Find Common Paths Forward

You may find, like most people do in times of conflict, that you both want the same thing but you're getting in each other's way. In this case, call up your skills on finding paths forward. Table 12.3 shows a couple of options for Fabrizio and Elisa. Working these options out together builds a sense of shared understanding and reduces the pain of reconsidering an idea to which you both may be deeply invested.

TABLE 12.3 PATHS FORWARD

What I Want	What They Want	Proposed Paths
To help and avoid travel	Someone in person	Elisa collaborates via video chat. Their company hires someone to help.

Finding mutually beneficial paths forward is ideal because both people can do what they want and get what they need. However, this approach isn't quite like a compromise, so it doesn't make for happy outcomes because both people lose something. It requires a bit of probing and good faith conversation.

There's always a chance that there's no mutually beneficial path forward, but it's less likely than you'd think. If you can't find one, this is a good time to call back everyone's top priorities and figure out which effort yields the highest reward. That list of priorities includes:

- Yours
- Theirs
- The team's
- The company's

Here's how a hypothetical conversation like this could go:

> Elisa: Tell me what you need here. This is the fourth time you've asked, and the fourth time I'm saying no. I'm being clear, so what's behind this? What are you trying to accomplish?
>
> Fabrizio: I need someone to be in person the whole week for our presentations and workshops with our client. It has to be in person.
>
> Elisa: What's beneficial about it being in person?
>
> F: I agreed to do it that way.
>
> E: Okay, we're going to need to dig a little deeper there.
>
> F: Being in person demonstrates our commitment to potential clients. There's shared context and facilitation help, too.
>
> E: So it sounds like you need another face to share context and facilitation.
>
> F: Yep.
>
> E: What if I came in over video chat and helped? That gets you to your goal and solves my issue.

Note here that Elisa could also distance herself from this by using "this person" instead of "me." She's also using questions framed in terms of what and how, not why, so that Fabrizio is less likely to make things more difficult.

Look Out For...

What's unfortunate is that despite Elisa's desire to help, Fabrizio is locked onto the idea of it being Elisa who comes, so he applied some additional, aggressive pressure on her. So, what's someone to do in a situation like this? Luckily, Elisa has options.

The Power Trip

Some people go on a power trip because they fear irrelevance. Some of them crave power and grab it any way they can. In general, people go on power trips and bully or push to make themselves feel important, mostly because they aren't.

Regardless of the motive, the situation can get dire when you stand between someone on a power trip and what they want.

This leads to the big reveal for Elisa's story, which may not come as much of a surprise to you now: "It was some kind of manipulation/power grab move. It didn't make sense to me why this would happen, but I just...hated it."

Become a Gray Rock

The best advice possible, at least by this book's standards, is this: you win by not playing. To do this, take a page from how psychologists advise people to handle others who love to manipulate and control. Make yourself really, really boring. It's called *gray rocking*. Here's how to do it:

- Keep a neutral tone in your responses and body language.
- Keep your responses to as few words as possible.
- Avoid engaging or asking them questions when possible.

This strategy works because the more boring you appear and the less likely you are to interact with them, the more your surface area for attack becomes reduced. This approach may mean being a little less like yourself, but the less you give to people who are on power trips, the less likely you are to become ensnared.

Another relevant example is that of a grease fire. If a grease fire flares up and you slam a lid on top of the fire or toss water on it, the fire flames back up. But if you starve it of oxygen by gradually sliding a lid over it, the flame goes out. That's what makes being a gray rock so effective: you give the other person less to work with.

Face It Head-On

What fun would it be to read a chapter on overcoming someone's pushiness without discussing how to directly address it? If you are intent on taking it on, there are things you'll want to know:

- The other person may come back with some force. People who are pushy don't like hearing no.
- Make sure your manager (or HR, if appropriate) knows what's going on. Tell them that no action is necessary at present; you're only informing them that something unusual seems to be happening. That way, if it gets too tense, they're aware of what's happening.
- Keep calm and be as factual and objective as you can so that they have less to work with. The less emotionally involved they are, the less they can push on.

In previous conversations, Elisa expressed her problems and objections clearly: she said travel was difficult, and she wasn't able to go. "I told him no. Multiple times, with no trace of ambiguity in my replies. I mean, what's clearer than 'no, I can't?' Did he just have too much wax in his ears so that he only hears what he wants?"

So when the topic of Elisa assisting came up again at one of their regular meetings, she was a little more curt than usual:

> Fabrizio: So, this sales event in New York really needs your help. Are you able to come?
>
> Elisa: Look, we've talked about this three times already, and I was clear that I can't make it. The timing doesn't work for me. My answer isn't going to change, so let's talk about our next item.
>
> Fabrizio: Hold on. No one else is able to help. Why can't you come? What's going on that you can't make it?
>
> Elisa: (pauses, is tired of being asked) Personal reasons.
>
> Fabrizio: Well, I'm having some strong feelings about [Elisa's response]. You should be there to help. I know you don't report to me, but I think you owe it to the team to be there. We need this win. We're on a team, and I committed us to this.

Elisa: I've been consistent in saying that I can't come. I have other obligations that I can't get out of. And I didn't commit to this.

Fabrizio: Okay, got it. Let's move on.

Here are a few other things Elisa could have said in that conversation:

- How this distracts her from achieving her goals.
- That his behavior harms their trust. Intended or not, there's harm being done.
- That she doesn't report to him, so leave it.

After the conversation, "I was relieved. I felt like I finally got him to relent and acknowledge what I said." Fabrizio, not surprisingly, didn't see it that way.

Shadier Tactics

Not everyone relents when they're told no. Some even make a good career out of being able to push past "no." Just ask any top-level sales executive who can make an art out of persuasion. Or a kid who hears no from one adult and goes to ask another, hoping they'll get a yes.

Others, however, resort to less savory tactics. Because life loves a good twist, there's one more surprise in store for Elisa. "A few days later, I got a call from someone in senior leadership. They weren't directly involved in the situation, so they didn't know my priorities. All they knew was Fabrizio asked them to talk with me.

"I had to explain again that this wasn't possible for me, and it conflicted with my priorities. It left me in a weird, very uncomfortable spot, having to explain myself to senior leadership. But right at that point, I decided to share what had been going on [that Fabrizio was unrelenting in his pressure after being told no], and that I only agreed to help find someone or assist virtually. Which I was doing." The call ended shortly thereafter.

Elisa was shocked at the lengths Fabrizio went to get what he wanted. These shadier tactics are difficult to prevent, owing mostly to their unexpected nature, but here are the best things you can do: remember that ambiguity works against you and that documentation works against them.

Pushiness Thrives on Ambiguity and Urgency

Unclear goals or those which are quickly thrust upon you can be a means of control or leverage for the other person. To counter this, try putting the work back on them to clarify their request, ideally in writing. (See Chapter 13, "When They Make Ludicrous Requests" for more information.) You may also try slowing them down: be busy when they interrupt you.

Documenting Helps

You're well-served to invest time documenting your decisions and agreements. A running record of your conversations and requests gives you a source of truth. Pushy people don't like truth: they thrive on urgency and rapidly evolving situations. Don't just leave important decisions or requests in an endless stream of emails or chats—put them in a single document. Bring this up to your manager so that they can know what's going on. (See Chapter 4, "Lying and Gaslighting" for more information.)

Final Thoughts

What ultimately happened here to Elisa? She replied: "I didn't do it. I didn't go. I was determined to stick to my guns after he got leadership to call me. That was pure manipulation. I don't put up with that. And as a recovering people pleaser, I'm not going to fall back into that trap again." Elisa knew that she might incur some kind of repercussions from her bout with Fabrizio, but she weighed the costs and chose what she felt was right for her and had no regrets. Here are some things to think about:

- Before saying yes or no, methodically think through what you have to gain and lose. You may come away getting something out of it.
- Think about which of your boundaries is being violated: Is it autonomy, relatedness, or competence?
- Try to find a common path forward if it suits your situation. Figuring out what you both need in order for you both to win is possible.
- Look out for power trips. Make yourself boring, or face the situation head-on. The choice is yours.
- You'll never regret sticking up for yourself in the long run.

CHAPTER 13

When They Make Ludicrous Requests

"Remember Sisyphus, the guy who kept pushing a rock up a hill forever? That was me. Every year I pushed a very valuable rock up a hill by convincing everyone that our design system team was worth it. And every year, someone who runs the budget kicked the rock back down the hill, starting the process over again."

That's Michael, who works at a big tech company. His team created his company's first design system for its warehouse software. If the term is unfamiliar, a design system is what companies use to make sure that the interfaces it creates are clear and consistent across its experience. Think of it like LEGOs, but for creating apps.

It was a huge success, saving the company vast sums of time and money by making it easy for new engineers to get up to speed quickly and reduce the time it took to launch updates and new features.

And at his company, it was standard practice for each team to justify their existence every year.

This particular year, Michael's boss Laurie applied more pressure to him than usual. It turns out that another design system emerged in the company. She said, "We can't fund two design systems. You either absorb them, or they'll absorb you." Michael felt like this was some unwinnable, zero-sum game. "I knew these two systems were way too different to merge. The request was going to be impossible to do and would be a very unpleasant lesson for everyone in the process."

Michael had a ludicrous request on his hands.

The Problem

Ludicrous requests usually fall into two categories: those made with intention, and those made unknowingly.

Those made with intention usually fall into two camps: people who anchor or purposefully suggest something outlandish to negotiate down to get what they want. The other part of the intentionally ludicrous crowd are people who could care less that they're dumping things on you. You're a little less likely to encounter these types of requests, but they do exist. (There's also a third, misguided type, which you'll hear about later.)

If you apply Hanlon's razor (covered in Chapter 1, "Before the Conversation"), you'll find that most people fall into the second camp: people who do so unknowingly. Plainly, they just aren't aware of the impact their request has. It doesn't mean that it won't gall you or confuse you, though.

The Solution

The best bet in these situations is to be direct and assume that they didn't mean anything by it. They are just a busy person who relies on you, another professional, to know how to help. Sometimes, you may find yourself at odds with them, but knowing how to navigate a situation to find a mutually beneficial way forward helps tremendously.

Or you can fold, of course. But perhaps you, like Michael, don't want that.

Be Direct

If you were in Michael's shoes, you might rightly feel uncomfortable. After all, your boss has just made a big, hard request for something you've already proven to be valuable. There's a power dynamic at play here, and you're going to want to approach this carefully. Still, the best approach here is to be direct.

Because Laurie is Michael's boss doesn't mean he can't be direct—it does require a bit more tact, however, given the power dynamic at play.

When Michael discussed the design system, he said, "It simplified so many complex problems. It was key to our accessibility efforts, too, as we were building that in from the start. It made deploying any changes much simpler, too. And engineers were able to start working in code three days sooner, which was huge at the scale we worked at."

Here are three ways shown in Table 13.1 that Michael could approach Laurie to discuss this situation. Each of these approaches takes the emotion out of it as much as possible and focuses on facts and trade-offs.

TABLE 13.1 THE DIRECT APPROACH

The Negotiation (Trade-offs)	Quant/Qual: Doing this means x can't be done. Are we okay with that?
Conflicting with other goals	Qualitative, these conflict. Bring up situation to other leaders. Trick: come in with potential solution.
Human impact	Anecdotes, qualitative stuff.
How am I supposed to do that?	Puts the work back on them.

Learn to See Behind the Request

Here's a universal truth: everyone's accountable to someone. The sooner you find out who those people are, the better your outcomes will be in tough situations.

When you've got a tense neck, a physical therapist may tell you that some of your pain "refers up" from other areas like your lower or mid back. The same is true with tense situations—what you see on the surface with the person in front of you is rarely the root of the issue. Enter stakeholder maps, which are a blueprint for how to navigate an organization and the people who run it.

Stakeholder Maps

For stakeholder maps to be successful, you need to know who could impact your project and what they need. You can customize this to your needs, but at a minimum you should include:

- Their name and position
- Their importance, relative to your project
- The impact they may have, relative to your project

How do you make one? First, look at your company's org chart. Look on LinkedIn or wherever your company congregates online. Ask your boss who they work with most often. These are things you'd do on a normal basis when starting a new job, but you're making a more tactical version for yourself. Then put this into a table or graph.

You can, and should, customize this to your needs (see Table 13.2). Other factors you could include would be:

- Risk of impeding progress
- Their outlook on your project or team
- Stakeholder's relationships to each other

In this case, Michael has four immediate stakeholders: himself, Laurie, Laurie's boss, and the other team's lead.

TABLE 13.2 STAKEHOLDER MAPPING

Stakeholder	Priorities/ Needs	Risk of Impeding Progress (0-4)	Outlook (0-4)	Relationship
Michael	Keep team alive	2	—	Self
Laurie	Satisfy boss	3	3	Boss
Laurie's boss	Reduce and justify costs	4	1	Skip-Level Boss
Other guy	Keep team alive	1	2	Colleague

Collaborate on a Way Forward

One more universal truth: people often just accept requests from their bosses without understanding why. No one's to blame for this, because:

- You're often busy.
- You don't see the whole picture.
- Accepting direction from authority is how you operate by default.

Further, leaders don't often explain why they make requests, which doesn't help matters.

But if you do try to understand, and you do it in a helpful way as laid out in Chapter 5, "Conflict with Your Boss," you can help navigate almost any kind of choppy waters at work.

You'll often find that when faced with a ludicrous request, the other person may have already tried to work it out in their head or made a few assumptions. Sometimes, they present the situation in a binary way: it's got to be this way or that way.

You should know that they may not intentionally be doing this to box you in. But you also know not to fall into that trap. Step back and find out the following:

- What do you need to succeed?
- What do they need to succeed?
- Where's the path where those meet?

So that's exactly what Michael did. He noticed Laurie was under pressure and making a ludicrous request, so he traced that pressure to its origin to address the root cause. Here's how he did it:

> Michael: "What's going on? We've had this discussion twice already, and I thought my team was safe, so what's changed?"
>
> Laurie: "We've got some extra pressure this year, and we just need you to justify why your team merits investment."
>
> Michael: "Tell me about this pressure. What's different? Anything more you can share?"
>
> Laurie: "There just isn't any appetite for funding two design systems. It's really coming down to who makes the better case. Winston [Laurie's boss] has got to show more profitability for our org because we had some rough quarters recently."
>
> Michael: "He knows that these teams do two mutually exclusive things, right?"
>
> Laurie: "Yeah, no. Wait, maybe not? I'd be willing to raise the issue with him again."

This was his opening. What Michael did next follows:

> Michael: "When's your next 1:1 with him?"
>
> Laurie: "Later in the week."
>
> Michael: "When you talk about this with him, what if I gave you some talking points? We can help Winston understand that these teams do two very different tasks and while we could collaborate more, we need to stay separate."

Michael continued, "I told her that we've got junior engineers who are coming to work on this, and instead of having them trawl through all kinds of components, we could have an agreed-upon library of what they build. Here's how much time it would save."

It's true that 99% of the time that a person makes a ludicrous request, the motivations and incentives aren't dictated by them. They are dictated by other people. If you can understand the ecosystem on a holistic level, you'll have a good understanding of what someone's motivations may be.

It took a couple of rounds, because Laurie's boss had to talk to someone else's boss, but this approach saved Michael's team. And, in an astonishing move, he saved his colleague's team. This just doesn't happen very often.

Look Out For . . .

You may encounter a couple of techniques when it comes to ludicrous requests. Top among them is using a manipulation technique to box you in. Another would be to avoid speaking up.

Not Speaking Up

You know by now that not saying something will almost always come back to bite you. Here's how that could happen.

In Michael's case, the cost was obvious: he would lose his whole team to the machinery of budgets and bean counters. And while the company may not have realized their mistake, they would surely feel the pain. "I knew that if I didn't say something, that if I lost my team, or my colleague lost theirs, my credibility could be shot." And at high enough levels in a company hierarchy, losing credibility can sink you.

Here's a simple and effective heuristic to use:

- What's the harm of not saying something?
- What's the benefit of saying something?
- If it went south, what would happen to me, no matter the odds, if it were traced back to me?

Michael knew that the impact of not saying anything was huge. And if it came back to him, "I'd be a fool. No way would I want to have that kind of shame hanging over me."

You may do the math and decide not to speak up. Or you may speak up and regret it. But either way, you will regret 100% of the times you should have but didn't.

Anchoring

Try this experiment. Answer one of the following questions quickly, without help, and within five seconds:

1. What do you think 1x2x3x4x5x6x7x8 is?
2. What do you think 8x7x6x5x4x3x2x1 is?

If you're like most people, you may have said the first question was around 512. The second answer has a higher average, around 2,250.

What you just did was nearly identical to a 1970s study by Amos Tversky and Daniel Kahneman to support their theory of anchor bias.[1] This is one reason why humans make flawed decisions with limited information.

Anchoring happens on much more subtle levels in daily life. Infomercials are notorious for these tactics. First, they show you something that they say can change your world, ask a high price for their product, and then they tell you that it's available for a limited time at a discounted price. This plays a subtle trick on your brain, making you think you're really getting one over on them. Really, you're paying for two products at full price, because the original price was only meant to help you see "value" in their sale.

In work settings, you'll find people asking for the impossible or unreasonable on purpose, hoping you'll compromise. They want to land in the middle. If you're faced with an anchor, try the following in Table 13.3.

TABLE 13.3 HOW ANCHORS WORK

What Anchors Use	How to Defeat Them
Biases	Recognize yours, ask someone else for input.
Poor or incomplete information	Research similar situations or outcomes.
Urgency	Slow it down, delay commitments.

NOTE ANOTHER EXAMPLE OF ANCHORS AT WORK

In another situation, Sophie wanted to go on a company retreat, but she didn't feel like she could. She'd been used to this kind of situation for so long, she didn't even think about it. However, after talking with her manager, the manager asked what would have to change in order for her to attend the retreat. When her manager floated the idea of childcare, Sophie said yes, that was the problem, and the manager agreed to take care of it. Sometimes all it takes is asking.

1 Amos Tversky and Daniel Kahneman, "Judgment Under Uncertainty: Heuristics and Biases," *Science* 185, no. 4157 (1974): 1124–1131.

Final Thoughts

There's one more class of ludicrous requests, and it ties back to football. Vince Lombardi, who coached the NFL's Green Bay Packers, historically set impossible goals and standards for his team. He said these goals allowed his players to achieve levels of performance they wouldn't have otherwise achieved and capped it off with this quote: "Perfection is not attainable. But if we chase perfection, we can catch excellence." Underneath the sparkly exterior of this quote is a noxious idea. It's one that enables exploitation and inhuman amounts of stress at work because a manager asks the impossible and sets unrealistic standards to get there.

So, unless you're a famous football player being paid millions of dollars a year with a support network that allows you to focus solely on winning the next game, this notion does not and should not ever be applied at work. Instead, follow these points:

- Be up front about the difficulty of accommodating ludicrous requests and don't take them personally.
- Finding out what you both need to succeed can be uncomfortable at first but will ultimately serve everyone best.
- Learn to see behind the request by making a stakeholder map.
- It's dangerous to blindly say yes or have a knee-jerk reaction and say no, because both can harm your credibility.

CHAPTER 14

How to Work with People Who Hate Change

Gemma, a seasoned engineer who built a career on helping companies boost their happiness and performance at work, has seen it all. Motivating slackers, exposing structural problems in both code and culture, and inciting big changes at companies were all part of her daily operations. She shared a story about Megan, another seasoned manager who was the immovable object to Gemma's unstoppable force.

Megan, who hired Gemma's company, worked as the manager in charge of a mobile app for a vending machine management service. Her app was used by drivers to keep vending machines accurately stocked and maintained, in order to ensure that the money was collected properly. The app also wrangled logistics, schedules, and route planning.

The problem, according to Gemma, was that "The app was broken and felt like an ancient relic from an Indiana Jones movie. It worked about as well, too. But Megan had ideas—strong ideas—about what needed to change and was pretty resistant to any change that didn't come from her brain." So Gemma was stuck and unable to help.

The Problem

So why is change so hard, even when the benefits are right there in front of you? Turns out your brain is generally opposed to anything that requires unnecessary amounts of energy.

That notion is compounded once a habit is formed in your brain. It's the equivalent of a worn path being paved. Going off-road to form new pathways becomes precarious and is something your brain is generally disinclined to do, even if it's on a flawed path already.

That's especially true if the path has some potholes and faults. Change also exposes faults in current ways of working, which aren't typically well received by those who have something to lose by the change you're bringing.

Our Brains Avoid Change

You can't really blame your brain here: it only wants what it thinks is best for you. But "best for you" is determined by the amount of energy (cost) an action requires now, not how much you'll save or benefit from later. Change requires more energy than sticking with the status quo, so it can be difficult to convince your brain to go through with it.

Gemma was used to change; it was, after all, her job. It wasn't Megan's job, though. "Our team did their usual," Gemma said. "We tried to understand the problems they were addressing so they didn't miss anything. We took a more exploratory, fact-finding, investigative approach. We wanted to talk to the drivers who used the app."

Gemma wanted to know, from the people on the ground, answers to questions such as "What takes you a long time to complete your work? What prevents you from doing your job? What would you like to see in the app?"

When she brought that approach up to Megan, "She looked at me like I had three heads."

> Megan: "That won't be necessary. I've got it all here. I know what we need."
>
> Gemma: "I get that. When we work this way, we uncover additional processes to optimize that aren't always apparent unless we talk to the people who use it. I can tell you about a couple examples..."
>
> Megan [interrupting, pointing to her requirements document]: "Look. I've got it here in black and white. I know what I want. Just build it."

Megan's response didn't allow for debate, nor did it allow for curiosity or questions. "She was very convinced that it needed to be a certain way, and it was pretty clear early on that there were problems with her requirements. But she wasn't willing to budge, even on things that we knew would fix a broken process." Gemma and her team took a step back to reconsider. What's causing this?

The Sunk Cost Fallacy

There's an old Latin proverb "nota res mala, optima," which, literally translated, means "an evil thing known is best." You may know it by its more modern (and, in your author's opinion, way less cool sounding) "better the devil you know."

The proverb references a cognitive bias called the *sunk cost fallacy*, in which people continue to invest time, money, or energy into something, even when it's no longer beneficial, simply because they already invested resources into it. People often use this bias as a way of justifying the continuation of a bad decision. In other words, "throwing good money after bad."

Carried to its extreme, continually falling victim to a sunk cost fallacy fits the definition of insanity: you keep doing the same thing over and over, hoping for a different response. That's what Gemma experienced with Megan. "In a conversation with her, I brought up a few issues we'd heard from their drivers and her responses were 'This is just how we work,' and 'We don't want to change that.'"

Change Exposes Faults

The primary reason that people resist change is that it exposes faults. When you bring deficiencies to light, you necessarily expose where people and processes aren't measuring up to what you need right now.

It's truly a double-edged sword (see Table 14.1).

TABLE 14.1 THE DOUBLE-EDGED SWORD OF CHANGE

Good	Bad
You stop doing unnecessary work.	Your position may be eliminated.
You save time and money.	Your budget might be cut.
Your team runs more efficiently.	You may have to relearn or readjust to something new.
You optimize processes.	If you aren't putting in your fair share, you might have to step it up.

The Solution

To convince people to embrace change, you have to be its advocate. Some people like to frame embracing change as an uphill battle, which isn't a helpful mindset. Yes, helping people embrace change may feel like work—and they may well resist it—but it isn't a battle. This point is important because if you frame "change" as a battle, you're likely to think more coercively about it.

Instead, it's more helpful to frame "change" in gardening terms, so that you're the gardener who is nurturing a new hybrid plant. It's got all the benefits of the old plant (way of doing things), as well as a few evolutionary or environmental adaptations. You need to tend the soil and ensure that each plant has what it needs to become something new.

Show Them the Value of Change

Your first action in this journey is to show people what's in it for them when they embrace this change. And don't shy away from the fact that it's hard, if that's the case. Being honest about the challenges you face gives you credibility and shows grit and determination, but it also gives other people the chance to contribute to the solution.

When deciding whether or not to go along with change, some people rely on data, some rely on impact, and some rely on gut feelings. Regardless, you can change your tack based on the person (or people) you're talking to and show them how they stand to benefit by trying something new.

One way to demonstrate the value of change and compare it with the pain of getting there is a 2x2 matrix (see Figure 14.1). It's an infinitely useful tool that lets you plot your ideas on an x and y axis, where each axis can be anything related to your situation. Some options could be the following:

- Risk and reward
- Pain and gain
- Time involved and value of opportunity
- Uncertainty and risk

FIGURE 14.1
The 2x2 matrix charts an item according to its effort on the y axis and reward on the x axis.

In Gemma's case, she listened to Megan and her biggest concerns, which were "wasted money, the certainty of the idea, and anything that deviated from the norm had to be worth the expense and trouble." "So the axes here were effort and reward," said Gemma. Next, they did the 2x2 exercise. After the pair generated a few ideas on sticky notes, it was time to put them on the matrix.

> **Gemma:** So let's chart a couple ideas from the team and talk about them a little more objectively.
>
> **Megan [puts her idea in the highest reward, medium-high effort quadrants]:** Okay, there. That's us.
>
> **Gemma:** Good to see what you're thinking. What we're hypothesizing may actually be less effort, letting us accomplish more for you with less time.
>
> **Megan:** I'm still not convinced. I'm not going to make a decision on this alone.
>
> **Gemma:** Let's get more specific. What are we missing? How are you seeing it?
>
> **Megan:** I can't retrain these drivers. They know how things are done. We can't lose more time.

After some conversation, Gemma took Megan's concerns about retraining to heart. "I wasn't super worried, because I got to the bottom of her concerns, which were losing time and money. I can work with that." So she designed an experiment to test things out.

Frame It as an Experiment and Build a Culture of Learning

People fear big change because they fear the unknown. For some, the unknown is a big, scary wilderness, and they don't want to venture out and get stuck in the dark with no way back.

But if you can take the process step by step, it's easier to backtrack or take a moment to recollect yourself if you think you're making a wrong move.

There's a tool that helps you do exactly that. It's called a *lean hypothesis*, and it's based on the work of Eric Ries and the lean startup methodology.[1] This tool has been used to help tiny startups grow to

1 Eric Ries, *The Lean Startup: How Today's Entrepreneurs Use Continuous Innovation to Create Radically Successful Businesses* (New York: Crown Currency, 2018).

large companies. It was even used by Zappos to validate whether or not selling shoes online would be a viable business. (It was, because Amazon acquired Zappos in 2009 for $1.2 billion.) The key parts are shown in Table 14.2.

TABLE 14.2 PARTS OF A LEAN HYPOTHESIS

Your Problem	What issue are you addressing? Who's having it?
What is your hypothesis?	How do you plan to address it? What do you think it will achieve?
How it will be tested?	What experiments will you do? Be detailed enough so that it can be tested.
How will you measure success?	Will it be quantitative (data-oriented) or qualitative (feedback-oriented)?

Put together, they look like Figure 14.2.

We believe `doing this` for `these people` will achieve `this outcome or impact`. We will test this by `experiments 1, 2, and 3`. We know the hypothesis is valid if by `this date` we get `this thing`.

FIGURE 14.2 Here's a template for what a lean hypothesis looks like.

So instead of building the entire app, Gemma could test ideas out bit by bit without exhausting all of Megan's time, money, and trust. These statements could be:

> "We believe adding a predictive restocking workflow for our app users will achieve less time restocking and fewer trips back to the warehouse. We will test this by making a prototype that simulates the proposed solution. We'll know this hypothesis is valid if we get a 20% reduction in time spent restocking with eight of ten participants."

By using a lean hypothesis, Gemma removed ambiguity and fear by setting clear expectations and parameters for her test. She made it much easier for Megan to go along with her proposal because both knew the time and money they were risking, and they could weigh these factors appropriately against their risk.

They could also repeat this process over and over again, making sure that each move was the right one. This process prevented the scenario of working in isolation and having a big, disappointing reveal. The longer you wait without validation, the higher the risk of being wrong will be. And what you risk is time, money, and more importantly, trust.

Look Out For . . .

You can do all the hypothesizing, mapping, and talking you want with someone who hates change, but it has to be done with incredible delicacy and tact, because you're tampering with the basic psychological needs of humans. If you push too hard, you risk outright resistance and sabotage. Which, unknown to Gemma, was exactly where she landed.

Pushing Too Hard

You've probably heard of the age-old metaphor of carrots and sticks (or incentives, as shown in Table 14.3). If not, picture a horse-drawn cart with a driver dangling a carrot in front of the horse with a whip in the other hand. If the horse keeps going forward, it gets a reward (the carrot). If not, it gets a punishment (the stick).

It's the go-to comparison for "leading" people: they do what you want, whether they take the easy way or the hard way. And that comparison is why "leading" is in quotation marks.

One, it assumes the horse, who trods these paths while the driver sits in relative comfort, knows nothing and has no autonomy. Two, it oversimplifies the situation: there is rarely anything so black and white in difficult situations. Hard conversations you need to have at work require a more nuanced approach.

A more accurate metaphor is found in working with wood. Each piece of wood has a natural amount of give built into it based on several factors. You must understand these factors before you can do anything successful with the wood, like make it into a guitar or a bench. To make something great, a little stress is required. But the stress needs to be proportional to the gain. In short: make it worth it.

For humans, these factors are the basic psychological needs discussed earlier in the book: autonomy, competence, and relatedness.

The woodworking metaphor highlights two universal truths:

- You can only push so much before hitting the breaking point.
- Only the inexperienced, incapable, or insensitive people push past the breaking point.

TABLE 14.3 INCENTIVES

Type of Reinforcement	Benefits	Drawbacks, if Overused	How It Looks
Negative	Only short term. Efforts stop once you stop pushing. Behavior will continue.	Morale can be crushed.	Threatens loss or damage
Positive	It's better for psychological safety, collaboration, and morale.	People can become entitled.	Shows benefits, praise, and recognition

Going exclusively one way is never a good idea. If your reinforcement is all too negative, it leads to a decrease in motivation, an increase in stress, and feelings of helplessness or powerlessness. You don't want to go overboard with positive reinforcement, either, which causes motivation to suffer.

Instead, strike a balance with clear, specific goals as well as what's at stake, like what you articulated in your lean hypothesis statement.

Here's how Gemma could have balanced things:

> "If we try this, we stand to help drivers gain more time to devote to maintenance, which has always been a pain for them to manage. It will take a small amount of retraining, but we'll minimize this with testing before we release."

Sabotage

What's particularly malignant about sabotage is that it's meant to remain unseen. And saboteurs count on their ability to make moves out of sight, which changes or prevents the outcome you're hoping to achieve.

If you're hoping this chapter gives you a surefire way to prevent sabotage, you're going to be disappointed. You will learn how to guard against it, though.

This story adds two new people, both working for Megan: Cora, an account executive, and Roy, one of Megan's direct reports.

One afternoon, Cora called Gemma in for an urgent meeting. She had just met with Megan. "Apparently, Roy had turned in his notice, saying he was going to come work for me because apparently I offered him a job. Megan was livid." The problem with this was, in Gemma's words: "Absolutely none of this was true. The shock was so huge that I felt like I'd been tased."

While Roy did want to work with Gemma's company, and he had approached her, Gemma said, "We both were clear that nothing would happen until my company's engagement was over. And that none of this would be done in secret. I can't risk my reputation or my company's. I'd even told Cora about it, too."

Cora told Gemma that she'd jeopardized their company's relationship with Megan's company and instructed Gemma not to speak to Roy again about this. Cora needed to resolve the tension herself.

Gemma stepped back as requested. "Then Roy called me, just as shocked as I was." Roy said he'd never said anything like that to anyone; he hadn't even mentioned approaching Gemma. Roy said he had no idea where it came from, and he'd never risk an opportunity like this by doing something so stupid.

"Something was up. This made no sense and didn't map to things I'd do or say," Gemma said.

So, Gemma reached back out to Cora. "I shared notes, emails, literally anything I could to show them that I wasn't doing anything shady. Absolutely no evidence supported I was doing what Cora's source claimed. There had to be some misunderstanding."

It wasn't clear until later that this scenario was fabricated entirely to discredit Gemma. She found out through a close friend at work that Cora and others had wanted Gemma out for unknown reasons and hoped this situation would do the trick.

Through her efforts at transparency and her past reputation, Gemma survived the ordeal. Not everyone will be so lucky.

Preventing and Spotting Sabotage

There's a difference between being paranoid and prudent. Paranoid behavior defaults to thinking you *are* or *will* be sabotaged; prudent behavior takes a measured approach and assesses potential risk. Even if the prudent person thinks there's a high risk, they exercise appropriate caution.

Try this exercise shown in Figure 14.3 for assessing the risk. Then read on for how to mitigate it.

Exercise: Sabotage Triage

For this exercise, you'll look at several factors and assign a score to each of them. Then you can decide what to do next.

The primary way to mitigate every part of this is to be transparent in your efforts, bring them along, and follow the recommendations from earlier in this chapter. In short, the more transparent you can be, and the more you can bring them along, the lower your risk of being sabotaged.

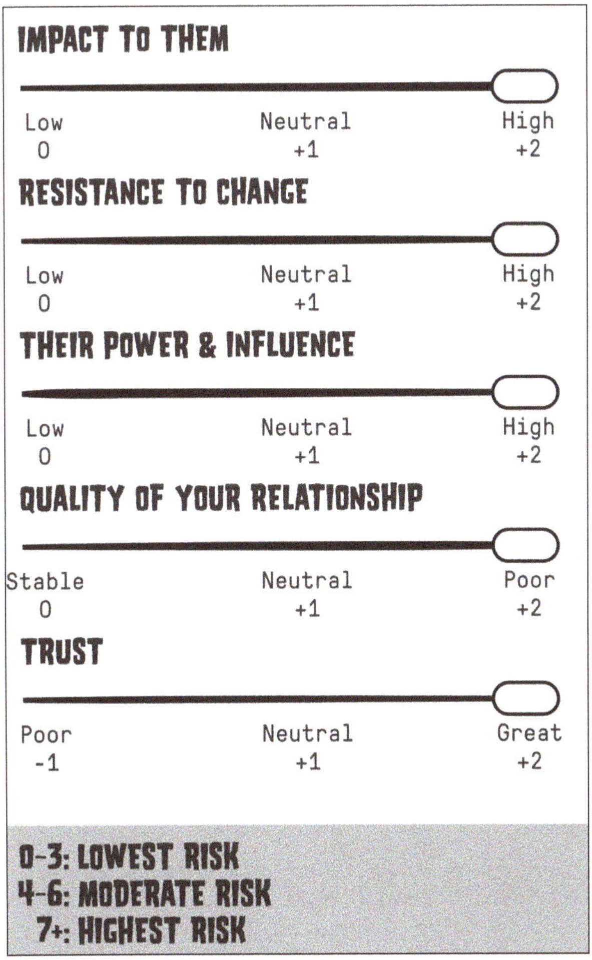

FIGURE 14.3
Sabotage triage helps you evaluate perceived risk so you can decide what to do.

Final Thoughts

Gemma's story concluded with her team doing exactly what Megan wanted. "Megan wasn't open to change, not even remotely. Nothing I could do would change that, and I think I created this whole conflict because I didn't read the room."

If you take nothing else from this chapter, make it this: short of coercive methods, there isn't any way to guarantee that someone who hates change will go along with you. You can only influence their actions.

- Change is difficult because our brains are wired to resist unnecessary energy expenditure and because it exposes faults in the current ways of working.
- The sunk cost fallacy is a cognitive bias that makes people continue to invest resources in something even when it's no longer beneficial.
- Using a 2x2 matrix to chart things like effort and impact are borderline magical tools to get people to see the benefits of an idea.
- To convince people to embrace change, you need to show them the value of it and frame it as an experiment.
- To mitigate sabotage, be transparent in your efforts and bring others along with you.

CHAPTER 15

How to Receive Feedback

Brad laughed and said, "You want to know the harshest piece of feedback I've received? That's easy. I worked on designing a record cover for a band and their manager, Janet, hated it and sent a searing stream of words back over." After seeing the initial designs, Janet said, "Are you [expletive] serious? It looks like someone vomited all over this. There's nothing good or redeemable here; this is complete trash. I hired you to make a good album cover, not this rancid cornucopia of horse shit." Janet clearly had a way with words and wasn't afraid to show it.

The Problem

Janet's feedback stood out as especially acidic, but the lead-up to it requires a critical examination. First, Brad didn't communicate frequently with Janet throughout the project. "I was a little younger in my career, so I wasn't good at asking questions. I thought I had all the answers, and I was always right, so I just asked them to send me a few demo tracks and tell me about the themes they wanted to explore, and I'd take it from there." He paused and laughed. "I know, I know. It wasn't the best start. I had a really big head."

Second, when doing presentations, Brad was a firm believer in the concept of the work speaking for itself. So, he didn't put much, if any, credence to those times when he did receive feedback. This, and the fact that his work as a designer in the music industry deals with high levels of subjectivity and big personalities, gives this chapter so much to work with.

However, when Brad got news that his client Janet absolutely hated his design, he was a little perplexed. It met all of the "goals" Janet wanted. Brad said, "It wasn't word for word, but you can't really do good work like that in this industry if you go to the letter with what they're asking. You want to take it one step beyond to really deliver something great."

A significant theme emerges here: how you receive feedback is just as important as how you ask for it. The remainder of this chapter focuses on getting you in the right, optimistic mindset. For more on this, see Chapter 1, "Before the Conversation."

The Solution

Before you attempt to receive feedback, you need to do two key things: set the stage by scoping your feedback request and engage the other person appropriately. If you neglect either of these, it's the same as expecting a table that's missing half of its legs to stay level as you eat on it.

Set the Stage for Good Feedback

Your first move here is to set goals for the kinds of feedback you're looking to get. Is it on a particular aspect of your project? The general direction of it? The more specific, the better. See Table 15.1.

What you ask for feedback on is just as important as what you tell them to ignore. Anything in progress, or anything that may distract from your goals, should be called out immediately.

For Brad, it would have been prudent to speak to the themes he was trying to convey in the album artwork. Instead, Brad said, "I just sent them an email that happily presented it as meeting every goal they had and ended it with what I now know is the worst way to end an email: 'thoughts?'"

Just like with the goals you set before having a hard conversation, you'll want to apply those principles of clarity here, too.

TABLE 15.1 GOOD FEEDBACK QUESTIONS VS. BAD

Do This	Avoid This
Is this in alignment with your rebranding principles?	Thoughts?
Do you find that this solution takes into account all of your technology stack's limitations?	When can we expect approval?
Does this address the key issue we set out to solve?	What do you think?

The better your transparency as you go along in your project, the higher quality your feedback will be. If you wait until the last moment to get important feedback, you're upping the risk factor for an upsetting outcome by an order of magnitude. Why? The work you're doing isn't just work: it's also both you and your stakeholder's reputation, time, and money. Showing them progress a little along makes any mistakes or missteps easy to correct.

NOTE WHAT IF THIS INVOLVES MULTIPLE STAKEHOLDERS?

If you're working on a big initiative involving multiple stakeholders, discuss everything you can with your primary stakeholder or the person who will be most influential in this conversation ahead of time. Their perspective will give you what you need to get ahead of potential issues.

Next, make sure to have a high-fidelity conversation. You learned about this in Chapter 6, "Conflict on Remote Teams" but as a refresher you want to use ways of communicating that give you the full range of verbal and nonverbal cues so that you don't misinterpret what someone says. Brad mentioned previously that he wasn't great at this. "Sometimes I'd send it right before the call and get their reactions right in the moment. That absolutely blew up in my face, but I didn't know what else to do."

Finally, make sure that you're in the right state of mind: one of openness and growth (see Table 15.2). Too often, people fear feedback. It's no surprise, as receiving negative feedback can potentially damage our personal standing, so we're hardwired to go against it. We always want to look and do our best, but we falsely assume that we can do it alone.

And the key to unlocking that mindset? Avoid tying your personal validation and worth to it. It's just work. Comedian Bill Hicks had a famous bit about how people take things too personally. He said, "The world is like a ride in an amusement park... when you choose to go on it, you think it's real. That's how powerful our minds are. The ride goes up and down, around and around, it has thrills and chills, it's very brightly colored, it's very loud, and it's fun for a while. Many people have been on the ride a long time, and they begin to wonder, 'Hey, is this real, or is this just a ride?'"

Others, he goes on, remind everyone that they don't need to be afraid because it's just a ride. It's seeing feedback on your work from this detached, objective perspective that makes all the difference. It's the difference in seeing feedback as a personal attack and an honest effort by someone to have the best work possible.

TABLE 15.2 THE RIGHT MINDSET FOR RECEIVING FEEDBACK

Pessimistic Mindset	Optimistic Mindset
An attack on you	An opportunity for improvement
Personal criticism	Constructive criticism
A threat to your reputation	A chance to learn and grow
A waste of time	Valuable information
Something to fear	Something to seek out
Unfair or biased	Honest and objective

It's true that not everyone is great at giving feedback. Some give unclear, biased feedback. Others can only see things from their perspective. But your tactics in how you engage them can yield something valuable from even the murkiest feedback.

Engage Them

After you've set the stage, now's the time to engage them. Remember that people didn't go to school to give feedback. It's your job—not theirs—to probe when feedback isn't clear or helpful. (You'll learn about other techniques to counter generally unkind feedback in the next section.) Generally, unhelpful feedback lacks one or more of the following characteristics: action, specificity, and kindness. Table 15.3 provides examples of each.

TABLE 15.3 UNHELPFUL FEEDBACK

Lacking Action	Lacking Specificity	Lacking Kindness
This is all wrong, fix it.	I'm just not feeling it.	Did someone vomit all over the page?
This isn't it, sorry.	I'll know it when I see it.	Are you serious?
My partner hates blue.	Can we make the logo bigger?	I'm giving this to so-and-so to finish.

Here's how Brad handled it:

> **Brad:** "Someone vomited on the page? What do you mean?"
>
> **Janet:** "There's no organization to any of this—it's jumbled, and the color palette is gross. Their music is bright and fun, not some sludge that seeped out of a drainpipe. And we need this in a week! I hope you aren't charging us for this crap."
>
> **Brad:** "I hear you. Let's figure out where we went wrong. So, we got the colors wrong, and it feels too messy. What does an example of something good look like to you?"

The conversation continued, and Brad got some clarity on what another round of updates might look like. Something brighter, poppier, and more fun. Janet was still heated, because she felt Brad was wasting their time and money. "We also wanted to communicate more frequently so that things wouldn't go wrong in a bigger way."

It was good for Brad to push for clarity, as the feedback yielded some valuable insights. Here are some additional tactics you can deploy when you're faced with unhelpful feedback:

- Ask for clarity about which parts aren't working for them so you can address them.
- Call back to goals and ask which of them is at risk.
- Probe to see if they have an idea in their head that wasn't communicated earlier.
- If you find it hurtful, tell them that feedback stung a little, and you want to get to the bottom of it together.

Aside from unhelpful feedback, people often mistake a client's, manager's, or stakeholder's desire to contribute for direction. But it's not always the case—generally, these people just want to help everyone have the best work possible.

One particularly helpful framework to parse situations such as this is Asana's "Do, Try, Consider" method. Here's Jackie Bavaro, who authored the Medium post about it:[1]

> A while back at Asana we noticed teams were laser-focused on shipping and would carefully ask if each piece of feedback was "launch blocking" at our launch reviews. Often non-blocking feedback would be brushed aside even if it was relatively

1 August 19, 2019: https://jackiebo.medium.com/do-try-consider-how-we-give-product-feedback-at-asana-db9bc754cc4a

> cheap and would really improve the quality of the product. We reflected on what was happening and realized that we didn't have clear language or norms on how to give or respond to feedback. And so, the Do, Try, Consider framework was born.

Brad shared that "Janet had a lot of ideas but hadn't really had good experiences with people before. I wasn't really on great terms with her after such a huge miss." While Brad's conversation with Janet didn't allow for this kind of back and forth the Do, Try, Consider framework did, and it's easy to hypothesize what might have happened.

Had Brad brought Janet into the process earlier, getting her ideas on what she saw working for them, he could have asked her to point out which aspects of any inspiration she'd like him to explore.

Putting it all together, here's what setting a good stage looks like:

- Identify what you're looking for feedback on.
- Share what you *aren't* looking to get feedback on (anything else will be noted but tabled).
- If this is your first meeting with someone, detail what good feedback looks like.
- Push for clarity when you sense subjectivity. Don't brush it off.
- Define a list of things you'll do, try, and consider.

Look Out For . . .

Feedback is a gift. As with most gifts, they often come wrapped, so its meaning and value can't be known until you open it. You may find that the other person giving you this gift is a good communicator, making it easy to open this gift. You may also find that they're insightful gift givers who give great feedback.

Not everyone's great at giving gifts. They mean well, but maybe their gift is harder to unwrap, or it isn't clear why they gave you this gift. However, anyone can ask questions to connect the dots of what's being conveyed with their feedback and show appreciation for the thought.

The feedback you receive may not ultimately have value, but everyone benefits from a thoughtful discussion. Even if the feedback isn't relevant or valuable, you've still received a gift from someone—treat it with respect and appreciation.

There's also a chance that the feedback you receive isn't meant to help you. It may be meant to cause harm. You may feel attacked when receiving feedback, but it's important to note that there is a valuable nuance when you get feedback that hurts: it may be negative but ultimately constructive, but it could also be malicious. You will quickly see how to spot the difference.

Brushing It Off

This is the worst way, hands down, to receive feedback. Brushing off feedback doesn't always look like ignoring it or saying "thanks for the feedback" while doing nothing, either. It can be failing to consider this piece of feedback in aggregate and noticing a bigger pattern.

Noticing patterns in your feedback requires a higher degree of self-awareness. (It's the opinion of your author that if you're reading this book, you've likely got a bit more of that than most people.)

For example, Brad got similar feedback twice before about his lack of communication to clients throughout the process. He only applied his manager's feedback to that specific instance, not how he communicated to clients overall. It really came back to bite him this time.

"Janet really did not want to work with me, and even went so far as to meet with the rest of my team without me." He was determined to get it right, so he persuaded everyone to give him one more shot. "We had to offer to do this one for free to keep her as a client, but it paid off. We finished the project successfully. We just had to do a hard reset."

It's important to call out that brushing off feedback isn't always the same as declining to implement it. There are times, such as when deadlines and budgets constrain you, that no matter how valid the feedback is, it can't be implemented. In those cases, clearly call out that you agree with this feedback but aren't able to address it.

Malicious Actors

Negative feedback can help you improve, but if that's all you're receiving, it might indicate malicious intent. However, it's possible that you're interpreting that feedback as malicious when it's not always intended that way (see Table 15.4).

There's a rare chance someone is acting out of malicious intent, however far-fetched it may seem. It's still worth considering how to react should you encounter it. You see malicious intent in the following two categories: vague or contradictory, and personal attacks.

TABLE 15.4 WHAT'S NEGATIVE VS. MALICIOUS?

Negative Feedback	Malicious Feedback
Gives constructive criticism for improvement.	Attacks the person instead of the work.
Provides insights for improvement.	Belittles and undermines both the work and the recipient.
Expresses a different perspective or preference.	Contradicts itself or is vague in a way that sets the recipient up to fail.

If you do receive malicious feedback, focus on these three things: becoming objective, gaining clarity, and responding appropriately.

For Brad, a perfect response to Janet's harsh feedback could look like this:

> "Okay, let's focus more on the work here. We'll work on the layout and get it more organized. It would help me if you could give more examples of what you're looking for. Also, what comes to mind when you say 'poppy and edgy'?"

Brad's response has several things going for it: it redirects to the work, asks for specificity, and reduces anything that might trip them up later (as "poppy" can mean anything to anyone).

To get objective, first determine that the feedback isn't too offensive; there's no need to dig through trash to try and find something valuable if it's too difficult for you. If you do want to process it further, try asking yourself this: if someone other than the original person gave you this feedback, what could you take from it?

If your feedback is a little murky, you can gain clarity by asking if there are specific examples that came to mind for this person. If they can't provide any, you may well be able to ignore it. You also have the additional option of asking someone else you trust if they have examples which fit with what this person told you.

Finally, decide how to respond. You may opt to avoid feedback from them in the future, set boundaries, or tell them that while you value feedback, their delivery wasn't acceptable. You can also discard it and move on. Remember, you aren't obligated to take and respond to every piece of feedback you get. For Brad, "I wasn't confident enough to tell her that I hated hearing this, and it felt like a personal attack, but my interpersonal skills weren't their best at that point. So, I just steered things back to work and seethed privately." While the former is appropriate, Brad (as well as you) would be best served by either telling the other person that the feedback wasn't helpful or letting it go without taking it personally.

For more on the topic of working with malicious people, see Chapter 4, "Lying and Gaslighting."

Final Thoughts

Feedback can be truly difficult to receive. People put so much of themselves into their work, that it's natural to take it personally or fear it. But reframing it makes all the difference. If you adopt a growth mindset, you will stop seeing feedback as a burden and embrace it as the gift it is.

- Set clear goals for the feedback you want to receive and communicate those goals to the person providing feedback.
- Be transparent about what you *don't* want feedback on and any works in progress that may distract from your goals.
- Engage with the feedback provider, ask for clarity, and probe when necessary to get helpful feedback.
- Avoid tying your personal validation and worth to feedback. Adopt a growth mindset to see it as an opportunity for improvement.
- Notice patterns in your feedback and take action to address them. If feedback is malicious, then become objective, gain clarity, and respond appropriately.

CHAPTER 16

Addressing Pay Inequality

"I really got lowballed with the salary for this job. I didn't know that's what I was doing. And naturally, the boss didn't say anything. I'm just a line item to them, anyway, so why would they pay me what I'm worth?" But before too long, Teresa and her team wised up and realized their boss wasn't paying them fairly according to what others like her were making in her area and line of work.

The Problem

Teresa's situation isn't unique. As a woman in tech who is also a person of color, this inequality is endemic. According to *Hired,* a 2022 report found that Black, Indigenous, and people of color (BIPOC) women earn 9% less than their white and Asian counterparts in the same roles. Put another way, men make nearly 10% more than people like Teresa. It's a massive gap.

A caveat before going further: this chapter isn't able to—and in fact, can't—solve pay inequality on a systemic level. There are too many factors, such as historical and structural inequalities, systemic biases, and cultural norms, to name a few.

Instead, this chapter gives you ways to advocate for yourself to address disparities in your compensation effectively and thoughtfully. It gives special attention to people who aren't white cisgender men, but these tactics work for nearly everyone.

The Solution

Knowing that you aren't making what you should sucks. It hurts your self-esteem, and it hurts your finances. But just knowing that you aren't being paid what you should be isn't enough: you have to have the confidence and data to prove it.

Make It About Data

Just like the Conversation Pyramid shows you in Chapter 1, "Before the Conversation," you'll want to start with facts and data. The first thing that helped Teresa determine that she was being underpaid were the invoices that her clients paid her company. Then she started seeing the occasional salary range posted on a job description for her company or a similar role at another company. "That's how I knew I wasn't being paid fairly. I was fuming. Partly I was mad at myself for being taken advantage of, but they shouldn't have put me in such a position."

That data, coupled with a very unpleasant working environment, made it clear to her that it was time to go. She said "Walking away from that job was terrifying, but I knew that I would rather put my time toward job hunting instead of being drained at this job and not earning a livable wage." Teresa made the right choice for her, but don't worry: this book is not going to advise you to quit as well, although you may well find it's the right choice for you, too. This book is, after all, titled *We Need to Talk*, not *I Quit, Bye Losers!* So, onward.

Publicly Available Data

Your first and best place to look for data is an open job description for a role at your company. The best ones contain salary ranges and clear job requirements. The more clarity there is in the requirements, the easier it is to understand how you're paid and how you contribute to the bottom line.

Job descriptions also make it easy to know if you're performing at, or even above, your level. If you're exceeding the requirements, making a case for a raise or a promotion is much simpler.

You can also look at sites such as Glassdoor and levels.fyi to get a broader picture of how people in roles like yours are being compensated. These sites typically list total compensation, including equity and any bonuses that people have.

Your Company's Financials

There is power in knowing how your company makes money, how much it burns each month, and what kind of growth it is experiencing.

If you're at a startup, they're likely more transparent with this kind of data. The larger your company gets, the less likely it is that you'll get a clear picture of everything. It isn't that your company is hiding the information. It just becomes more complex, and you're only likely to hear about it during a quarterly update.

Bear in mind, earlier stage companies like those being funded by investors typically pay a little less in cash and more in equity. This approach typically inverts as a company matures, giving people more cash and a little less equity.

"How money gets made is the biggest thing I ask about when I interview," Teresa said. "I need to understand that there actually is vertical growth for my salary." She also uses this to help her understand if she's being paid fairly off the bat.

If you can show how your work contributes to the company's bottom line, you may be able to make a stronger case when it comes to remedying any pay disparities. Knowing the company's financial goals and metrics can help you make data-driven arguments for fair compensation.

Use Other Trusted Sources

It may not be entirely possible to determine if you're being paid fairly using the information stated previously. It may not even exist. But it's virtually certain that others have gone down this path before you.

Your first stop should be with a recruiter or staffing agency. "I ended up talking with a recruiter," Teresa said. "She told me 'oh no, you're asking way too little. You need to be asking this much.' Then she showed me three other roles she was trying to fill and what they offered."

Folks in this line of work must know what the market supports. It's quite literally their job to know that information. After all, they can't place someone in a role if they're asking too much, and they can't get people to their clients if they aren't paid enough. They won't get you the absolute best pay, but they'll help you establish a baseline for what to expect.

Online communities are also a treasure trove of information. Most communities, such as Leading Design and Rands Leadership Slack communities, have dedicated groups that help people understand and compare salaries and equity without the pressure of a manager looking over their shoulder. It's also a great place to find a mentor who has done your job before.

"I used the information I got from this recruiter to avoid companies that were going to pay me too little. And at my next job, I asked my boss about a raise when the time was right."

Teresa used an existing meeting with her boss, Bruce, to bring up the topic. Here's how the conversation went:

> Teresa: "Okay, next item on my agenda. I wanted to have a conversation about my compensation. Sound okay?"
>
> Bruce: "Sure thing."
>
> Teresa: "I've been looking over my job description and the contributions I've made these last six months. I've gone above and beyond my duties by creating a new marketing campaign that's brought us 20% more paying customers and reduced the

customer support's call volume. I know that's something typically done by people with higher titles and more responsibility than I have, so I'd like to ask you to consider a raise or title change for me."

Bruce: "What were you thinking?"

Teresa: "I've compared data from two sources we use for new hires and other job descriptions, and I think asking [this much, or for this title change] is appropriate. How are you seeing it?"

Bruce: "You're right, and those are some huge contributions that have made a meaningful impact. Let me go see what I can do."

Teresa: "Thanks, I really appreciate you advocating for me."

Your conversations don't have to look exactly like this one. You can try these other ways of addressing it:

- "My salary isn't competitive with market rates. Are you aware? Can we adjust this?"
- "I'm performing above my level according to my job description, so can we discuss promoting me?"

Lastly, avoid bringing other people directly into the conversation, as everyone's compensation is unique. Focus on your role, your contribution, and what value you provide.

Negotiate Up Front

Negotiation is a fascinating art, especially around salaries. It's too bad that so much of the advice and techniques revolve around what amounts to baseless superstition, leading to unnecessary frustration. "Never give a number first!" some people crow. "Have that conversation in the first round" others sagely advise. Still others say "talking about salary early is gauche" and "ask for 20% more and settle."

As the old saying goes, an ounce of prevention is worth a pound of cure. The same is true for pay disparities: if you can address the problem before it becomes one, you'll have a far easier time. The place to do this is during salary negotiations when employers ask you about your salary expectations.

Until more pay transparency or other kinds of workplace standards resolve this for everyone, it's time to demystify negotiating. Here are the universal truths of salary negotiations.

They Want as Much for as Little as Possible, You Want the Opposite

Companies must have a budget for new hires as a function of yearly and quarterly financial planning. Each company allots money for hiring early on in its financial plan for the year and that grows or shrinks depending on a lot of factors. Sometimes the amount available is per role, and with others it's a set amount per team per year. A quick and informal survey of smaller startups (fewer than 20 employees) showed that the prominent way of budgeting for this was a set amount for the team.

So, companies like this, bluntly, want to pay as little as possible to get someone in the door. It's not you; it's just how the system works: less money spent on talent is more money for other things like runway and bonuses. This does have a side effect of unfair pay.

It Doesn't Matter Who Goes First... Mostly

A common superstition you'll encounter concerns who goes first when it comes to talking about money. It's possible that by making your employer go first, they'll give you a higher number than you expect. In truth, it doesn't matter much.

What *does* matter, however, is the information mentioned earlier, and how you bring it up.

What about fairness? An employer has already decided if they're going to be fair or not, so that also doesn't matter much. If, when presented with evidence, they're unwilling to budge or try to use Toilet Paper Logic (read on for more on that), you either take what's offered or walk. If they're unable to budge, that's a different story that you can negotiate through by asking for more equity, perks, or time off.

There's also the chance that some employers will tell you if you're asking too little. It's not common, but it happens. Transparency and fairness is important; if it feels like a steal, it probably is, and smart people like Teresa will figure it out and respond accordingly (recall that she left her first job over this).

Close Enough Is Good Enough

There's an old saying that close only counts in horseshoes and hand grenades. It also counts in salary negotiations.

If you obsess on getting every single dollar you want, and it's certainly your prerogative to do so, you might end up harming yourself in the end. Say you have a current job offer on the table for $95,000, but you're holding out for a position that pays $100,000. If your potential employer isn't able to make that happen, you could walk away and hold out for another offer.

So, $5,000 isn't anything to sneeze at, but be sure to weigh the risks and opportunity costs of walking. What if it takes an additional three months to get another offer? What about (God forbid) six months?

If it takes you an additional three months to secure that slightly higher offer, you've forgone a quarter of the year's salary from the first offer (nearly $24,000). Holding out for an extra $5,000 would actually only benefit you by about $3,750. Here's how that works out (see Table 16.1).

TABLE 16.1 OPPORTUNITY COSTS

Description	$95,000 Offer	$100,000 Offer (3 Months Wait)	$100,000 Offer (6 Months Wait)
Monthly salary	$7,916.67	$8,333.33	$8,333.33
Earnings forgone in waiting	—	-$23,750	-$47,500
Earnings after waiting period	—	$75,000	$50,000
Total earnings in 1 year	$95,000	$98,750	$95,500
Difference in earnings in 1 year	—	+$3,750	+$500

If you're in a situation like this, and it's close, do the math and see if you'd be better off waiting. You likely aren't, so establish what you need and give yourself an acceptable amount of wiggle room.

If You're Unsure, Defer or Seek More Information

If you're still unsure, and someone asks you a question like "Can you tell me about your salary expectations for this role," you can use these replies to get you through the conversation:

- "I'm flexible. I know some companies are heavier on cash compensation while others are heavier on equity. How does that typically break down for you?"

- "What did you budget for this role? I don't need exact numbers, just a rough estimate is fine to make sure that we're in alignment."
- "I'm interviewing at places that have a pretty wide range, so can you tell me where you're landing in terms of budget for this role?"
- "I don't want to hinder these conversations prematurely. Can you tell me a ballpark figure of what you're looking to pay? Then we'll see if that makes sense for both of us."
- "It depends on the total compensation package. Can you tell me a little more about it?"

You'll find people generally respect your line of questioning. There are some who won't, and it's a red flag. Either hold your ground or bow out gracefully. But for those who do respect your questions, you've just made sure that you've got the best offer you can get without a whole lot of fuss.

Look Out For . . .

It can be a tricky business to have conversations with people about pay disparities. That's especially true when it's your pay and your job on the line. Some employers intentionally confuse the issue, and some employees take the wrong tack in addressing it.

Toilet Paper Logic

Some companies consciously add to the problem of pay inequality by not adhering to standards or saying they're somehow different from everyone else. While it's true to a degree, it's also unnecessarily complicated. It's a lot like shopping for toilet paper. Sure, it sounds weird, but hang on, and you'll see where this is going.

When you're browsing the aisles for toilet paper (or bathroom tissue if you aren't in America), you'll see some products include bonus rolls. Others advertise extra big rolls or mega rolls. Pricing is shown per sheet on some (not all sheets are the same size), while others list price per roll.

There are admittedly other factors that affect price, but it doesn't have to be this needlessly (and comically) confusing. If companies priced by standards, such as price per square inch or centimeter, this would be a simpler exercise.

Here's where companies come in: those who use meaningless distinctions to insist you can't make direct comparisons between them and their competitors (who are very much like them) use what this book calls *Toilet Paper Logic*.

Here's what Teresa could say if Bruce were using Toilet Paper Logic:

> Bruce: "I see that you've looked up these other companies, but they aren't like us. You can't make a direct comparison."
>
> Teresa: "I'm seeing a lot of similarities with stage, size, and revenue models. Our company's numbers are up. What am I not considering?"
>
> Bruce: ". . . we just aren't like them."

Bruce's Toilet Paper Logic is flimsy and falls apart under scrutiny or when you apply standards to meaningless distinctions. You can see through it, though. Here are the factors to consider (see Table 16.2).

TABLE 16.2 SETTING STANDARDS

Factor	Description
Stage and size	Early stage and young companies typically pay at or below market value in cash and rely on other benefits and equity. Later stage and more mature companies typically pay at or above market value in cash and rely less on other benefits and equity.
Profitability and revenue	Companies with stable income streams (e.g., subscription models) and high profitability may be able to support higher salaries. Companies reliant on less stable, seasonal revenue (e.g., retail) may not be able to support higher salaries but give more in bonuses.
Specialization and market competition	The supply and demand for a particular role in the job market can influence the pay scale. If there's a shortage of people with certain skills, companies may offer higher salaries to attract talent.

The last item in this table is worth your focus, because it contains common wisdom about how to leverage competition in the job market to counter pay gaps.

Getting Another Job Offer as Leverage

This move seems like a surefire way to get you what you want, right? It's certainly a compelling idea: pay you more, or risk losing someone who's done so much for your company and knows all the inner workings of it.

While there is a chance you'll get a counteroffer, they are anorexically slim. And the benefits will be short-lived at best because you'll be identified as someone dissatisfied with their job and will be the first on the list to go if layoffs occur.

The most likely outcome here is you're going to be told "Good for you! Best of luck out there. When is your last day?" That's because you've used a hostile negotiation move that played on people's fear of loss with a clear threat: "Pay me more or I'm leaving." While that notion isn't bad in and of itself, the delivery certainly is. Threats and negotiations don't go well together. Some companies even have policies that prohibit them from making counteroffers. Lastly, it's not kind to the people on the other team that you were "considering" joining.

The best route here is if you've gone to the trouble of getting another job offer, take the new role and don't waste your time with this tactic. Tell your soon-to-be-former employer that your compensation wasn't up to market rates and let them take the hit right on the chin.

Maybe after all of this, you think presenting another job offer is still the right move. If so, here's a list of factors that will likely affect your success rate (see Table 16.3).

One final note: in researching this book, only one person out of the dozen or so people interviewed was successful in pulling off such a move. She was a high-powered design consultant, and she doubled her salary. But it came with strings so onerous that she ended up leaving a few months later. She counted it as a win and moved on.

TABLE 16.3 CONSIDERATIONS WHEN MAKING COUNTEROFFERS

Factors	Increased Chances	Decreased Chances
Market competitiveness	High demand for your skills and experience in the job market.	Low demand for your skills and experience in the job market.
Your value to the company	You have unique, specialized skills or knowledge that would be difficult to replace.	Your role is relatively common, or your skills could be easily found in another candidate.
Your performance	You have a strong track record of success and high performance in your role.	Your performance has been average or below average.
Company resources	You work for a large company or well-funded startup with resources for salary negotiation.	You work for a smaller company or startup with limited resources for salary increases.
Company culture and policies	The company has a culture of negotiation and flexibility around salaries and benefits.	The company has strict policies around salaries and benefits or a culture that doesn't encourage negotiation.
Precedent	The company has accepted counteroffers in the past.	The company has never accepted a counteroffer or has a policy against them.
The other offer	The other offer is significantly more attractive in terms of salary, benefits, or other factors.	The other offer is only slightly more attractive, or it is comparable to your current compensation.

Final Thoughts

Pay disparities are a transparency, equity, and inclusion problem. And, as Teresa put it, "Having knowledge about how much people at your company and industry get compensated is true power." Imagine what could happen if everyone had that level of transparency. If you work at a company that has pay transparency standards in place, that's great. If you don't, consider becoming an advocate for them. At the time of this writing, many states in America, such as California, Colorado, and New York have laws on the books supporting this. More are sure to follow. Meanwhile, consider these factors:

- The gender pay gap is a systemic issue in many industries, including tech.
- To address pay disparities, it's important to gather and present data to support your case.
- Publicly available data, such as job postings and salary ranges, can be a starting point.
- You can also look to recruiters, online communities, and your company's financials for additional information.
- When negotiating salary, it's often best to let the employer state the first number so that you don't leave good money on the table.

CHAPTER 17

How to Build Psychological Safety on Your Team

Lisa worked at design agencies making websites for most of her career. The last agency she worked at was something special. "I could share any idea. Some were great; some sucked the air right out of the room. But everyone just respected where we were coming from and tried to see the merit in those ideas." In other words, it felt safe, even if you were wrong.

It wasn't always like this, she said.

The Problem

For example, Lisa said that previous agencies had "people getting ridiculed for the tiniest misstep, getting called an idiot if you disagreed, and passive-aggressive team members that drove off half the team. I was always in fear of losing my job or saying the wrong thing." She once saw someone cry in the bathroom after a meeting.

You've probably got your own horror stories, but the effect of these are chilling and prevent psychological safety from taking root and thriving. The rest of this chapter focuses on how to build, restore, and fortify that safety so that you can be your best selves at work. And hopefully put those horror stories far away from your mind.

The Solution

First, a note: psychological safety doesn't mean just being nice to everyone. It means being able to say constructive things, even hard things, and still feel like you've got the goodwill and support of your team. It's safe to fail, experiment, and disagree.

Set (and Model!) Clear Expectations

Every company has cultural norms, explicit or otherwise. They're spelled out in policies, onboarding documents, and in myriad other ways. But what's rarely explored is how people prefer to be communicated to and how they communicate with each other. There's an overwhelming amount of minutiae to this, but if you boil it down, three areas emerge: how you prefer to communicate, what you find motivating, and what is a no-go for you (see Table 17.1).

TABLE 17.1 COMMUNICATION

How you communicate.	Think about frequency, directness, and channels you use.
How you want to be communicated with.	Do you prefer written? Slack? Real-time?
What is motivating.	Do you find motivation in identifying areas to improve, or where you've done well?

Defining your communication preferences may be tricky, but it's work that pays dividends later. Because when you work with other people, knowing what makes everyone tick means easier communication because you've already established some common ground.

However, the dynamic changes and is a little different when you're working in a larger company. It won't make sense to spend every first conversation with a new person going over your preferences—no one's got time or energy for all of that. So how do you make this work on a larger scale? One answer is called a user manual.

User Manuals

Every time you get a new product in your life, it usually comes with instructions. Charge it this way; don't use it that way. Each one's a little different, hence the instructions. If that sounds like people, that's intentional: the best way to make them feel safe at work is to ask them what makes them feel that way.

Here's what's contained in a user manual that will give you insights into who you're working with:

- What motivates them?
- What demotivates them?
- What are fun, human things they like to do?

You can have as much fun as you want in writing your own user manual questions. If you're a documents-type person, okay. If you're visual, you can use whiteboard software like FigJam, Freeform, or something entirely different (see Figure 17.1).

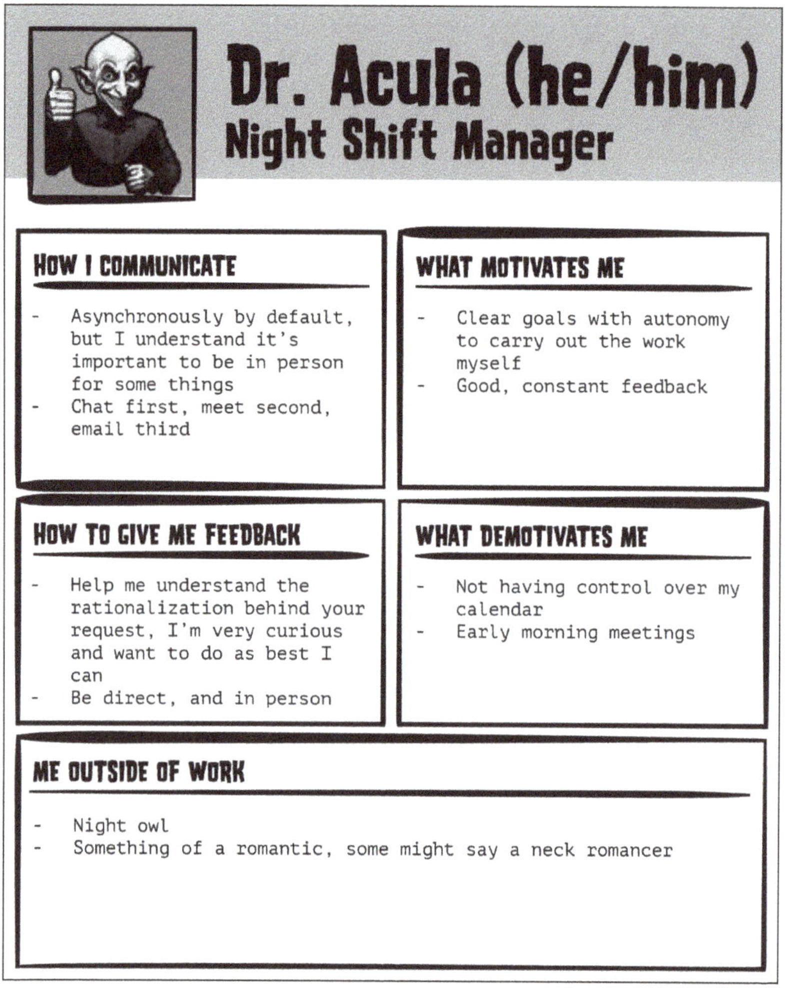

FIGURE 17.1

An example user manual that includes information about how a person prefers to be communicated with, what helps them thrive, and more.

Make sure that you include things relevant to your team and company, but here are some other ideas:

- Please do/don't.
- What you like to do outside of work.
- How you prefer to receive feedback.
- How you communicate, which is important when everyone has differing communication styles.

Whatever you choose to include, customize it and make it meaningful for your team. It also helps to periodically review these, as teams, needs, and even the person changes over time. What's relevant today may not be up-to-date in a year or so.

Making a user manual also serves to set up boundaries. Humans in general aren't great at stating boundaries, for fear of losing their standing with the team. But if you help your team create their own user manual, you're giving them a voice and helping people contribute in ways that make the most sense for them.

You'll also want to make them public. Use whatever collaboration tool you have. At the time of writing, you could put it in your bio on Slack, on a page in Notion, or use something else like a whiteboard software.

Lisa said, "When I first met one of my teammates, I felt a little unnerved. I like to know someone's listening to me. Usually, they do active listening and say 'mmhm,' but he kept quiet." When they talked, Lisa found out that her teammate usually kept quiet during conversations and maintained a neutral expression as a sign of respect for the other person. Keeping quiet is how he showed that he was paying attention. Once Lisa knew that fact, she felt more at ease.

There's one other perk to this: you're building a firewall. Making a user manual inhibits any kind of dehumanization. Here's why: when people are just numbers or fairly anonymous people, it's easy to gloss over the nuances of personal communication styles. For example, how often do you yell at someone who cuts you off in traffic? They are just a silhouette in another faceless vehicle, and you assume they're probably careless or got in your way. But it could also be that they hadn't slept the entire night because they had a sick kid, or they were going through a really stressful time. When you see the richness of someone else's personality, it's much, much harder to be unkind. That's just what these manuals do.

Remove the Fear of Being Wrong

Few people enjoy being wrong. It isn't all bad, as being wrong usually comes with a deeper understanding of the thing you were wrong about; it can, however, bring on feelings of embarrassment, shame, or even anger. But if you can remove the sting of those emotions and reframe it as learning or getting a richer context that you didn't have before, it's much easier to swallow when you didn't get it right.

When you do this, both you and your team are going to feel more competent, because a failure or misstep isn't the end of the world but is helping you create a better one. You'll experiment more, and you'll come up with novel solutions to problems that you wouldn't have thought about if you were still trying to avoid being wrong.

"I remember my boss making a decision that didn't go like he'd hoped it would. He'd pushed for a twist on a standard kind of component. It wasn't in line with what the rest of the team wanted, but he felt like it was the right move, so the team supported him." Afterward, it failed. Pretty spectacularly, actually. "He laughed a little and said 'well, this wasn't my finest moment' or something with a little humor that just made me think how it's okay to be wrong. And he got to work on an alternate idea that fixed things."

Here's what you can do:

- Use a little humor.
- Discuss it in terms of what you hoped to achieve and the gap between: I tried to design a smarter sorting and filtering function for our mobile app by adding multiple filter options per page, but I ended up getting feedback that it was confusing because we put too much on a small screen.
- Make sure that you're grounded in the same principles, just so things don't go off the rails.
- Try testing things. Lots of sites and apps use multivariate testing, so it may take a little bit of extra time to set things up, but it's worth it if it's important.

Embrace Different Perspectives

There's a saying about opinions that goes "strong opinions, loosely held." The idea is that you strongly believe something but can be swayed. It's a good starter because it encourages a zero-sum game where one person's opinion can easily get discarded should another person argue a better case. Or, more accurately, do so with more passion or determination.

It's time for something else: strong opinions, graciously welcomed.

Making this change is subtle, but it's game-changing. What you're doing is welcoming other opinions, and you're going to take them into account to form a more informed perspective. The more you can see things from different perspectives, the better and fuller your own will be. And that's how discussions should work.

Here's how:

- "I'd love for someone to poke holes in this."
- "What am I not considering?"
- Don't come in with a full list. That changes the mindset to "what's missing?" instead of "what can I add?"

One thing you'll want to avoid is tokenizing. Sometimes it can be difficult to spot, as shown in Table 17.2.

TABLE 17.2 HOW DO I KNOW IF I'M TOKENIZING?

Type of Tokenization	Description	Ways to Counteract
Viewing someone primarily through the lens of their identity.	This involves simplifying an individual's identity to just one aspect (e.g., race, ethnicity, gender, or sexual orientation), thereby overlooking their other characteristics.	Recognize and appreciate the complexity of each individual's identity. Try to know people beyond their group identities and challenge your own stereotypes or biases.
Expecting them to represent or speak for their entire group.	This places an additional burden on the individual, asking them to represent or provide insights about their entire group, which assumes homogeneity within the group.	Understand that each individual's experiences and perspectives are unique. If you want to learn about a group's experiences, seek out various sources and don't rely on one person to educate you.
Including them only in certain situations to create an appearance of diversity.	This involves inviting or including individuals in certain situations, not for their unique skills or contributions, but for creating an image of diversity.	Value individuals for their unique skills, talents, and contributions, and not just for appearances of diversity. Promote genuine inclusivity in all situations.

Put people with experience in accessibility issues on your team. People who live with disabilities are perfect candidates. This is, admittedly, easy to say and harder to sell. But who knows how to help those with disabilities better than those who live with them every day?

If you're building a moderation team for a new social network, broaden your team to include people who are routinely on the receiving end of things that need moderating.

If you're building an app, go test it with people who live with accessibility issues. There's no substitute for real human feedback.

Look Out For...

Here are some of the biggest ways that psychological safety gets nuked. Sometimes the past invades the present, and sometimes people are unintentionally (for the most part) undercutting someone else.

Letting Past Trauma Inform the Present

This is a particularly tricky section to write as an author who's experienced some hard times and trauma at work before. If you've ever been fired, laid off, harassed or worse at work, that's trauma. Past trauma, especially when unresolved, can affect your ability to feel safe in new work environments.

Situations at work don't often allow for closure. Most situations end with extremely difficult conversations, abrupt resignations, and terminations or layoffs that then seep into your personal life. This sudden blow leaves you in a state of suspended animation, unable to fully know *why* or *how* this happened, much less how it could have been avoided.

Those past traumas taint new opportunities and relationships and can sour them before they have a chance to mature on their own. They also make it difficult to distinguish the past from the present, so you project negative past experiences onto current situations. This leads to a lack of psychological safety, decreased productivity, and morale.

Why is that? Mostly, it's due to a lack of closure from previous traumatic situations. More extreme forms of this present as complex post-traumatic stress disorder (CPTSD). This book isn't equipped to tackle CPTSD, that's for the work of therapists and other trained professionals. It is, however, prepared to offer some first aid and a little preventative maintenance.

Lisa recalled being laid off. After getting some strange signals at work where her accounts didn't work, she said, "I called my boss and said, 'I think I'm about to be let go. Did you know anything about this?' He said 'no,' and then stopped mid-sentence. 'Oh shit, me too. I got laid off too.'" What followed was a meeting where HR read them a script, told them what they'd get from the company, and ended the call. She didn't get to say goodbye; she was quarantined and removed.

Lisa's experience isn't unique. It's hard on anyone going through something like that. And if you go on to the next company with that unresolved trauma, the cycle repeats.

Here's how to start healing from those past traumas.

Acknowledge the Past and the Pain It Caused

Past trauma at work isn't something people talk about a lot either—there's a sizable stigma attached to it. Common arguments against this are that when you are talking about it, you aren't being a professional, or you aren't being resilient enough. And your "complaining" can hurt future opportunities by seeing you as a liability.

Make sure that you're talking to someone if you need to. It doesn't have to be a therapist; it could be someone you respect or has been through something similar before.

You may also need to allow yourself time to grieve and admit that yes, you were hurt deeply by what happened. Work is a support system for life, and when that support system is threatened, it hurts you personally.

Ask yourself in what ways you can protect yourself in the future. Maybe it's having a bigger emergency fund saved. Maybe it's having new boundaries.

If you've been harassed and still need to be reachable by phone, consider having a "burner" number that only people from work can have. There are services and apps that offer this for a next-to-nothing fee, and you can use it on any smartphone or computer. If you're in the United States at the time of this writing, most states have protections for the personal information of those who have been victims of harassment and worse. Many in the United States offer something similar to California's Safe at Home program, which protects the mailing information of victims of domestic violence, stalking, and other situations.

Know Your Triggers and Try to Push Ahead

Once you've worked through the first two sections, ask yourself this: Can you be aware of your triggers and manage them so that you give these new people a chance to succeed or fail on their own? It won't be easy work, but it's how you can move forward.

Depending on how severe your past trauma was, you may want to consider talking with a therapist or other behavioral health specialist to manage the trauma. Regardless of your choice, give yourself some grace in dealing with the situation. There's a parallel to draw from here to old sports injuries. They can be reactivated and aggravated just as your trauma can, and you treat it accordingly. Sometimes that's rest; sometimes it's another kind of intervention.

Weaponized Positivity

Everyone wants to be happy at work and talk about the good things that others are doing. Some people and companies take it to the extreme and *only* talk about the good stuff, hoping the bad stuff will magically go away. If you don't talk about the bad stuff, it isn't there, right? Wrong.

Here's the thing about this kind of positivity: the harder that people seem to cling to positivity and happiness, the more likely it is that there's something truly rotten underneath that isn't being addressed. It's also textbook delusional behavior.

Sure, no one likes bad news, but you can't force happiness or manifest only good things in the world. It's important to recognize and address the bad, the negative, and the uncomfortable, or it leads to counterbalances like nervous breakdowns, extreme depression, and unethical behavior. By tackling these issues, you're going to build psychological safety and insulate yourselves from future problems.

Lisa put it well: "If you only tell me good things, I'm not going to trust you as much." She said it goes for coworkers as well as leadership. "One of my CEOs was a guy who thought he was the most effective if he was hyping up his team. It turns out that's all he knew how to do. He handled bad news poorly, if at all. And when things went south, he was absent or absolutely callous about it."

Plus Deltas

"Plus deltas" is a feedback practice that involves identifying the positive aspects (pluses) and areas for improvement (deltas). This is helpful in providing honest, candid, positive, and constructive feedback. Here's what it looks like in practice:

- Share what you perceived as positive aspects or strengths (pluses) and be specific about the impact they have. Don't just offer empty compliments.
- Identify areas where you believe improvements or changes could be made (deltas).

This practice highlights positive elements that you want to reinforce and the areas for growth to foster improvement. It promotes a balanced and constructive approach to feedback by recognizing strengths while addressing opportunities for development. For example, here's how Lisa worked with her boss on a design system:

> Lisa: "Let's talk about the design system and presentation I gave earlier. What were the pluses you observed?"
>
> Dewayne: "I thought the way you organized this was clearly thought through, and I wouldn't have a moment's trouble finding what I needed. The iconography also looked really cohesive and was a big step up from what we had before! You clearly communicated the value of having a design system and tied it back to business goals."
>
> Lisa: "Thank you! I tried really hard on that. Now for deltas, did you see areas where there could be improvements?"
>
> Dewayne: "One delta I noticed was that you got really deep into the details, which made it challenging to absorb so much information. It's clear that you've thought it through, but maybe take a step back from the details for the executives as things were lost. Additionally, incorporating more real-life examples could enhance the audience's understanding."
>
> Lisa: "Thanks for that feedback. I think you're right about the pace. I was feeling rushed and wanted to show that I did my homework. I'll work on slowing down my pace and not getting so deep into the weeds."

Or, if you find that you don't agree with the feedback, you can try this:

> **Lisa:** "I hear you, but it was really important to put all that info in there. I could tell it was a bit much, but I had some previous conversations that indicated the execs really wanted to know about how we'd tackle accessibility. Maybe I could have called that out more."

If you aren't one for sticking to formats or that feels too foreign to you, that's just fine. The main goals are to share what truly went well (remember, be specific about the impact those decisions had) and what could be improved.

Compliment Sandwiches

It's amazing that compliment sandwiches still exist. If you're unfamiliar, a *compliment sandwich* is when someone tells you two good things with something not so great in the middle. It's got a lot of other great names, but my personal favorites are a *shit sandwich* or a *turd taco.* Alliteration and teenage humor can really do a lot for you.

Compliment sandwiches are hostile for psychologically safe relationships because they're built on the idea that people can't handle the truth. Nothing says you can't be trusted like having to be told two positive things for every negative thing you're told.

It isn't that the person telling you this has nefarious intentions necessarily. They most likely aren't thinking about what it means when they use one. The impact is the same, regardless: it makes any positive thing coming out of the other person's mouth lose nearly all credibility.

Compliment sandwiches also fall into "nice" territory, which this book expressly avoids. Having hard conversations at work isn't about being nice, because nice isn't authentic—it's about being kind. And the kindest thing to do is get directly to the problem without beating around the bush.

Here, you'll find two other, kinder methods.

Build on Their Strengths

Also known as *appreciative inquiry*, this technique helps people excel at what they're best at. Appreciative inquiry is an approach to organizational development and problem-solving that focuses on amplifying strengths. Developed by David Cooperrider and Suresh Srivastva in the early 1980s, it's a positive and strengths-based approach to organizational change and development.

It applies perfectly to helping people get better at what they're already good at. Here's how a conversation about Lisa not being great at user interviews could play out:

> Dewayne: Okay, bit of a curve ball coming your way about this project. We want to make sure you're doing what you're best at, and conducting user interviews isn't it because you've had a tendency to jump to solutions instead of listening. So, we want to have you focus on something else. We saw you were great at distilling insights and actionable items from those interviews, so we'd like you to focus on that, and we'll get someone else to handle the actual interviews.

Offer Other Support

It may not be an option to have another expert come in to handle something, and you've got to work with what you have. Here's how that conversation could go:

> Dewayne: We're seeing you struggle with user interviews and being too leading with your questions, and we want to support you. We'd like you to work with Martin, who's really good at this. And, just as a reminder, this isn't a reflection on you as a person or the work you do. Those insights are very valuable, but we want you to continue growing, and Martin will be a big help here.

The final recommendation for this section is to put the compliment sandwich where it belongs: buried between two layers of dirt, six feet underneath the ground.

Final Thoughts

In closing, a note for leaders: You are the best model and biggest make-or-break point for psychological safety on your team. You're the team's safety net, so make double sure you do your best to make them feel safe by following through on what you say you'll do. By neglecting to do that, you cut little holes in that net. If that becomes a pattern, your team won't be able to trust that net to help them, and they'll look for other ways of getting the support they need. Or they'll pancake when they walk a high wire. After all, you can't trust a safety net that isn't there.

- Set clear expectations and communicate preferences to establish common ground with coworkers.
- Create user manuals to understand what motivates and demotivates each team member and customize them to make them meaningful to the team.
- Remove the fear of being wrong to encourage experimentation and novel solutions.
- Embrace different perspectives and welcome other opinions to form a more informed perspective.
- Avoid letting past trauma inform the present and focus on building on strengths and offering support.

CHAPTER 18

When You Don't Have Time to Prepare

While typing away at his desk, John's boss, Winston, walked up, and without breaking stride said, "John, we need to talk." John was usually a fairly level-headed guy, but he'd been feeling some tension with his client, and his stomach sank when Winston spoke.

"I read between the lines a lot; you kind of have to in my line of work. Sometimes I see things that aren't there, but Winston's one-liner 'invitation' to a conversation didn't help matters at all with me."

The Problem

Everyone's had a similar moment when they had to jump into action (or reaction, rather) without preparation. Maybe it was an ominous invitation like John's, or maybe a temper flared up in the middle of a meeting. Regardless, think of this chapter's focus as "what to expect when you aren't expecting a fight."

"I got a little too nervous in those moments when I didn't have time to prepare. I'm fairly methodical and can give you a thoughtful reply if I have a moment, but I could never have seen this conversation coming." What Winston had to tell John was that his client called with news that John wasn't contributing to the project he was working on. John's client alleged he wasn't showing up to meetings, not delivering work, and not being available to talk.

The problem with this is that we're at the mercy of two things: our amygdala and ingrained habits. This response even extends to self-professed methodical people like John, but it is possible to train yourself to respond calmly when put in a stressful situation. It takes practice, but it is possible.

The Solution

You've heard the old Latin phrase "know thyself." It's critical when you're dropped into a situation with no prep. If you can know how you respond to stress and how to stabilize yourself, you're going to be miles ahead of where you are right now.

Know How You Respond to Stress

Earlier in Chapter 2, "Having the Conversation," you learned about the safety spectrum. Figure 18.1 builds on that concept and adds both abrasive and avoidant behaviors opposite each other (yelling, for example is the opposite of clamming up). It also adds detail to the sweet spot by identifying the ideal behaviors. Those behaviors are defined as those which help you function best when you're subjected to sudden stress. Later, you'll learn how to move toward being centered, regardless of where you are.

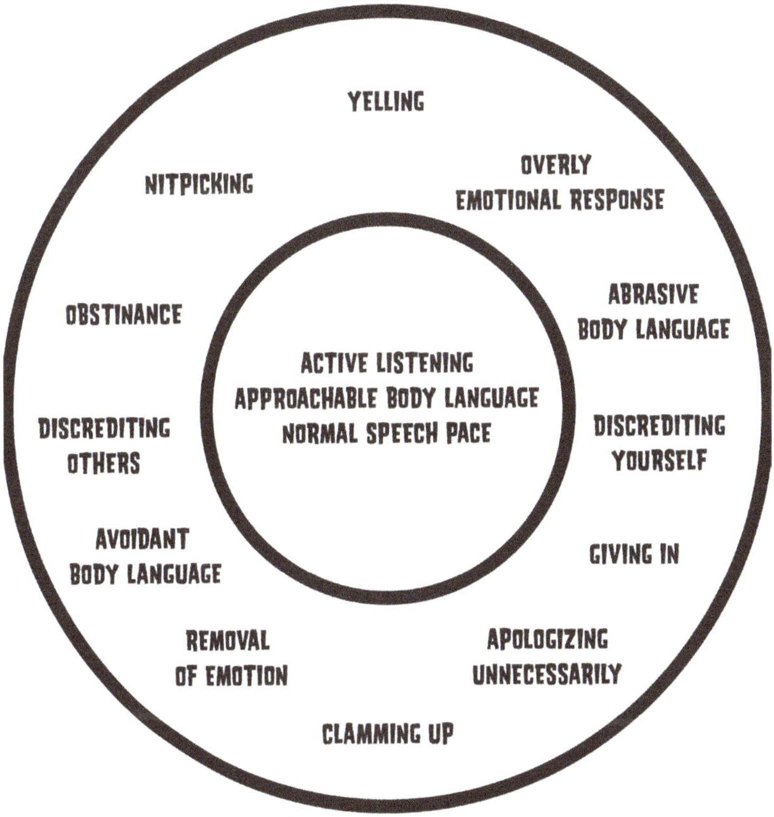

FIGURE 18.1
Here are some common abrasive and avoidant behaviors arranged in a circle. The center shows a behavior that is healthy and balanced.

Everyone is going to respond to stress differently based on their upbringing, culture (see Chapter 10, "Understanding Cultural Dynamics"), and previous life experiences. It may well be unpleasant to see (or have) a heated knee-jerk reaction, but most people aren't even aware it's happening—this isn't to excuse any harm caused by said reaction, but it does explain it.

Think about a recent time when you were ambushed with a situation. How did you react? What did you do? Understanding your default response to stressors is helpful, as what follows helps you determine which activities can best help you return to center.

NOTE ABOUT THE CENTER OF THIS DIAGRAM

> The emotions on the outside of this diagram do not mean they're invalid or incorrect, they're only a starting place. We're humans. We're wired to be emotional and should normalize the healthy display of emotions, just not in a way that's going to harm another person.

When John saw this diagram, he said, "I'd feel my legs start bouncing, and my hands get a little shaky." He went on to say he primarily "apologized out of hand for things because I hate conflict. I come from a culture where 'talking back' to authority is a sign of disrespect." And apologizing, he said, was the quickest way to get someone off his back. "It wasn't the most genuine thing I've ever done, but you do what you have to do to get by when you've got a situation brewing."

Because of his upbringing, John also removed all emotions and assumed whoever brought this to him (Winston, in this case) was correct. "It was one of those times that my cultural defaults put me at a disadvantage, because I wasn't prepared for my client to outright fabricate stories."

Winston, by the way, was more direct and aggressive when it came to conflict. You can tell by his cold "we need to talk" and subsequently not stopping to allow John to ask questions.

Center Yourself

Before continuing with John's story, imagine being dropped into the middle of a dense forest without a compass or a map. It's dark. In the distance, you hear some strange critters deep within, and it spooks you a little. You also can't see the sun or stars, so you have little sense of direction. Lost and alone, it's easy to panic.

If you take a deep breath and focus on your surroundings, you can begin orienting yourself and remember what to look for. Maybe you hear a stream (streams lead to rivers, and rivers lead to people) or see a distant mountain peak (higher ground gives you better vantage points). By focusing on what's around you, you can begin to find your way out.

The same is true with conversations that you don't have time to prepare for. For John, centering himself meant focusing on his breathing and taking it slowly—this way he wouldn't get overwhelmed, and he could find his stream or mountain peak.

The conversation, however, didn't go so well.

> **Winston:** Your client says you aren't delivering on what we promised them. They haven't seen any research for this app they're building, nor have they seen any market positioning documents. They're threatening to pull our entire engagement with them unless you step it up. What in god's name are you doing over there? This isn't like you.
>
> **John:** [visible panic] I'm sorry, what? That's insane.

John said he panicked. He doesn't remember much of the rest of the conversation, owing mostly to his nervousness and shock.

> "Instead of taking it slow, I got anxious and just blurted out a bunch of things I did and asked what the hell they were talking about. Never mind that I didn't like the project or the people, but business is business sometimes. Either way, it wasn't a really good look for me, because I came off frazzled."

Remember to Box Breathe

For more on this, see Chapter 3, "People Losing Control."

John had three opportunities to center himself, focus on his breathing, and get himself out of his own head:

- When Winston "invited" him to a conversation
- When he sat down after coming into Winston's office
- After Winston delivered his opening line

John could have also asked for a moment to go get something and collect himself. Then the conversation could progress as such:

> **John:** [takes a deep breath] Okay, hang on. I'm not contributing? Can you give me some specifics to help me understand?
>
> **Winston:** I only know that they aren't happy and that you aren't showing up.
>
> **John:** You know me, Winston. I've got a lot of time in with our company and have had nothing but happy clients. Why would I do something like this? Can we look at what's not being delivered?

Even though you can't always prepare for an entire conversation ahead of time, you can (and arguably should) have a few go-to phrases at the ready. Practice them in smaller settings so that they come naturally to you. When you're presented with a situation like this, your brain's survival circuits activate and trigger an amygdala hijack (see Chapter 3).

Having a go-to statement can provide you with valuable time to cool down your—and potentially their—amygdala hijack while you center yourself. Here are some useful phrases to help you center yourself during a difficult conversation:

- Give me a moment, that's a lot to process.
- I need a second to get my head around this.
- Can we pause for a moment so I can collect my thoughts?
- Let me take a minute to consider what you've shared.

Work Your Way Out of the Forest

When you're on the receiving end of a sudden burst of conflict, your first instinct may be to solve it with the same urgency in which it was presented. Resist this urge.

Instead, treat this like a grease fire in a kitchen. Your first instinct may be to toss water on it, which only makes matters worse—getting sucked into the heat of the moment or rushing to a conclusion will only do likewise.

Instead, you need to contain and starve this fire of oxygen. This happens by combining a slower pace with the reflecting technique you learned in Chapter 2. As a refresher, reflecting includes echoing (repeating their words), labeling (assigning an emotion to their words), and summarizing (recapping their statement).

Using reflecting here forces a more objective conversation about your situation and encourages everyone to focus more on the issues underlying the conversation, not the urgency that people typically respond to.

For John, his goal would be to get Winston to explain things a bit more.

> **John:** [takes a breath] Hmm, they aren't happy? This is confusing to me, but we can figure it out. What other information or context do you have? Who said this?

Notice while Winston has smaller amounts of information, he may have more context on the client or broader situation, which could provide a foothold for you. It also gets Winston into problem-solving mode, as he's thinking holistically.

Going deeper, John and Winston can also probe to find out more objective aspects of the conversation, such as seen in Table 18.1.

TABLE 18.1 AREAS TO INVESTIGATE

Questions to Ask	Possible Solution Areas
What specifically is at risk?	Look at your deliverables, timeline, budgets. Also consider the relationship.
What are your options to remedy?	Bring in additional team members, adjust the scope of the work, offer a partial refund.
What issue may underly this one?	Mismatched expectations, poor communication, misaligned goals

After doing this, they'll be able to find a way forward to satisfy their client. "I talked to Winston, who got more context from our client. They weren't able to get very specific, outside of saying I wasn't available for this meeting or that event. Even with prompting, they couldn't provide a lot more detail which was a red flag."

John was able to provide a defensible response to their problems, notably that he was indeed at every meeting and had contributed several things to their project. But something changed after his first day that slipped past him until that moment: "I declined to do some out-of-scope work. They asked me to do personal tasks for them and other unrelated business tasks, which wasn't at all related to my line of work. I'd declined to do them, and that's when things changed."

Before Winston went to speak with their client to smooth things out, John mentioned that what might be best was to swap personnel as their client seemed to have a misunderstanding of his role. Or maybe they plainly just didn't like him. "I also said to Winston that maybe I should go because they tried to assassinate my character," he laughed. Winston agreed, and they swapped John for someone else.

Look Out For...

When tense situations crop up, you've got to keep a clear head. That means you've got work to do to counter the default knee-jerk tendency to get caught up in a situation, overcorrect it, or dismiss the issue entirely. Any of these can tank a relationship or project. Getting caught up in it makes progress impossible, overcorrecting sets everyone up for failure, and dismissing it is a recipe for failure.

Getting Caught Up

When you get caught up in a situation, no one wins. This takes innumerable forms, but typically they fall into two categories according to the safety spectrum you read about in Chapter 2: abrasive and avoidant. Each of these chips away at (or eliminates entirely) mutual trust and the best possible outcomes for everyone.

It's obvious that no one likes to be wrong, and when people perceive a higher cost for being wrong, they act against their best interests. And much of common wisdom tries teaching you to be a completely logical, unfeeling computer that makes the perfect decision every time. This book doesn't want that for you, and its author does not believe that is possible. The best thing you can do is generate awareness of these emotions so that you can steer yourself back to center when you think they may be getting the better of you.

John was prone to operating out of the avoidant camp. Instead of really probing to see what the issue was, he would simply apologize and do what the other person asked. It undermined his competence and ultimately was a disservice to himself, the project, and his client, but he didn't see any way forward.

Here's a quick checklist in Table 18.2 that you can use to see if you're prone to getting caught up in things along with some remedies.

TABLE 18.2 COMMON WAYS PEOPLE GET CAUGHT UP]]

Type of Issue	What It Looks Like	How to Remedy
Abrasive	Interrupting	Take five: what are three things you can see, two you can smell, one thing you can touch? This helps you stay anchored in the moment and not in your head.
	Yelling	Step out of the conversation. "I'm having some really strong emotions here, give me a moment."
	Focusing on assigning blame rather than finding out how to fix it	Ask yourself: "What if we're both right?" "What can I learn from this?"
Avoidant	Saying this isn't an issue	Ask "how is what I'm doing preventing us from reaching our goal?"
	Planning your next response instead of listening while they speak	Take notes when they speak. This will naturally slow down the conversation, allowing for pauses and thoughtfulness.
	Giving in immediately and doing whatever they ask	Remember you are also a professional and have a wealth of experience to draw from. Bring them along and create a solution together.

Overcorrecting

John's business is client services. And sometimes he and others in his line of work need to make concessions to keep their clients happy. It doesn't matter how great your employees are, if you don't have happy clients, you don't have a business.

Being in a situation with an unhappy client makes the proposition of swooping in, offering a soothing tone, and a few freebies seem extremely tempting. While it may seem generous or magnanimous on your part to ensure that everything goes smoothly, avoid this notion. The more you overcorrect, the more you overcomplicate.

"Winston didn't do this in this particular situation, but he had in the past promised to do something for a client that our firm didn't do: marketing. He was convinced that we could do it for them, but no one on staff had that specialty. And certainly not for a client in that industry and of their size." It was a nightmare, and Winston had to walk back his promise to that client, which they subsequently lost.

Developing awareness of whether or not you're overcorrecting is an art that takes time. And you will have to overcorrect a few times to get a feel for what's right. Table 18.3 can accelerate that growth for you.

TABLE 18.3 TYPES OF OVERCORRECTION

Type of Overcorrection	What It Looks Like	Appropriate Remedy
Are the solutions causing more problems?	Winston offers to extend the project for free, causing John's next engagement to start later and risking that new client's business.	Understand the issue in more detail and offer an appropriate response.
Are you making decisions based on emotional responses?	Winston's client gets angry, and he does whatever they ask.	Ask yourself if you would advise someone else to do what you're proposing.
Are your actions more extreme than is warranted?	Winston fires John on the spot.	Ask them what the ideal scenario would be for them and work from there.
Are you promising something that you can't deliver?	Winston offers for their company to do the marketing for their client, but their company doesn't have that specialty.	Ask a colleague if they would view your response as appropriate.

A "Fake Yes"

While you read about dismissals earlier, there's one more malignant form of dismissal that needs covering. It's called a *fake yes*.

John had a nasty habit in tense moments that caused him unnecessary amounts of stress. "I was really good at telling people yes, and then hoping they'd forget about what they asked. Sometimes I'd get annoyed when they came back and asked again." John's motivations weren't trying to show craftiness or underhandedness; instead he acted out of fear of displeasing them. That's a fake yes.

A fake yes occurs when you agree to something in the moment, with no intention or capability of ever actually doing it, or with the hope that you will never have to follow through. Sometimes these incidents occur accidentally: maybe you weren't clear on the agreement, perhaps you didn't establish a clear outcome, or you didn't define any type of accountability.

Regardless of intent, the impact is the same: someone will remember you agreeing to do something and not doing it, and they won't trust you as much (or at all) in the future. Anyone can agree and say yes, but trust is made or broken on your follow-through.

To that end, there are two ways you can avoid giving a fake yes: follow through to ensure accountability and bring in the client on creating a solution.

John, as he said earlier, was prone to just agreeing and hoping people would forget. It did work for him on occasion, though not always. And with Winston, it wouldn't have been advisable, since he felt stress from his lack of communication and that he delivered some poor quality work.

You can make your own phrase, but here are two starters:

- I get that this is a problem and am so sorry we missed this. I'll work to fix this right away. Can I let you know what I think the best way is by tomorrow?
- Okay, we definitely want to address this. How do you see this working?
- Let me take a moment to think about the best way to proceed.
- I need a little more info in order to make an informed decision. Can we discuss this further and bring in the rest of the team? I'll schedule some time later this week if that's okay.
- I absolutely get your concerns. Let me review the situation and get back to you with a plan of action for you to approve tomorrow.

You'll notice each of these statements contains an acknowledgment of the issue, which validates their concern. They also give concrete next steps, which demonstrates transparency and works to restore any lost trust.

Final Thoughts

There's one last trick to help prevent an amygdala hijack, and it's a personal favorite.

First, find a little item that will serve as a reminder to stay centered and focused when tense situations flare up. It doesn't have to be anything fancy. It can be a cute little rubber duck, a fun sticker, or even a piece of paper.

Then, with whatever object you choose, spend a little time studying it and reminding yourself that you can navigate any unexpected situation with ease. Maybe even look at it and think about your go-to phrases if you get stressed.

Finally, when those situations arise, and they definitely will, you can look at this object and remind yourself that you've got what it takes to work your way through this situation.

- Know thyself. Understand how you respond to stress.
- Center yourself by focusing on your breathing and taking it slowly.
- Avoid getting caught up in the heat of the moment by using a few go-to phrases at the ready.
- Resist the urge to solve a tense situation with the same urgency it was presented.
- Avoid giving a fake yes by following through to ensure accountability and bringing the client in on creating a solution with you.

CHAPTER 19

When You Can't Agree

Norman and Lila are cofounders for a new social network. They're currently going in circles about whether or not their new social network should have direct messages (DMs). It's a core feature of every other social network, but allowing it also allows a lot of harassment and bullying.

Lila doesn't want them at all, but Norman thinks they're essential to helping them meet expectations they and their investors have for this new network. Every time the idea of DMs comes up, the situation becomes more fraught and tense each time. They've punted it down the road as long as they could, and they're at the point where they have to make a decision.

Lila said, "I've been harassed on other social networks through DMs, and so have my friends. I don't want to build a network like this." If they do add this feature, which she doesn't want, she believes they shouldn't do it like everyone else. But she's stuck.

She goes on. "Moderation on big social networks either relies on unpaid moderators like Reddit does or a contractor on the far side of the world like Facebook does." There are also well-intentioned codes of conduct, but harassment still persists. "I just want to build a place where no one's getting death threats on a daily basis. That's not too much to ask," she concluded.

Norman is a veteran of the social networking space. He's also got a good track record—two of his previous startups were acquired. Norman really wants to do right by the people on his platform, but doesn't see a way to exclude DMs and still meet the goals they and their board of directors set. He also hasn't experienced the harassment Lila has and is a little less sensitive to it.

The Problem

The core of Lila and Norman's disagreement is the trickiest: balancing ethics and business.

Both parties could agree to take the easy way out and shift responsibility. Placing the mandate to prevent harm on individuals makes it effortless to ignore it when harm inevitably occurs. Those people with fewer scruples might choose to hold their nose and look away in hopes of avoiding the consequences of their decision.

So how do you balance ethics and business? Throughout the book you've gained tools that help you mend safety in tense situations. But in situations where agreement seems impossible, you need something bigger. Think of this chapter as the "break glass in case of emergency" toolkit.

The Solution

Problems like the ones Norman and Lila face are thorny, fraught with issues, and have high stakes. Both people care deeply about doing the right thing. They also have obligations to meet, and simply talking it out won't solve this one. They need to find ways to elevate their viewpoints and reframe the problem.

Get Out of the Trench

When you've dug around for ideas and solutions and continuously came up empty, you may find you've dug yourself into a trench. It can be hard to see your way out of it. Good news and bad news: there's always a way forward, but you might get a few scratches and bruises along the way.

First, examine your motives and potential biases. You may find that you're injecting bias, be it a cognitive, experiential, or confirmation bias (see Chapter 20, "Mediating with Multiple People"). For Norman and Lila, it's easy to examine the other's motives and look for biases. Norman may identify that Lila could be injecting an experiential bias. She may note that Norman is exhibiting a cognitive bias, having never experienced the level of harassment she or her friends have.

Norman and Lila could also opt to consult with an expert. In their case, they might look for social or clinical psychologists who could offer insights into behaviors, motivations, and emotional responses. Combining their experience with Norman and Lila's, they could come up with a novel solution that inhibits any potential harassment on the platform.

If it's tricky to find one of those, you can also browse a host of scholarly articles on sites like Google Scholar and PubMed.

Reframe It with Lateral Thinking

Back in 1974, Brian Eno, a musician, and Peter Schmidt, an artist, created a set of cards called Oblique Strategies designed to issue challenging constraints to help musicians break creative blocks (see Figure 19.1). The idea was that if you can introduce a seemingly opposing or unrelated idea, it can break you out of your rut.

Norman and Lila's stakes here aren't the same as a musician making a record, admittedly, though they still apply because what Eno and Schmidt did was to apply lateral thinking. If it's a new term for you, *lateral thinking* is an approach to solving problems that forces you to look at your issue from a different, sometimes non-sequitur angle, to come to a solution. You'll do things like challenge your assumptions, reframe the problem, and consider alternative perspectives.

WWW.ENOSHOP.CO.UK/PRODUCT/OBLIQUE-STRATEGIES?FILTER=OBLIQUE STRATEGIES

FIGURE 19.1
Here is an example from Oblique Strategies of how to apply lateral thinking.

Here are a few from the deck, which don't always apply but just go to show you how . . . unexpected they can be:

- Instead of changing the thing, change the world around it.
- Imagine the music as a moving chain or caterpillar.
- Change instrument roles.
- Idiot glee.

To help, Table 19.1 has a few other more, erm, practical yet lateral ideas.

TABLE 19.1 LATERAL THINKING

Strategy	Description
Change the scale.	Think about the issue on a larger or smaller scale. Does the problem still exist?
Poke at what you're ignoring.	What aspects of the problem have been overlooked or undervalued?
Question every assumption.	Challenge the underlying assumptions. What if the opposite were true?
Promote the mistake to a solution.	What if the mistake or problem was intentional? Can it be turned into an advantage?
Invert the problem.	Reverse the problem or challenge. What if the problem was actually the solution?
Switch roles.	Switch roles among team members. How does a different role change your perspective of the issue?
Embrace negative space.	After someone speaks, pause to allow time for reflection. New ideas often emerge during periods of silence.
Seek inspiration from unlikely sources.	What's the last thing that inspired you? Go see what the latest scholarly article has to say. See if it is fertile ground for planting your problem.
Explore how they'd do it.	Write out how you think the person may solve the problem. Then talk about it.
Imagine if this technology didn't exist.	Think about how you'd perform this action in real life. How would our prehistoric ancestors handle this?
Create a paper machete.*	Ask for the most outrageous solutions. This can lead to novel and innovative ideas that break through deadlock.

* Not literally, paper machete is only a play on words meant to illustrate a point. Or heck, maybe it is literal; that's half the fun of lateral thinking anyway.

For Norman and Lila, it would be helpful to change the scale. Earlier, Norman said that his data indicated a very small number of users were harassed and bullied. For argument's sake, say it's 1%. What if it was 10%? 100%? Changing the order of magnitude changes how you perceive the problem in a very literal way.

The pair may also want to imagine how they'd solve their issue if some (or all) technology didn't exist. This frees them from the constraints and issues DMs present.

A personal favorite is seeking inspiration from unlikely sources, hoping they'll yield inspiration for how they address an issue. Doing this is tricky work at first because it runs counter to your instincts to define something and see it clearly.

Instead, you've got to squint and remove some definition. For example:

- Clearly defined: allow one-to-one messaging without harassment or bullying.
- Less defined: let people converse without it being weird.

Table 19.2 shows how this can work in practice.

TABLE 19.2 ANALOGS FOR LETTING PEOPLE CONVERSE WITHOUT IT BEING WEIRD

Idea	Description	Application
Hollywood actors and agents	You don't talk to them first, you talk to their agents. They vet you first and pass you along.	A gatekeeping method screens messages and prevents weirdness from making its way over.
Business cards	You get their contact information and can continue the conversation if you'd like. You apply your own vetting.	The sender requests to chat and provides a standard set of info to the receiver, who decides what to do next.
Pubs	You interact mostly in a semi-public space, semi-private conversations happen in booths, private conversations happen elsewhere. Vetting is distributed, as is action: anyone can spot and eject anti-social actors.	No private conversations on the app, people can chat in threads. If you want to chat privately, sender and receiver agree where to do so.

Whatever resolution they come up with will still require some planning and collaborating. However, Norman and Lila were able to step back from their problem and see it from a few different angles. Now they have new perspectives to help them better understand their problem.

Reset Yourself

If you're tired, have low blood sugar, or you've stared at the problem for too long, your brain isn't going to make great decisions. So find something that rejuvenates you.

You'd be surprised to know basic things such as having a nap, getting a snack, or going for a walk can help. Naps and walks help your brain focus on other things while it works on the problem in the background. Snacks give your brain the glucose it needs to make decisions.

Carl Jung provides an excellent example here. It's well-documented that he found great inspiration and solace in nature. He often took long walks, which he considered a form of meditation. These walks were a key part of his daily routine and thought process. Having quiet moments in nature provided him with the tranquility and space to ponder deeply, allowing him to formulate many of the theories that we still use to consider human psychology.

Making sure you're rested is key to (please pardon the following) "dreaming up" new solutions. While you're sleeping, your brain unconsciously works through problems as it processes thoughts.

If you aren't getting enough sleep, your brain has much difficulty in navigating the unexpected, revising plans, competing with distraction, and communicating effectively. A study titled "The Impact of Sleep Deprivation on Decision Making: A Review[1]" is one of many such examples that establish that a sleep-deprived brain is really only suitable for doing mundane, monotonous tasks. Not breaking deadlocks.

If such a notion sounds impractical or silly, ask yourself: what are the odds of you being in a situation requiring an immediate decision? Pretty long, most likely.

Lastly: snacks. Yes, there really is a section in this book telling you to get a snack.

Ohio State University psychology researcher Brad Bushman coauthored a study about the link between low blood sugar and

---

1 Y. Harrison and J. A. Horne, "The Impact of Sleep Deprivation on Decision Making: A Review," *Journal of Experimental Psychology: Applied* 6, no. 3 (2000): 236–249, https://doi.org/10.1037/1076-898X.6.3.236

aggression between couples using pins and voodoo dolls.[2] "We need glucose for self-control," said Bushman, lead author of the study, which was released April 14, 2014, in the *Proceedings of the National Academy of Sciences*. "Anger is the emotion that most people have difficulty controlling."

The study followed over 100 married couples for three weeks. At the end of each day, Bushman measured their blood sugar glucose and asked participants to stick pins in the voodoo doll that represented their partner, which indicated levels of aggression.

Not surprisingly, Bushman found that more pins were pushed into the dolls when blood sugar was low. Here's a fun twist: those with the lowest blood sugar levels pushed *twice* the number of pins in as those with higher blood sugar levels.

It's easy to connect the dots here: if you're decently rested and well-fed, you're going to be able to make better, more informed decisions.

Look Out For...

Being in an unbreakable deadlock with someone may seem like some worst case, ninth circle of Hell in Dante's *Divine Comedy* situation. "What more could go wrong?" you wonder. Reader, every circle has its outer edges. And you're at one such place.

Whirlpools

Imagine yourself getting caught in a whirlpool while swimming. If you don't find a way out, you're going to get sucked right down to the bottom. Going against it will tire you, while doing nothing will likely sink you. Indecision in the face of a deadline is exactly that. You need to find a way to swim sideways. Enter "disagree and commit."

This axiom originates from Amazon's leadership principles. It's a clever idea—one that neatly sets out that you must move forward because staying still isn't an option. It's no small act, despite how pithy "disagree and commit" sounds.

---

2 Brad J. Bushman, C. Nathan DeWall, Richard S. Pond Jr., and Michael D. Hanus, "Low Glucose Relates to Greater Aggression in Married Couples," *Proceedings of the National Academy of Sciences of the United States of America* 111, no. 17 (April 2014): 6254–6257, https://doi.org/10.1073/pnas.1400619111

When you disagree and commit, your viewpoints are shaped by your lived experience and expertise, making the process of disagreeing and committing more akin to being stung by a murder hornet. Navigating this is more nuanced than simply saying "Okay, do it your way" and letting things unfold.

Disagree

First, examine everyone's goals. How clear are they? If there's something fuzzy, consider clarifying it. Unclear goals mean they're subject to interpretation and disagreement on tactics. Be careful not to overly define a goal in a way that doesn't allow for flexibility. It will work against you.

Second, assess the validity of everyone's arguments. Are the facts, data, and precedents they're based on solid? Do said elements ignore conflicting facts and data? If not, you're likely arguing an emotional or biased viewpoint.

Third, know that humans are emotionally-driven. It's okay to have emotionally-influenced arguments because that's where empathy and caring come from. Arguments can't be decided by data all the time. Informed by? Yes. Decided entirely by? No. Remember that the more you look for data to support your point of view, the less you're able to see the other's side or competing information. Be open to data that runs counter to your beliefs.

Commit

Here comes the hard (hardest?) part.

After looking through the cases everyone made, integrate what you can, if it makes sense, to form the strongest, most actionable plan. You'll then unite and move forward.

It's valuable in these moments to have a contingency plan in place in case the original plan goes sideways. You don't need to fully define it, as that will waste valuable time and energy that you could be spending on achieving your goals. You'll want to save that for what comes next: uniting.

To unite is to set aside the disagreement and go forward. You've got your plans, you've got your goals, and it's time to move. This means no malicious compliance, or doing only what's explicitly agreed to with the hope that you're vindicated or it goes your way in the end.

If you find yourself in that position, it's nearly certain that you will want to reexamine your motives or ask yourself if you really did let it go. Disagreeing and committing can hurt, especially since you put so much of yourself into your work. That doesn't mean you should take that hurt out on everyone else.

For Norman and Lila, it may look like Table 19.3.

TABLE 19.3 DISAGREE AND COMMIT PROCESS

1 Disagree	
Examine goals.	Consider how clear the goals are and clarify any fuzziness.
Assess arguments	Determine if the facts, data, and precedents are solid and if conflicting facts and data are being ignored. It's okay to have emotionally-influenced arguments, but be open to data that runs counter to your beliefs.
Assess motivations and emotions.	Are you holding on too tight to a viewpoint despite data or solid arguments to the contrary?
2 Commit	
Combine strengths.	Combine the arguments made by each party to create a plan that is both strong and actionable.
Form a contingency plan.	Create a plan in case things don't go as expected. Don't fully define it, as that will waste valuable time and energy.
Unite and move forward.	Set aside the disagreement and work together toward the agreed-upon plan. Avoid malicious compliance or doing only what's explicitly agreed upon. If you find yourself struggling with disagreeing and committing, take a moment to reexamine your motives or ask yourself if you truly let go. Remember not to take out your frustrations on everyone else.

Seeking Perfection

The other inhibitor here is chasing perfection. Everyone wants perfect, so they polish over and over, usually abandoning it. At its root, perfection is a fear of failure. And you're going to break that fear.

At some point, the people making the watches you wear, the books you read, and apps you use daily reached a point and said, "Okay, that's good enough." Then they pushed it out into the world.

What drove that decision? It may have been that they met the goals established with their team. Maybe a deadline arrived. Or they might have decided it was perfect. Whatever happened, the point is this: instead of endlessly polishing, they called it good and released it.

There will always, without question, be something to improve. Knowing and accepting that what you do will have a few warts and rough patches can be a difficult feeling. It's vulnerable and uncomfortable. Let this book acknowledge and validate those feelings while also nudging you toward something productive.

If Norman and Lila remain deadlocked, all of their back and forth does no one a bit of good. It's also actively harmful for them as they aren't making progress and are burning money every day they delay.

Snapshot in Time

To loosely quote a pearl of wisdom from this book's editor (who did not mandate its inclusion), the book you're reading is a snapshot in time. When it was written, your author composed all of these words with every bit of knowledge and skill he had at that time. But times change. So does the author, and so do you.

Accepting this frees you from the constraint of making the perfect thing. What you make may not be perfect for all time, but it's perfect for now.

Norman and Lila's startup will be smaller at launch. Their size works to their advantage because they can gather enough information to see how people actually use DMs before they get big. This way they can formulate a thoughtful plan of action before the problem becomes too big to manage.

Bit by Bit

The joy of startups and the internet is that nothing is truly final. There are always updates you can make. Instead of a big reveal, Norman and Lila could choose to launch smaller pieces of their company. This helps them learn quicker, launch quicker, and reduce the cost of errors.

Launching bit by bit goes by many names. The *MVP* (*minimum viable product*) is a common one. Whatever method you choose, you're divorcing yourself further and further from the siren call of perfection because you're always sending something out in the world. It's consistent, it's always moving, and you're always learning.

Join the Cult of Done

In 2009, Bre Pettis and Kio Stark came up with a manifesto for the makers and doers of the world, one designed to give people a creative jump-start in their endeavors. The key idea: get it done. They came up with a cleverly named "Cult of Done." It is, for the record, not a real cult. Here's a poster that lays out all the tenets (see Figure 19.2).

Focusing on "done" isn't an invitation to move fast and break things. By no means should you do that, as it enables careless, thoughtless decisions that ultimately cause more harm than good. Do something better instead: move quickly, with intention.

Norman and Lila ultimately decided to launch their network with a feature that allows off-platform communication. "This let us launch quickly and get data on how people communicate and interact with this feature. If we find this feature is really popular, we'll evolve it based on feedback from our users. If it flops, we decide to go with the standard DM approach and look to develop other safety toolsets."

NOTE THE CULT OF DONE TEXT

Step 1: There are three states of being. Not knowing, action and completion. Step 2: Accept that everything is a draft. It helps to get it done. Step 3: There is no editing stage. Step 4: Pretending you know what you're doing is almost the same as knowing what you are doing, so just accept that you know what you're doing even if you don't and do it. Step 5: Banish procrastination. If you wait more than a week to get an idea done, abandon it. Step 6: The point of being done is not to finish but to get other things done. Step 7: Once you're done you can throw it away. Step 8: Laugh at perfection. It's boring and keeps you from being done.

Step 9: People without dirty hands are wrong. Doing something makes you right. Step 10: Failure counts as done. So do mistakes. Step 11: Destruction is a variant of done. Step 12: If you have an idea and publish it on the Internet that counts as a ghost of done. Step 13: Done is the engine of more.

FIGURE 19.2
The Cult of Done poster, designed by Joshua Graves after Bre Pettis and Kio Stark, shows their 13 tenets.

Final Thoughts

You may wonder how (or why) you made it all the way through a chapter about breaking deadlocks without talking about compromise. It's a fair question, and here's why: compromise isn't a tool to find paths forward, it's a tool to distribute pain. With compromise, everyone is some varying degree of miserable. Why would anyone want that when successful ways forward always exist, even if you have to work for them?

Lastly, if you want to send this "Cult of Done" poster to George R. R. Martin to encourage him to finish "A Song of Ice and Fire," you'd have the eternal gratefulness of a large number of *Game of Thrones* fans.

- When faced with a deadlock, it is important to step back and examine potential biases and motivations, possibly with the help of an expert.
- Use lateral thinking to reframe the problem by considering alternative perspectives and challenging assumptions.
- Take care of yourself by getting enough rest and nutrition to maintain decision-making abilities. And, to the degree it's possible, create the conditions for others to do the same.
- In situations where agreement seems impossible, apply the "disagree and commit" approach to move forward.
- Rather than compromising, seek paths forward that work for everyone and launch quickly to gather data and evolve based on user feedback.

CHAPTER 20

Mediating with Multiple People

Vicaria and Donald used to be deeply collaborative leaders. They'd disagreed in the past, as is common for engineering and product management leaders, but the tension was healthy and pushed their teams to deliver incredible work that landed them a boatload of new funding from their investors.

The Problem

Then a miscommunication involving a botched product launch and significant wasted funds for an ad slot during a major sporting event ruined everything. The product, an app, which was focused on giving baseball fans exclusive access to players before the playoff games, missed its launch window. Each blamed the other's team for the problem, and neither could come to any kind of agreement about how to handle the issue moving forward.

The weekend before launch, Vicaria's engineering team uncovered a bug with some legacy software. It presented them with two bad choices: completely gut the app's features or switch codebases at the last minute. They switched codebases, but didn't communicate that, and didn't make the launch. Vicaria said, "The design and marketing team did a quick turnaround and put up a sign-up page that got an okay response, so it wasn't a total loss. But it sure felt that way."

Donald's product management team felt like Vicaria's engineering team wasn't communicating with them (they weren't). Vicaria said Donald's team was changing feature requirements after they were in development without giving time to test and adapt (they were). "We also felt really micromanaged, which made it worse," Vicaria said.

But they still had an app to launch. And it was a hot mess. Tensions boiled over in a meeting about when they could launch with the features required. "I don't remember everything that happened leading up to it, just that it was tense. We were yelling." Then someone, the CEO, heard Donald and Vicaria yelling.

The CEO, Jada (a former product manager), called them into her office for an on-the-spot mediation session. She hadn't had any actual mediation training, so it went poorly.

Vicaria said, "Our boss said she'd had enough of our infighting, and it was spilling over into our teams. It was time to work it out so we could launch. But it was a terrible experience for me. Instead of hearing both of us out and helping us find common ground, it became pretty clear that our boss was on Donald's side, and I was being told to get in line. I think calling it an ambush would probably have been a fairer term."

In the retelling of it, Vicaria's mediation session was a failure for multiple reasons: her boss wasn't impartial, the setting wasn't neutral, and she wasn't prepared for it. Since this session was a train wreck (Vicaria's words), this chapter is a healthy mix of what-did-happen and what-if and what-shoulda-happened.

The Solution

Being a mediator is like being a seasoned trail guide for two hikers caught at a crucial fork on a mountain trail with an impending storm looming overhead.

One hiker is absolutely convinced the left path leads back to camp, while the other is just as convinced the right path is the way. Neither can hear the merits of the other's positions and each is focused on being right and getting their way. Their insistence on being right is blinding them to the fact that if they don't decide, they're going to be caught in a storm.

The mediator, like the trail guide, doesn't simply point out which path is correct. Instead, they delve deeper, trying to understand why each hiker believes so firmly in their chosen direction. Is it a landmark they remember? A gut feeling? Past experience? Or perhaps a bit of pride?

By bringing clarity to each hiker's perspective, the mediator helps them see the merits and pitfalls of both paths, and most importantly, the potential of forging a new path together.

This trail guide doesn't force a consensus or choose sides, but instead illuminates the terrain, helping the hikers make more informed decisions and encouraging collaboration toward a solution that gets both safely through the storm.

Get the Right Mindset

What comes to mind when you think of someone in a mediator role? Maybe someone negotiating a bitter divorce or refereeing a cage match with two MMA (mixed martial arts) fighters going at each other. Mediating is generally much, much less intense than that. Although some conversations can get pretty tense, with the right mindset—being neutral, patient, insightful, and outcome-focused—you can handle whatever level of tension you encounter.

People need mediators when collaboration is broken and they can't find a way out of things on their own. It could be a communication or cultural issue, but regardless, they need help, and you're there to provide it.

When you mediate, you're there to help people find a way forward together, not to ensure that everyone gets what they want. After their session with you, both sides should leave feeling heard, respected, acknowledged...and a bit disappointed. You can't have one side too happy or getting everything they want. If that's the case, then you've failed.

Be Neutral

You're dealing with a complex, high-stakes issue, so you need to keep a level head about you. This means not favoring one person over the other. It also means letting them express themselves without taking on their emotions. It's difficult work to check your opinions, biases, and emotions at the door, but it's necessary nonetheless.

Vicaria's boss wasn't neutral here, as she was previously a colleague of Donald's and a current friend. In the conversation, Vicaria said, "Something felt off, because when I pointed out where communication failed, or there was something amiss with how we managed our launch plan, it got dismissed. I know I wasn't perfect. I'm human, and I got upset, too. But I found her agreeing with Donald time and time again."

If you're going to mediate for people, you'll need to make sure that you ground yourself appropriately beforehand. These conversations need to let people fully express themselves to get to the bottom of an issue. That can be thorny, and you need to let them do this without personally taking on their emotions. You're no good to anyone here if you find yourself too caught up to guide them.

Picture yourself acting like a lightning rod in a storm. You can take whatever lightning is flying around in the room, capture it, and return it safely into the ground. You aren't responsible for the lightning—you're just redirecting it, and not taking on any of it.

If you can't be neutral, and the parties don't perceive you as such, you shouldn't be mediating. Full stop.

Be Patient

When a plant's roots get tangled, they can kill the plant if left untended. And untangling them takes time. You may need to cut a few of the roots, or you may just need to massage them a bit so they can relax. It's much the same with mediating: to succeed you'll need patience to help co-workers separate those roots so the entire plant doesn't die.

Patience builds on the skill of neutrality. Where neutrality lets people express themselves fully, patience lets them express themselves at length. This is a circular process, as some topics and themes come up over and over in your conversation. You may spot it immediately, but it takes time for others to realize it.

Mediation sessions aren't like a dentist visit where you deal with some unpleasantness and a fake promise that you'll keep up with your flossing, and then you're done. Sometimes these sessions can take a few hours. Or multiple sessions. Or both, depending on how complex it is.

Be Insightful

Finally, after letting people express themselves fully and at length, you get to leverage your insights. Reflect what you're hearing and help everyone dive a little deeper to uncover what may be motivating their positions. As you learned earlier, most issues come down to three things: autonomy, relatedness, and competence.

Take special care in these sessions to note body language, tone of voice, and other nonverbal cues. This way you'll be able to see if what someone says matches what they believe. This also helps you guide the conversation and address hidden issues that may be pivotal in finding a way forward.

NOTE MAKE A GUIDING PRINCIPLE

> After reading this section, consider creating a guiding principle. This way, you know what you're about as a mediator. Here's a great starter that encompasses all the values mentioned here:
>
> "I'm here to help two smart, capable people work through a difficult situation. I'll keep a level head, be patient with them, and reflect what I see so that I can shine a light on a way forward together."

Set the Stage

Now that you've readied yourself, it's time to help them. That includes having each person do a little homework, finding the right place to have the conversation, and setting some ground rules.

Define the Problem

There's a thought experiment related to what happens when an unstoppable object meets an immovable force. Often, those forces and objects are the entrenched positions.

While it sounds like the setup for something cataclysmic, skilled mediators see it for what it is: a logical fallacy. Both things can't exist in the same universe. If a force is unstoppable, there can be no such thing as an immovable object and vice versa. One or both may be particularly strong, but there's always a way forward. (Yes, always.)

The following table helps each person define how they see the situation at hand. Work with them individually beforehand to fill this out. It should never happen in the presence of the other person. Here's why: Let's say Vicaria believes Donald is lying. She wouldn't want to tip Donald off to that. Should he find out, Donald may delete records that prove he is, or take action against her for that assumption. Instead, you will use Vicaria's belief to get information from Donald that can prove or refute her belief without Donald being the wiser about it.

There's one additional benefit to doing this ahead of time: writing things down helps add much needed clarity for everyone. Use Table 20.1 as a starting point.

Table 20.1 gives both parties the chance for the careful choice of words without the pressure of immediate responses to what may be extremely complex situations. This method also provides you with a clear understanding of both people's perspectives.

And the emphasized "*one* item?" It's a forcing function. It's unnatural that there may be just "one thing," especially in highly complex situations, but your goal as mediator is to help them avoid what they see as a certain catastrophe. Managing beyond the top issue also adds an impossible level of difficulty and encourages one side to see how much they got vs. the other person.

TABLE 20.1 SETTING THE STAGE

	Vicaria	Donald
Situation	Due to unexpected issues, the engineering team made a last-minute, unplanned switch of codebases to meet feature requirements that were slated for launch.	We were coordinating the big launch of the app. It involves strategic planning, coordinating marketing efforts, and communicating with stakeholders.
Behavior	The engineering team, despite knowing the risks, decided to switch codebases without communicating it to anyone, hoping it wouldn't be a problem.	We were unaware of the codebase switch until it was too late. So, we had to adjust plans accordingly and manage the crisis with stakeholders. They expressed their frustration about the late communication from the engineering team.
Impact (on you, the team, and the project)	The team felt micromanaged and pressured to meet a deadline. They also felt that the project was mismanaged and lacked support to do the job right.	The PM team feels extremely stressed. We have upset stakeholders, had financial losses, and foresee a potential damage to our reputation. It's hard to trust the engineering team.
Why might the other person be unwilling to work with you?	Donald's team may be upset because their launch was blown, and it cost the company.	Maybe they felt like they didn't have a choice, and this was very high stress. Maybe they thought they could make the deadline without making it worse.
What is the one item you need to happen to be successful?	PM must let us do our work and *not* change things last minute unless it's critical.	We need regular updates from engineering. We can't be in this situation again.
What's the worst that can happen?	We lose our jobs.	Loss of investment, confidence, and jobs.

If you don't push someone to prioritize, you won't make forward progress. Should you see multiple key items, require your coworkers to put their criteria in a numbered list and tell them the session will only focus on the top item. And sorry, but you can't make everything number one.

Set Up the Conversation

You'll also agree on a time and place, making sure that it's blocked out on everyone's calendar. Aim for one session that is two to three hours max.

Avoid multiple sessions at all costs, even if everyone's busy. No one needs to prolong the issue, and you don't want to give anyone an opportunity to take action until you're out of the session.

You may find that hesitant participants use being busy as a barrier, and that's not a bad thing. Take it as a signal that they want boundaries and reassure them that you will respect every moment of their time.

You'll also need to consider how acidic the situation is. If you're dealing with two feral cats who can't talk to each other, you will want to separate them. This chapter focuses on mediations where people can still talk with each other, but will show you what to do in case they can't.

The location where you have the conversation cannot be an afterthought. You'll want to choose a private space where you aren't going to be disturbed. And this place cannot be either person's office or workspace because you want to preserve that neutrality.

How the room is arranged is also important. Vicaria and Donald can't be on unequal footing, with one person behind a desk. Both need to sit facing each other with you in the middle.

Establish the Rules

None of the work that's done in this session will have any value if there aren't some rules laid out ahead of time. Without them, your mediation session will almost certainly turn into a useless venting session without a clear outcome.

Here's a starter set of ground rules:

1. **Establish purpose:** Everyone is here to solve a problem (you articulate said problem) and craft a resolution. That means hearing different perspectives and things you may not want to

hear. You will also state the time limit for this and what happens should no one reach an agreement (e.g., escalation).

2. **What the stakes are:** Lead off with "What's the worst that can happen" to show that both parties believe leaving without an agreement can cause great pain.
3. **What your role is:** You reflect, moderate, and facilitate. You're going to stay neutral. You aren't here to babysit or clean up a mess. You're here to help two intelligent dedicated people find a path forward.
4. **One person at a time:** Only one person speaks at a time. This includes making sure that your devices are muted. No distractions. Do one thing, this thing.
5. **What's out of bounds:** Always start with a rule against personal attacks. You may need to add other points, especially if one person is prone to yelling or other inappropriate behavior.

NOTE WHAT IF I SPOT PERSONAL ATTACKS?

If you spot personal attacks, you don't have to defuse them or solve them. This is where you act like a referee and simply say "that's out of bounds, as it's a personal attack." If they continue, they're taking a break.

If you find that the parties can't talk with each other, you're doing what's known as "shuttle diplomacy" or "caucusing" and working with each party individually. In that case, you can omit steps four and five.

Facilitate Conversation

After you've read the rules, bring up their homework. It's up to you how it's shared: each person can read their own, they can read each other's, or you can read them yourself. If you do end up reading and summarizing what each person says, make sure to use *their* language and words, not yours. Using their phrasing positions you as a neutral conduit, not a biased interpreter.

Your involvement and guidance depends entirely on the relationship between the people involved. Higher tension, stakes, and toxicity mean more structure. Your skills with insight should guide you here (see Table 20.2).

TABLE 20.2 HOW MUCH GUIDANCE MEDIATORS NEED TO GIVE

Situation	It's Not Great, but Manageable	It's Volatile
Structure	Lower structure	Higher structure
Participation	Actively participate more	Questions and responses, only let them take the reins if it feels like they won't get too heated
Time	Soft limits on time	Timed responses
Facilitation	You guide and facilitate, highlighting commonalities	You'll read or summarize their statements

Reflect

What you do next depends on one thing: is the animosity between the two parties preventing them from listening to each other at all? If it isn't, you can point out that they share more common ground than not.

Your motivation for saying this is to highlight specifically how they have a shared vision and let them bridge the gaps where it diverges. (Hint: the shared vision is always there, but it's usually just hidden under a bunch of junk, like resentment and blame.)

Here are a few things you can say to highlight common ground:

- "It sounds like you're aligned on the core issues and core goals. That makes this way easier. The work you have before you is working out the details, so. . . ."
- "It seems like those goals don't fully line up. Let's call back to those. Where do they overlap?"

If you aren't seeing it, you could try:

- "It looks like you two are trying to achieve two opposing goals. What were the overall goals for this project?"
- "It sounds like you each have different ideas of what success looks like. Can you talk more about that?"
- "It seems like there are some fundamental differences in how you approach this issue. Can you explain those differences? Let's try to find some common ground."

If you noticed, these statements are phrased tentatively (see Chapter 2, "Having the Conversation"), and you should use this format here, too. By speaking tentatively, you demonstrate you aren't forming the conclusions or making value judgments on the people involved. You're just reflecting what you see.

If they can't stand each other, take emotion out of it entirely, like this: "If we reach an agreement on this today, what will this mean for everyone?" You can also remind them that anger can come and go, but consequences are permanent. Is this really what they want?

You can also focus on the consequences of *not* reaching an agreement. Usually, that means escalating the situation and having someone else make a decision for them. That person usually doesn't have to live with the full impact of it, and they'll lose faith in them to do their job.

Here's why you want to take the shared vision out of it: it can further entrench people's positions. If this were somehow more tense, Vicaria and Donald could agree that there was a shared vision, but the other was too dimwitted to see it, and that's why they're doubling down.

Mediators also need to use reflecting here to probe and uncover the motivating factors or causes for tension. Try these:

- "What's behind that?"
- "When did you first notice that?"
- "How did it impact you?"
- "What do you see as the core issue?"
- "Okay, sounds like you're saying [this thing], is that fair? Want to add anything to that?"

It's preferable to have structured questions that you ask, and then give them sound boundaries for time to talk. If someone is prone to go on at length, you can limit everyone's response time. But do not do this to just one person—it's got to happen for everyone or no one.

Build to a Resolution

Managing the back and forth isn't all you have to do. A mediator needs to keep nudging the participants toward a resolution. This resolution may not be perfect, and that's fine. Perfection is the enemy of good, and good enough is great.

You may find it helpful to do other exercises with each other, such as charting the effort and impact of each request, and brainstorming how to move forward with those constraints.

While you aren't responsible for the final outcome, you deal in trade-offs and consensus building. It's helpful to know what you want to aim for here, as well as what you want to avoid (see Table 20.3).

TABLE 20.3 CONSIDERATIONS

Considerations	Goals	Anti-Goals
Who benefits	Mutually beneficial, meeting the needs of everyone involved.	One party wins, leading to resentment. May not result in a lasting, effective resolution.
Outcomes	Actionable and specific, with clearly detailed steps that ensure everyone knows what is expected of them.	Vague or unmeasurable, leading to confusion, misinterpretation, or noncompliance.
Communication	Open, everyone expresses their thoughts and feelings honestly and respectfully, now and in the future. This fosters understanding and collaboration.	Suppressive, inhibiting open communication and silencing other voices. Undercuts understanding and further deteriorates conditions.
Perspectives	Understood and welcomed; acknowledging other perspectives leads to better outcomes for everyone.	Ignored and discouraged, exacerbating misunderstandings and conflicts.
Interests vs. positions	Focus on interests and positions, creating more opportunities for creative problem-solving and mutual gain. Focusing on the underlying interests (the needs, desires, or concerns that are important to a party).	Strict adherence to positions, (focusing only on things like policies), inhibiting exploration of alternative solutions. Leads to deadlock.
Relationships	Long-term relationship focused, improving or preserving relationships between parties, setting the foundation for future collaboration.	Win-lose mindset, focusing on one side winning. Strains relationships and hinders constructive resolution.

Look Out For...

Mediating is tricky business. If mediators aren't careful, they can unconsciously bias and prevent what could have otherwise been a mutually beneficial situation. And because mediators are often walking into tense situations, they need to ensure that participants stay in the conversation.

Your Own Bias

Regrettably, you don't magically become a neutral party when you assume the role of mediator. You've still got work to do, mainly in the form of combatting your own biases. Everyone has some, even the most enlightened people. These biases can negatively influence outcomes, discredit others, and tank what might otherwise be a good path forward.

As a mediator, you can't, absolutely *can't*, make it look like you're siding with someone. The only side you're on is the resolution of a problem with mutually beneficial outcomes.

Cognitive Biases

These types of biases find you unconsciously favoring one party, due to similarities you share. For instance, if Donald and Jada attended the same university or came from the same hometown, Jada might unknowingly lean toward Donald's side due to this shared commonality, creating a cognitive bias. Should Jada focus mostly on only negative or positive information, or she jumps to conclusions, it could also indicate she has a bias.

Experiential Biases

You may also have had previous experiences that make it difficult for you to be neutral. If Jada had been in a situation similar to Donald and Vicaria's, she may be inclined to nudge Vicaria and Donald to follow the path she did. She may also relate more strongly to one person's experience more than the other. That's, once again, a reason why neutrality is key.

Confirmation Biases

If Jada has a pre-existing belief, such as engineers are lazy and uncommunicative, she may look for opportunities to lead the mediation in such a way. She may ask leading questions that lead them toward her idea of what should be done, dismiss contradictory evidence, or favor evidence that supports her view. Call back to the metaphor of the trail guide and hikers from before and remember this: you aren't here to decide for them, you're here to help them decide for themselves.

Communication Breakdowns

This chapter would be woefully incomplete if it didn't cover what everyone fears the most about mediation: things crashing and burning.

After all, you're dealing with adults with free will and wildly divergent approaches to conflict, so there's no surefire way to success here. The only thing that comes close is a stakeholder (like someone's boss) demanding a resolution, and even that isn't a guarantee. Chapter 3, "People Losing Control," takes a more in-depth approach to when people reach their limit, so this section focuses more on how to bring people back to center in a group setting.

Vicaria said of her quasi-mediation session that "Things really broke down. It got heated. I got mad, I felt like I wasn't being heard. So did Donald. He said something implying I had a lack of expertise that had me feeling personally attacked. I almost left. I can handle my work being picked apart, but not me personally."

Her boss didn't step in, either. It wasn't clear if she wasn't skilled in mediation, or wanted to let things play out. Either way, the impact was the same: Vicaria wanted to disengage and felt like she was on her own. And by not stepping in, her boss let the worst happen: Vicaria threw in the towel.

Here's what happened:

> **Donald:** I just can't understand why we're still talking about this. It's perfectly clear, as I've laid out, how we ended up here. I told you multiple times we needed those features and the others weren't important. We're here because you missed that and didn't want to tell people you blew it.
>
> **Vicaria:** Okay, but you didn't tell *me* anything. You posted something in a product management–specific Slack that I don't check. Do you know how many channels I have to read? I can't keep up. You didn't even mention me or tell me about it. Had you communicated with me directly, I could have shifted our plans and helped reduce the scope or at least told you that what you were asking wasn't reasonable. Now we've blown a lot of money and goodwill because *you* didn't communicate.
>
> **Donald:** DO. NOT. TELL ME HOW TO DO MY JOB. I communicated it! It isn't my fault you don't read that Slack. Or can you even read? Your job is to give me the code I need to launch this. I don't have time to manage another incompetent person. Roll with it or quit. I don't care and don't want to deal with this trash anymore.

And here's what a skilled mediator would have done: jump in, call back to the rules they established, specifically the ones about personal attacks.

> Jada: Wait, wait, *stop*. Donald, that's out of bounds. Personal attacks are not acceptable and are against our rules. If you do that again, we'll separate, and I'll have to reflect this in my report.

Jada now has two options: separate them, or give Donald a chance to apologize so they can move on. Then Jada would reflect some of what she heard Vicaria say. Namely, that they weren't communicating directly. She then can ask if there's a way to solve that.

> Jada: I heard Vicaria say you two haven't communicated about this. What's your communication cadence like in general? How would establishing this benefit everyone?

If you're wondering "why didn't Jada shut Donald down and say it wasn't alright to talk to someone like that," this example hews closely to the ideal of neutrality for the sake of making a textbook case to follow. You can and should use your own judgment on what to say, and use words that are authentic to you so long as you too don't get drawn into the fray. (Donald was totally over the line, by the way. No one should talk to another person like he did.)

Not Establishing Accountability

As established earlier, mediators need to be outcome-focused. Getting the participants to come together on—and stick with—their agreements involves establishing accountability and documenting it. Just like a project can't succeed without goals, neither can mediation. If you don't have accountability, you don't have committed action. And lacking committed action, no one's bound to do a thing. And more than likely, they won't.

Here's what you need to establish:

- **Who agreed to do what?** This needs to be as clear as the most perfect crystal. Use bullet points if necessary, but at a minimum you need to list what commitment each person made in explicit and unambiguous terms. If there's wiggle room, the agreement is likely to fall apart.
- **What time frame?** Establish clear timelines for every task or outcome to be completed. This creates a sense of urgency and provides a specific point in time to check on progress or completion. This ensures that there's no ambiguity about when someone will know the outcome.

- **How will everyone know that the issue's been resolved or is actively being addressed?** Define how progress and fulfillment of those agreements will be tracked and evaluated. This may include regular check-ins or progress reports. This aspect also outlines what will happen if the tasks aren't completed as agreed, which can serve as an additional motivator and create a culture of accountability.

Vicaria ultimately got the blame for the missed launch pinned on her, which was a big blow. "It was an even bigger blow to their credibility, honestly. I was going to agree to whatever and start looking elsewhere." Outcomes aren't always ideal, much like Vicaria's. But imagine for a moment what could have been.

Any mediation needs to end with some sort of artifact and documented outcome, successful or not. This includes whether or not people participated in the mediation, and what agreements were or weren't made (see Table 20.4).

TABLE 20.4 AGREEMENTS AND ACCOUNTABILITY

The Agreement	Donald and Vicaria will have regular syncs focused on monitoring the backlog and identifying any blockers.
The time frame	Daily until next big launch and then weekly
The proof	Email a spreadsheet with progress and any blockers to Jada.

After people reach an agreement in the mediation, the mediator then documents it and notifies the appropriate people. This could be an email to their boss or stakeholder, a company-wide email, or just to the people involved. The important part of this is making the agreement official and establishing accountability.

Final Thoughts

Mediation is hard. Really, really hard. Not only are you managing yourself, but you're managing multiple other parties. That's why this chapter was so much longer than the rest. To put a finer point on the message of this chapter: you need to focus on providing a safe environment for people to be heard and respected if you hope to achieve any reasonably decent outcome. This isn't fundamentally different than your one-on-one conversations, but it does require a little more effort.

- Define the situation, behavior, and impact of the problem before the conversation to add clarity.
- Set up the conversation in a private space that is free from distractions.
- Establish ground rules for the conversation to ensure a productive outcome.
- Use reflective listening to probe and uncover underlying interests or causes for tension.
- Work toward building shared goals and an actionable resolution with clear timelines and accountability.

CLOSING

There are two more things I'll share before closing.

First, change is inevitable. The future may alter the specific situations you find yourself in as well as the techniques and approaches you take. No matter what the future brings, you will always be able to step back and ask yourself "What's the kindest thing I can do right now?" and find a path forward. And that's the key to finding the path out of whatever haunted house in a horror movie you find yourself in.

Finally, a theme revealed itself in the stories that people shared with me at workshops, interviews for this book, and day-to-day work. They had difficulty accepting the situations they were in and the feelings surrounding them. "Are my feelings valid? Is it acceptable to have felt this way?" they would say in one way or another.

My answer was almost always the same: yes, your feelings were valid. Let me share a quote from my childhood that's always stuck with me. It's from *Mr. Rogers' Neighborhood*: "There's no 'should' or 'should not' when it comes to having feelings. They're part of who we are and their origins are beyond our control."

In short, feelings are always valid—it's just the acting on them and how they influence your response that's the tricky part.

It's a freeing notion: once we accept and validate our feelings, we're practicing a form of kindness, which is the core of this book. Kindness and acceptance are distinct concepts, but they are so deeply intertwined that it's difficult not to mention them both in the same breath.

And the situation I mentioned in the introduction? I had a hard conversation with that particular team and that research became the foundation of the framework of this book. We got it sorted out and went back to the originally approved version. It ended up helping a lot of patients have meaningfully better experiences with our client. The team communicated a bit better, too, but wasn't ever close to perfect. And that was fine.

Why was it just fine? It wasn't anything compared to the confidence and peace I felt: I'd been through hell and found a way out. And then I knew how to get myself (and anyone else) out if I ever found myself there again.

INDEX

C

D

E

F

G

H

I

J

K

L

M

N

O

P

S

Dear Reader,

Thanks very much for purchasing this book. There's a story behind it and every product we create at Rosenfeld Media.

Since the early 1990s, I've been a User Experience consultant, conference presenter, workshop instructor, and author. (I'm probably best-known for having cowritten *Information Architecture for the Web and Beyond*.) In each of these roles, I've been frustrated by the missed opportunities to apply UX principles and practices.

I started Rosenfeld Media in 2005 with the goal of publishing books whose design and development showed that a publisher could practice what it preached. Since then, we've expanded into producing industry-leading conferences and workshops. In all cases, UX has helped us create better, more successful products—just as you would expect. From employing user research to drive the design of our books and conference programs, to working closely with our conference speakers on their talks, to caring deeply about customer service, we practice what we preach every day.

Please visit rosenfeldmedia.com to learn more about our **conferences**, **workshops**, **free communities**, and **other great resources** that we've made for you. And send your ideas, suggestions, and concerns my way: louis@rosenfeldmedia.com

I'd love to hear from you, and I hope you enjoy the book!

Lou Rosenfeld,
Publisher

ACKNOWLEDGMENTS

I have this habit of jumping into a new and exciting thing without realizing exactly what I've signed myself up for. That is, until I've bonked my head several times on the way to the end. Those endeavors usually yield a fun story or two, and if I'm lucky a little knowledge I can use in the future. This one, though, was a doozy. The stories, the learning, the work required to get to the finish line. It's been the most rewarding, challenging experience of my career so far.

There's no possible way I could have done this alone, and I am deeply grateful to everyone who's helped me along the way. I'd like to thank a few people specifically, though, as their contributions were monumental in one way or another. Bryan Zug, whose unshakably merry spirit and grizzled sherpa counsel supported me when the waters of life became too choppy to sail alone. Marta Justak, for encouraging me to push myself and giving me the hard truth especially when I didn't want to hear it. Lou Rosenfeld, for the opportunity and unfailing kindness. Rosenfeld authors, for support and encouragement. Everyone who contributed to an interview especially against the advice of their therapist. (I'm keeping your names out of it, but you know who you are.) Reviewers, whose insights made this book so much better.

I acknowledge the great contribution of experts who graciously gave of their time and patiently answered my questions: Susan Weinschenk, Karen Catlin, Darren Hood, and countless others whose research and wisdom inspired me.

The authors of the countless horror stories I read when my brain short circuited, you all showed me that people can face cosmically horrible, scary things and come out the other side (mostly) okay. Go Get 'Em Tiger, who unofficially sponsored this book with their delicious coffee. My dog Charlie, for reminding me to get out of my head by taking a walk and getting some treats (sage advice we all could use). My cat Frankie, for making sure we both got some relaxing time together. I couldn't have done this without you, my little loves.

ABOUT THE AUTHOR

Joshua Graves is the founder of Lost Horse Labs, a human-centered design company. He is an expert in human-centered design and communication. With over 15 years of experience studying how people interrelate, navigate challenges, and solve complex problems, Joshua has become a recognized expert in human-centered design and communication.

His extensive background includes building and leading design teams, conducting in-depth user research, and exploring the psychology behind interpersonal dynamics. In his work with high-profile organizations and his workshops, Joshua helps hundreds of professionals navigate complex workplace dynamics and build stronger, more effective relationships. Joshua's approach combines insights from psychology, neuroscience, empathy, curiosity, and years of practical experience facilitating difficult conversations. He lives in Joshua Tree, California.

www.ingramcontent.com/pod-product-compliance
Lightning Source LLC
Chambersburg PA
CBHW041125180926
51615CB00021B/3076